D1546327

STARDUST
BY THE BUSHEL

HOLLYWOOD ON THE CHESAPEAKE BAY'S EASTERN SHORE

BRENT LEWIS

SECANT PUBLISHING
Salisbury, Maryland

First Edition Published by
Secant Publishing, LLC
P.O. Box 4059
Salisbury MD 21803

ISBN: 978-0-9997503-3-9 (hardcover)
Library of Congress Control Number: 2021919099

Cover design by Beaux Arts

Dedicated to my cousin Kenny Kerchner, my friends Terry Alley Smith and Mala Burt, my wife, and my parents, who could never gauge which movies might be inappropriate for younger viewers.

FOREWORD

The title of this book is, admittedly, a bit of a puzzle. *Stardust* is the glamor of the marquee, the mesmerizing sheen of the starlet and the leading man. A *bushel* is a wood-sided basket with wire handles, best known in packing sheds as a container for fresh fruit, or blue crabs.

Stardust and bushels – what in the name of Louis B. Mayer does the one have to do with the other?

Turns out a watery, agrarian land settled by farmers and fishermen, divided by an entire continent from Hollywood and Vine, has been singing its siren call to movie directors, movie stars, and award-winning screenwriters since celluloid became a thing. Maybe that's precisely because the Eastern Shore is a little bit different than most anywhere else.

In his classic *Rivers of the Eastern Shore* (1944), author Hulbert Footner memorably pictured the Shore as "a peninsula shaped roughly like a bunch of grapes. It hangs down from a stem in the north, where only a few miles of land separate the waters of the Delaware from the Chesapeake, spreads out in a wide shoulder, and tapers off to a point (Cape Charles) at the south." The fact that it includes parts of three states – Delaware, Maryland, and Virginia – gave rise to the portmanteau *Delmarva*, often used interchangeably with *Eastern Shore*.

Even more than it is a fertile peninsula, rich with seafood and poultry, soybean fields and roadside farm stands, the Eastern Shore is a state of mind. Its historic remoteness from the mainland and all those meddlesome state bureaucrats in Annapolis and Richmond lent the Shore its distinctive character.

Eccentric. Independent. Even a bit gnarly.

First ferries and stagecoaches, then steam engines, now suspension bridges and the Internet have dragged this once-inaccessible peninsula from its archaic roots into modern times. But life remains a bit slower in Bay Country. Charter boat fishing and hunting for waterfowl remain dependable lures for visitors.

Every summer, Ocean City attracts tourists by the millions to a classic beachside resort experience, but the human tide retreats after Labor Day, the umbrellas and lifeguard stands come down, and shutters are drawn across many a window until Memorial Day.

There's a saying on the Eastern Shore that folks who retire here (aka *come-heres*) can do one of three things: sail, paint, or write. It's not literally true, but close enough for a certain kind of corporate refugee or federal retiree. For those who come seeking their own little stretch of waterfront or woods, the Shore can be a kind of Eden.

With that as background, it is perhaps less surprising to learn that for much of the past century, the Eastern Shore has also been a recurring draw for the great American dream factory.

It has served both as a charming location for major feature films like *The Runaway Bride* and *Wedding Crashers*, and as a secluded getaway for some of our best-known marquee idols, including the likes of Annie Oakley and Tallulah Bankhead.

Who knew that Fay Wray was married in St. Michaels (for the first time) with Gary Cooper standing witness in his work duds? Or that Robert Mitchum and his friend Yul Brynner once dented a country gate near Trappe, racing their twin Aston Martins like fugitives from a James Bond movie?

Brent Lewis knew.

In *Stardust by the Bushel*, he recounts this whimsical history in an incomparable, knowing voice. Brent is tenth-generation Eastern Shoreman, and he knows this land, this water, in his bones. He also is a passionate consumer of popular culture who loves comic books and collectables, music, and comedy from nearly every genre. For him, extended research on cinematic history was a personal pleasure, and he shares his findings in this generous book.

Lights, camera, action ... *Stardust*!

Ron Sauder
Publisher
Salisbury, Maryland

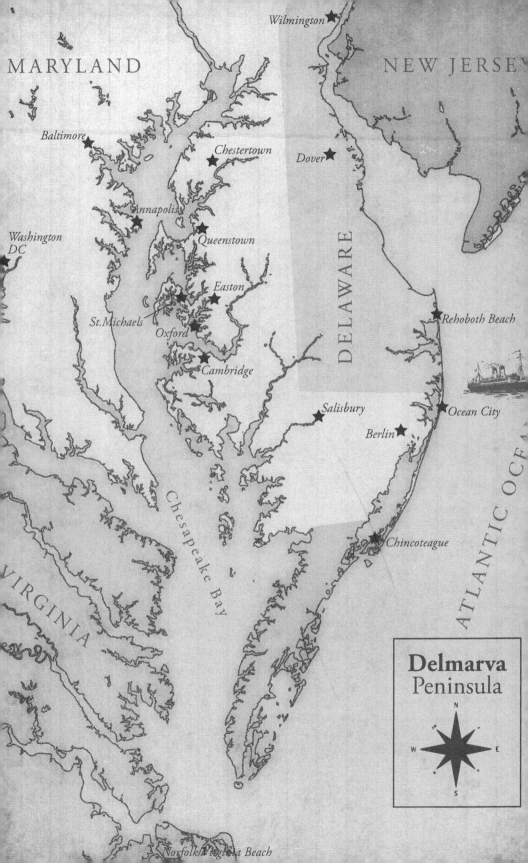

CONTENTS

FOREWORD V

OPENING SCENE 1

    THE WHIP (1917) 3

ON LOCATION 13

    BERLIN 15

THE STARS 25

    ROBERT MITCHUM 27

    LINDA HARRISON 43

    LINDA HAMILTON 63

    TALLULAH BANKHEAD 83

ON LOCATION 103

    EASTON 105

BASED ON A TRUE STORY 117

    HARRIET TUBMAN 119

    ANNIE OAKLEY 141

    ROBERT KEARNS 157

    MISTY OF CHINCOTEAGUE 179

ON LOCATION 201

    ST. MICHAELS 203

BEHIND THE SCENES   217

    JAMES M. CAIN AND FILM NOIR   219

    EDNA FERBER AND THE JAMES ADAMS FLOATING
    THEATRE   243

    LUCILLE FLETCHER AND DOUGLASS WALLOP   259

ON LOCATION   281

    DELMARVA AND OCEAN CITY   283

FEATURE PRESENTATIONS   317

    THE FIRST KISS (1928)   319

    VIOLETS ARE BLUE (1986)   329

    CLARA'S HEART (1988)   337

    SILENT FALL (1994)   345

    RUNAWAY BRIDE (1999)   349

    WEDDING CRASHERS (2005)   355

    FAILURE TO LAUNCH(2006)   363

ACKNOWLEDGMENTS   369

BIBLIOGRAPHY   373

INDEX   399

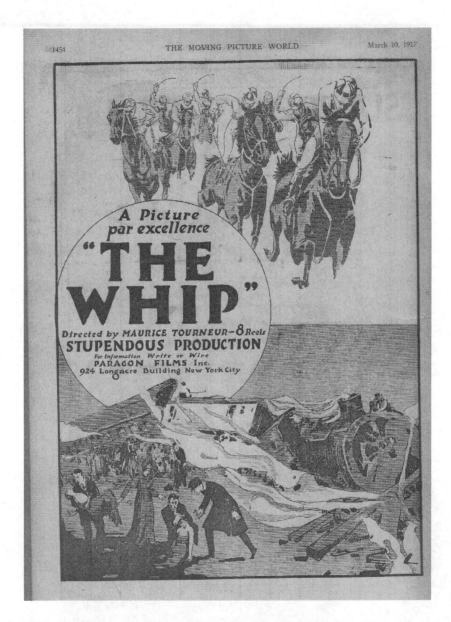

Featuring an eye-popping train crash staged near Queenstown, *The Whip* brought the big-time silver screen to Maryland's Eastern Shore in 1917.

THE WHIP
(1 9 1 7)

"I was exposed to The Whip just short of forty years ago. I've never recovered."

—*Tallulah Bankhead*

The Centreville Observer, January 6, 1917:

When the rushing train struck the box-car . . . [t]he freight carrier reared high in air, seemed almost to turn a somersault and then crumpled into a pile of splintered, shattered timbers. Its roof was torn off and hurled through a clump of small willows beside the track. The train ran on a few feet, amidst a cloud of smoke and dust, then the engine left the rails, rolled over and gave up its "ghost" . . . the rails were twisted up almost into knots and the ties were scattered to the four winds . . . the express train crash[ed] into a box-car . . . and smash[ed] it to flinders. The engine left the rails, plunged down an embankment and buried its nose in the bank beside a marshy ravine . . . the engine lay on its side, a battered, torn and twisted heap of scrap metal from which the steam escaped in clouds with a loud hissing.

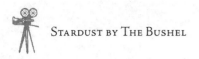

The year 1917 was a banner one for the movie business. Not only did Buster Keaton, Technicolor, and full-length, animated features debut onscreen, so did the Chesapeake Bay's Eastern Shore.

From the lighthouse at Cape Charles, Virginia in the south to the Chesapeake & Delaware Canal in the north, the Eastern Shore, home to some of our nation's oldest communities, was still a rather isolated part of the country when America's romance with cinema began. Besides occasional advancements in work or play, life here remained virtually unchanged for generations. Most Eastern Shore folk were farmers or worked on the water, or their occupations supported those traditional industries. Though its residents were generally self-sufficient, life on "The Shore" did require interaction with the outside world. Supplies, mail, news, and even entertainment—as evidenced by the famed James Adams Floating Theater—were shipped in; seafood, farm products, and the occasional prodigal son or daughter "craving the world" shipped out. By 1917, rudimentary movie houses, and even a few fancy theaters, had opened for business in a growing number of Shore towns.

The waterfront village of Queenstown, Maryland, located about 10 miles from the eastern terminus of the Chesapeake Bay Bridge, was established on April 1, 1707. Originally known as Queen Anne's Towne to honor the reigning queen of England, Queenstown was the seat of Queen Anne's County government until those jurisdictional institutions were moved north to Centreville in 1782.

British troops attacked here in the War of 1812. In the 1800s, Queenstown was a Chesapeake Bay region steamboat and railroad hub, transporting both goods and passengers to and from the area. In the first decades of the twentieth century, the population of Queenstown proper stayed consistent around 275, give or take. Today, even with an expansion of construction and the ever-encroaching influence of the Baltimore-Washington metropolitan area, there are still fewer than 700 in-town residents. Queenstown was, and, according to its motto, still is "Parvus Urbs Ad Is Aqua" —the Little Town on the Water.

In 1917, the big-time came to this little town.

William Aloysius Brady (1863–1950) was a colorful and charismatic showman and boxing promotor with an only-in-America backstory and a reputation for flashy promotional skills. A high-stakes gambler in every regard, his great skill in life seemed to be earning and losing fortunes.

Brady's life story, what he called his "dim and spotty past," began "when the nineteenth century was still a going concern." He was kidnapped in San Francisco at the age of three by his father and brought to the gang-ridden and poverty-stricken Bowery neighborhood in New York City where Terence Brady, a freelance writer of ill temperament and bad habits, eked out the barest of existences. Raised on Shakespeare and near-starvation, young Brady found fleeting joy in the theater. Whenever he could scrape together the twenty cents for a seat in the Old Bowery Theater's nosebleed gallery, the designated section for the exuberant and sometimes violent hoi polloi, Brady had no doubts where his money would be spent.

As a teenager, after his father died falling under an El train, Brady headed west, where he hustled employment at every opportunity. He was particularly suited for work calling for "cockiness, a loud voice, presence of mind, and a sense of the dramatic." He stumbled into a theater gig, where he made himself useful by learning every job in the house, both onstage and behind the scenes. Later he admitted that his move into the upper levels of the entertainment industry "had a good deal to do with the old-time tradition of piracy and plagiarism," but in the end he produced more than 260 plays and 40 films. There had to be more substance to William A. Brady than his self-deprecation allowed.

In 1892, Brady hired boxer James J. Corbett for a role in *After Dark*, a play he'd bought the rights to from a man who didn't own them. Convinced he'd found a winner, despite never having managed a fighter and having attended only one boxing match in his entire life, Brady helped convince Boston's retired champion John L. Sullivan to get in the ring with his "Gentleman Jim." Corbett won with a knockout in the twenty-first round. Brady went on to become one of the most influential behind-the-scenes characters in modern professional boxing's early days.

A man of many talents, said by a contemporary to have "more charm than was right for any one man to have," Brady would be ringside at a boxing match in Coney Island one night and on Broadway opening a production of *King Lear* the next. He had money and prestige, and he knew how to get what he wanted.

In early 1917, what he wanted was a train wreck.

Brady owned the rights to *The Whip*, a horse-racing melodrama that featured the era's standard-issue, firm-jawed hero, damsel in distress, and devious, mustache-twirling bad guys. Originating in London as an elaborate and highly successful stage play, *The Whip* opened on Broadway in November 1912. Over that winter season, one of the show's audiences included a ten-year-old Tallulah Bankhead, who was celebrating the holidays with her sister and widowed father, Alabama politician and future Speaker of the House, William B. Bankhead. Little Miss Bankhead, of course, would grow up to be one of her generation's most heralded actresses and remains to this day an icon of flamboyant overindulgence. She also happens to be one of the Eastern Shore's eternal residents. Tallulah Bankhead is buried at St Paul's Cemetery in Kent County.

Of seeing that production of *The Whip*, she wrote in her 1952 autobiography:

> *The Whip* was a blood-and-thunder melodrama....It boiled with villainy and violence. Its plot embraced a twelve-horse race on a treadmill, a Hunt Breakfast embellished by fifteen dogs, an auto smashup, the Chambers of Horrors at Madame Tussaud's Waxworks, and a train wreck with a locomotive hissing steam. . . . It was a tremendous emotional dose for anyone as impressionable and as stage-struck as our heroine.
>
> The curtain hadn't been up five minutes before Sister and I were on the verge of hysterics. By the end of the first act both of us had wet our pants....At the final curtain, I was a wreck, frantic, red-eyed and disheveled....Nothing I had ever seen or heard or read had made such an impact on me.

The Whip's story centers on the villains' efforts to keep the equine title character—"as ugly as sin" with "a temper like the devil" —out of an important race. In one last-ditch effort, they sabotage an express train, causing it to smash into a boxcar they believe is transporting the horse. The train wreck was a sensational and central part of *The Whip*'s theatrical productions. It's a huge and expensive scene to produce on stage, and though Brady possessed the cinematic vision, even creative types as trailblazing as Maurice Tourneur (1876–1961), *The Whip*'s director—a pioneer of filmmaking techniques, style, and story—hadn't yet figured out how to feign all of what could be imagined.

To capture *The Whip*'s train-wreck sequence on film, Brady flexed his considerable capital, influence, and charm. He arranged for the use of an abandoned section of track that ran from the junction in Centreville to the Queenstown pier and belonged to the Maryland, Delaware, and Virginia Railroad. Then he purchased an out-of-commission steam engine and some other cars, including a couple of passenger coaches. According to a December 30, 1916, issue of the *Centreville Observer*, "rapid fire photography" would be used to make the upcoming crash sequence so realistic that movie audiences would believe "they are witnessing pictures of an actual running together of powerful trains."

Harry C. Rhodes (1914–2014), one of Queenstown's most distinguished born-and-raised residents and superintendent of Queen Anne's County schools from 1952 to 1967, included in his book, *Queenstown—The Social History of a Small American Town*, the following headlines from the January 6, 1917 issue of the *Centreville Observer*:

CAMERA BATTERY FILMS REALISTIC RAILROAD WRECK NEAR QUEENSTOWN
SPEEDING EXPRESS TRAINS CRASH INTO BOX CAR

William A. Brady, Millionaire Theatrical Magnate, Directs Collision Scene for "The Whip," Racing Melodrama to be Shown on Moving Picture Screens.

Large Crowd Sees First Filmdom Views Ever Taken on Eastern Shore.

Irving Cummings Plays Leading Part in Saving Horse

The newspaper reported that "under the personal direction of Wm. A Brady, a New York millionaire theatrical magnate and producer of photo-plays, the famous railroad wreck scene in *The*

Whip, a racing melodrama filmed by the Paragon Film Co. was taken Thursday afternoon at Queenstown" and that "under the dreary gloom of a leaden sky, the midnight scene of a thrilling incident" was recorded "by a battery of eight cameras."

More than 500 spectators showed up to watch the filming of the spectacular sequence that started with the train puffing down the track at about 35 miles an hour. G. E. Eckstrom, a "well-known engineer," leapt off after sounding "a long drawn whistle blast as the swan song of locomotive engine No. 4," which, upon collision with the obsolete rolling stock purchased for the sole purpose of maximum wreckage, performed acrobatics never before staged for the screen. Estimates of costs for the 100 feet of film shot that day range from $10,000 to $25,000, quite a considerable pile of dough back then for a minute or so of screen time.

As soon as the scene was in the can, the moviemakers hopped on a "special train driven by Engineer Winfield Roe" and "made a speedy nine minute run to Centreville," where they "caught the afternoon train to New York City."

Advertising for *The Whip* promised filmgoers: "Big race scenes, wonderful hunting scenes, the best train wreck and the most thrilling automobile accident ever seen in pictures . . . combined with a powerful and attention-riveting story, make this the world's biggest screen play." Seen through modern eyes, the film sags, but the action sequences are among the most exciting of the era, and cinephiles would be hard-pressed to find earlier examples of such tropes as a villain tampering with the hero's brakes or a car racing to catch up with a runaway train.

The stars of *The Whip*—Alma Hanlon, June Elvidge, and the horse-saving Irving Cummings—left behind diverse legacies.

Alma Hanlon (1890–1977) acted in twenty-three silent movies between 1915 and 1919, *The Whip* probably being the most noted, and then she retired. Her daughter from her first marriage, Dorothy Kingsley, grew up to be one of the screenwriters behind such Hollywood hits as *Seven Brides for Seven Brothers* (1954) and *Valley of the Dolls* (1967). June Elvidge, on the other hand, had seventy acting credits to her name from 1915 until she retired in 1924.

Irving Cummings, born in 1888, began his career on Broadway, was acting in short films as early as 1909, and appeared in movies with such stars as Buster Keaton and Roscoe "Fatty" Arbuckle. He showed up in 145 films from 1910 to 1927. After the advent of talkies, Cummings transitioned into directing and became known for helming Technicolor 20th Century Fox musicals with stars like Betty Grable and Carmen Miranda. He also directed Shirley Temple in four popular movies.

After producing *The Whip*, W. A. Brady continued to live a life straight out of the movies, winning and losing wealth in a cycle that would drive lesser humans cuckoo. As a symbol of his time, the brash Brady made millions in the stock market and was wiped out in the crash of 1929. Always in character, however, he rebounded almost immediately by scraping together enough money to buy a play that all his competitors had passed on. *Street Scene* ran 600 performances, won the Pulitzer Prize, and made Brady half a million bucks. The night Brady died, his wife of 51 years, the actress Grace George, left his bedside to perform in *The Velvet Glove* at the Booth Theater. Being a show-must-go-on kind of guy, everyone who knew him agreed: it's what Brady would've wanted.

The Whip premiered at the Centreville Opera House in September 1917. Its initial run was extended when hundreds of curious hometown moviegoers showed up to see the Eastern Shore's inaugural onscreen appearance.

Everyone has their favorite movies. Some people love lowbrow slapstick comedies, while others prefer exquisitely presented Oscar-bait tearjerkers. Action flicks might be their cup of high-octane tea, or maybe they prefer to shiver through horror movies, sing along with musicals, or swoon over iconic romances from yesteryear.

No matter what kind of movie fan a person might be, turns out there's one kind of movie almost everybody enjoys.

The kind filmed in their backyard.

ON LOCATION

Berlin is a red-brick charmer of a town that has played host to two major movies. Its name is believed to derive from the 19th century hostelry *Burleigh Inn*, not the capital of Germany. *(Author)*

BERLIN

It was the summer of 1999.

Back in February, President Bill Clinton had been acquitted in his impeachment trial. The Columbine High School massacre took place in April. John F. Kennedy Jr., his wife Carolyn Bessette-Kennedy, and her sister, Lauren, died in a plane crash off the coast of Martha's Vineyard on July 16. Nine days later, Lance Armstrong won his first Tour de France. The win would later be stripped away when he was disqualified for doping.

There were wars, acts of terrorism, and natural disasters.

Prince had been singing about a party-time apocalypse for years, but that didn't make folks any less Y2K-edgy. Boy bands ruled the music charts. Somehow, overalls held up by one strap, M. C. Hammer pants, and lots of flannel-on-flannel were in fashion. Reality television was beginning to take over what we still called the "airwaves." Jar Jar Binks and *Star Wars: Episode 1—The Phantom Menace* were disappointing movie fans worldwide.

While we all braced for what might come next, hoping for a bright spot, a little fun, and a little romance, a little town on Maryland's Eastern Shore that had been angling to remain relevant was now about to get famous.

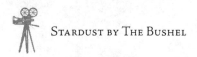

Berlin is in Worcester County. Fewer than ten miles west of the Ocean City Boardwalk, the village developed over the years around a 1677 land grant called Burley. Main Street was once part of a forest trail that linked the native tribes of the area. In the eighteenth century, that ancient pathway became part of the Philadelphia Post Road, connecting Eastern Shore colonists to the centers of commerce in the north and west. There was a crossroads tavern along about here called the Burleigh Inn. Shorefolk have a documented lackadaisical attitude toward spoken English, so it's been speculated that "Berlin" might have evolved from a habitual contraction of that establishment's name.

Incorporated in 1868, Berlin remained a crossroads of sorts for regional travelers, sporting visitors of the hunting and fishing type, and salesmen—"drummers" who used inns and boarding houses like the Atlantic Hotel (c. 1895) as home base while going out into the countryside to "drum up" business. In those days of steamships and railroads, such lodgings dotted the small-town landscape of the Eastern Shore. By the turn of the twentieth century, Berlin offered travelers more choice of accommodations than were available in Ocean City.

Prominent figures Berliners claim as their own include icon of the U.S. Navy Stephen Decatur (1779–1820) and the Reverend Charles Albert Tindley (1851–1933), the influential Methodist preacher and pioneering gospel music composer who wrote the hymn that inspired the civil rights anthem *We Shall Overcome*. Linda Melson Harrison, born in 1945, a member of two of Berlin's most prominent families, won teenage beauty contests before moving to California and making her mark playing the sexy primitive called Nova in 1968's original *Planet of the Apes* and the first sequel *Beneath the Planet of the Apes*, a role enshrining her in the hearts and minds of fantasy and sci-fi fans across the universe.

There's a headstone in Berlin's Saint Paul's Episcopal Church Cemetery with the name Indiana Jones on it. The deceased was a lady, and her married name was Henry, but still.

Man o' War (1917–1947), considered to be among the all-time champion racehorses, is also one of the town's favorite adopted sons. Foaled in Kentucky, Man o' War was sold to the textile manufacturer Samuel D. Riddle, who brought the horse to his farm near Berlin for training in 1918. Man o' War raced twenty-one times and lost only once—to a steed named "Upset." In 1920, the *New York Times* named Man o' War and Babe Ruth co-athletes of the year. He appeared in three films, two documentaries about horse racing, and once as a fifth-billed actor in the 1925 silent movie *Kentucky Pride,* directed by the legendary John Ford. In 1937, one of Man o' War's progeny, War Admiral (1934–1959), was the fourth-ever winner of the Triple Crown. A year later, War Admiral was the favored rival against his nephew in the sensational "Race of the Century" at Baltimore's Pimlico Racetrack, as portrayed in the *Seabiscuit* films of 1939 and 2003. The earliest version used newsreel footage of the actual race, so in that one, War Admiral appears as himself.

As Berlin thrived, its biggest industries were the Berlin Milling Company, Phillips Cannery, and Harrison Nurseries, publishers of a popular nursery and seed catalog. Harrison was a dominant force in US peach production and the biggest worldwide distributor of fruit trees and ornamental shrubbery. The Globe Theater, originally a horse-and-carriage garage, was converted and opened as a silent movie house in 1917. The Globe later made the conversion to sound and prospered for most of the next fifty years.

But times change. Ocean City was growing into a vacation destination. Modern highway bypasses were built. Homegrown businesses shut their doors, and in 1960 there was a peach blight that wiped out an industry that had provided hundreds of jobs. In the mid-1980s, a group of concerned citizens, politicians, and business leaders decided to stanch the town's decline and were making efforts to revitalize. By the late 1990s, Berlin was working its way out of a long slump, making strides toward a more prosperous future and looking for its moment to shine.

Julia Roberts was not in any kind of a slump whatsoever.

It took Roberts only two years—from her debut in 1988's *Satisfaction* to 1990's *Pretty Woman*—to become a top-tier, world-famous movie star. Since then, she'd delivered hit after hit with only the occasional box-office slipup, yet regardless of her leading man, she was never quite able to capture the screen chemistry she shared with her *Pretty Woman* co-star Richard Gere. Gere had clicked with audiences in 1980 and 1982 with *American Gigolo* and *An Officer and a Gentleman*, but when *Pretty Woman* came along his career needed a winner. Teaming up with Roberts in her breakout role was just what the success doctor had ordered. Nine years later, another victory couldn't hurt. Once both stars were onboard, *Pretty Woman* director Garry Marshall (*Beaches, The Princess Diaries*) signed on to helm their second rom-com collaboration.

Then, as now, the Maryland Film Office's goal, under the longtime leadership of its director Jack Gerbes, is to "attract film and TV production to the state, so Marylanders can benefit from the immediate positive economic impact of the production, as well as the long term positive impact from tourism and good public relations." In service to their mission, the film office is the first point of contact for studios and independents looking to shoot on location. Filmmakers describe what they're looking for with regard to locales, landscape, and architecture. The film office then identifies locations that may suit. A scout takes inventory and photos of potential sites. Once it's decided to film in an area, the local tourism offices and the film office help studios get permission to use private properties or public spaces and help with accommodations and support services.

When it was decided by the powers-that-be that Berlin would be perfect to portray the quaint and quirky fictional hometown of Maggie Carpenter, Julia Roberts's runaway bride of the title, a deal-clincher was that the town in the movie would be called Hale—after Hale Harrison, one of Berlin's most prominent native sons and owner of much of the real estate that would be in the picture once cameras started rolling in late October 1998.

Taking on a role like any actor would, Berlin, now Hale, was subjected to costuming and makeup. Old storefronts, some vacant, were temporarily converted into such locations as the Carpenter family hardware store, the Hale newspaper offices, and the beauty salon, Curl Up and Dye. Debbie Parker's Victorian Charm gift shop was turned into a dress store for one important scene.

The house where Maggie lived with her widowed father (Paul Dooley) is still a private family home. Some interior features were changed to accommodate the actors and camera crews. Scenes shot inside include Gere's Ike Graham ambushing Maggie with a visit, a confrontation Maggie has with her dad, and one of Maggie's unconsummated weddings, the one with the Grateful Dead fan. There's also a scene filmed here where Roberts, movie star gorgeous, runs outside and sits on the porch to read a newspaper.

Though preparation took weeks, the stars of the production were in town for just five days. Gere kept a low profile, but Roberts, warm and down-to-earth, seemed to have charmed everyone she met. She'd ride her bike through town and when she visited the bazaar at Buckingham Presbyterian Church, she "bought everything those ladies had made." The studio celebrated Roberts's birthday one night after filming, and she gave roses to all the little girls who were on set.

A gifted artist, Patrick Henry owns Henry Fine Arts in Berlin and he's Eastern Shore–hospitable in an easygoing manner that reflects his nature and upbringing. He grew up in these parts and has watched his surroundings change dramatically through the years. Prior to the start of filming, the late Rex Hailey, Berlin's mayor at the time, called Henry to discuss purchasing four framed prints to present as gifts to Roberts, Gere, Marshall, and the town of Berlin. Henry agreed, but he had a lot going on, so what he did was add remarques, new hand-painted art to his existing prints of soon-to be iconic Hale landmarks: the Falcon Diner (now Rayne's Reef), the dress shop (Victorian Charm), the Atlantic Hotel, and the house on Baker Street where the Carpenters lived. Then Henry got a second phone call.

"I was busy working on an exhibition," Henry says, "when Mayor Hailey called. He told me that everyone was ready for the presentation of the framed prints I'd prepared, and that he wanted me to do the presenting. I was in work clothes. I called my wife and said Velda, I need you to come uptown because they want me to present the prints."

When Henry got to the shooting location, the dress shop, "they were all in there filming. A big crowd was forming and here comes my wife being led by a police officer, with my daughter Stephanie tagging along. Velda's eyes were all big, like what have you gotten me into. They, the actors and Garry Marshall, came outside. I came up from [the] other side of Mr. Marshall and found myself this close to Julia Roberts. She looked like an angel. She turned around and said, 'Oh, I never met you before. What's your name?' And I said, 'Puh...puh...puh.' That wasn't like me. I'm not really a stargazer and until that moment I was cool as a cucumber. But I wasn't

20

prepared for her to just speak to me like that. Richard Gere came over and he's this handsome guy, a real movie star. And he said, 'Hello, what's going on over here?' I told him about the paintings, explained the remarques. Now, they had just gotten done doing their thing after what was probably a long day. They could have easily been standoffish, but they weren't."

The positive good vibes and front page publicity Berlin reaped from *Runaway Bride* were immediate, immense, and long-lasting, and though the film is still the best-known local production, it wasn't the town's last encounter with Hollywood filmmaking. After *Runaway Bride*, Berlin changed its name again, this time to Treegap, for Disney's 2002 fantasy romance *Tuck Everlasting*, a remake of an under-the-radar 1981 movie based on an acclaimed novel by author Natalie Babbitt (1932–2016).

Endearing but nowhere near as successful as *Runaway Bride*, *Tuck Everlasting*, directed by Jay Russell, featured *Gilmore Girls* star Alex Bledel in her first movie. It takes place in 1914, and Bledel plays the rebellious upper-class Winifred (Winnie) Foster, who falls in love with an immortal teenager named Jesse Tuck, played by Jonathan Jackson. Jackson was cast at the last minute after Jared Padalecki, Bledel's love interest in *Gilmore Girls*, bowed out of the role. Others in the cast include three Academy Award–winning actors: Ben Kingsley as The Man in the Yellow Suit, William Hurt as Angus Tuck, and Sissy Spacek as May Tuck.

To transform Berlin into early-twentieth-century Treegap for the four-day shoot, producers removed all modern fences, sidewalks, and electric lines that might show on film, and dumped tons of dirt on the streets to accommodate old-time carriages and horse and buggy rigs. A wide shot of the town kicks the movie off, and for a few seconds Berlin goes back in time. There are a few other glimpses of the town in its early days, including a stickball

21

scene, and toward the end, there's a contrasting bookend shot of modern Berlin that's an effective storytelling device.

The mountainous rural sequences where most of the film takes place, however, are in reality far and away from any Eastern Shore locale. In fact, the film was made almost entirely in other parts of Maryland, with scenes shot in Havre de Grace, White Hall, Bel Air, and the Fair Hill Natural Resource Area in Cecil County. For outside shots of the Tuck family cabin, an exterior façade was constructed near Baltimore's Loch Raven Reservoir.

Today Berlin is an Eastern Shore success story. Captivated visitors amble down tree-lined streets populated with eateries of every type, art galleries, unique shops and antique stores, and such landmarks as the restored Atlantic Hotel, and the Globe, now a popular restaurant and music venue. There are forty-seven structures here on the National Register of Historic Places, including those located in the downtown commercial district. In 2019, Berlin celebrated the twentieth anniversary of *Runaway Bride* with guided walking tours and a town-movie night featuring toasts and a wedding cake.

At a mid-shoot meet-and-greet held at Berlin's Globe Theater on November 1, 1998, Garry Marshall told attendees about the reasons he chose their town—the mix of the old and new, the layout of the streets, the fact that there were so many businesses in close proximity that could be adapted to fit the needs of the story they wanted to tell. He chatted with guests, took photographs with them, and signed copies of his recently published memoir. What most endeared him to his audience were perhaps his final words to the gathering that evening.

"Good night folks," said the affable and famous out-of-towner, "and may the good Lord bless you enough to live in a small town. That," he concluded, "is my salute to Berlin."

After all these years, there's still something special between Berlin and *Runaway Bride*.

They make a wonderful couple.

THE STARS

Robert and Dorothy Mitchum met as teenagers in Delaware and married in their early twenties. At the height of Mitchum's renown as a leading man in Hollywood, he frequently retreated to a secluded horse farm near Trappe, Maryland, where he and Dorothy raised their family in the 1960s. (*Zuma Press Inc./Alamy Stock Photo*)

ROBERT MITCHUM

"Simply by being there, Mitchum can make almost any other actor look like a hole in the screen."

— *David Lean, director*

Cape Fear. The Longest Day. El Dorado. The Sundowners. The Grass Is Greener. Home from the Hill. Two for the Seesaw. These are just some of the movies that Robert Mitchum, the screen's foremost symbol of macho post–World War II antiauthoritarian disillusionment, made between 1960 and 1966.

It was also during those years that he and his family called the Eastern Shore home. Why here? "Maryland isn't that remote," Mitchum explained to Baltimore's *Evening Sun* newspaper, "I can fly anywhere in no time at all. But when I'm there it's like being in a different world. My unsocial nature is well known. In Maryland I can be as unsocial as I want and nobody gives a damn."

Robert Mitchum's life got off to a rough start. He was born in 1917, and before he was two years old his father James was killed in a railyard accident. His widowed mom struggled to provide for their three kids—firstborn Annette, Robert, and the infant John, born after James's death. Robert and John eventually ended up on their maternal grandparents' farm near Felton, Delaware. Robert later told the *Saturday Evening Post* that back then the locals thought he was "some kind of degenerate. They ran me out of town so many times," he said, "it finally took."

Ann (Gunderson) Mitchum's second husband was a World War I veteran named Major Hugh Cunningham Morris. After they were married, the whole family moved to New York City, where Robert attended Haaren High School in Midtown Manhattan's infamous Hell's Kitchen. Always the brightest student in school, he was also the most consistent troublemaker. Robert was impossible to discipline, and though he wasn't a big or strong kid, his favorite pastime seemed to be getting into fights. He also wrote poetry. Those who would know Mitchum the man would come to understand that his lifelong antagonistic behavior was often protective, a type of camouflage that shielded his literary and artistic leanings.

While in New York he befriended an orphan named Manuel Barque. The two outsiders ran away and got as far as New Haven, Connecticut, before getting caught. It would be Robert's first real run-in with the law. It wouldn't be his last.

The Great Depression now entrenched, Robert and his brother were sent back to the family farm in Delaware, where he completed his high school curriculum at the age of fourteen. He was voted valedictorian, but split town before graduation. He spent the next few years hopping freight trains across America, finding work where he could, "rolling drunks," and living the life of a boy hobo.

Arrested in Savannah, Georgia, for vagrancy, he was sentenced to a chain gang for 180 days. He escaped after serving "maybe as much as 30" and hitchhiked to Baltimore.

He met Dorothy Spence when he returned to Delaware for a visit. Tall, good-looking, and popular, Dorothy was dating his brother, but from the moment they were introduced both she and Robert knew, as Dorothy put it, "That was all she wrote."

"I was 16 years old when I met her," Robert said in an interview. "She was 14. I met her in Camden, Delaware, on a blind date in the back of a model A Ford. . . . I kept coming back. . . . Every time I came back, they'd button up the town. They'd say, 'God, here it comes again.'"

The two of them would sit together on the lawn of Caesar Rodney High School. It was scandalous. She'd been May Queen. He was a "bum." Dorothy told *People* magazine in 1983 that everybody was against her and Robert being a couple. "The principal of my school gave me a lecture about not seeing him."

"I had to wrestle half the school for her," her husband added.

Robert then hit the road again, making his first cross-country train hop to visit his sister. Annette had changed her name to Julie and moved to California to become an actress. Attached to the Long Beach Players Guild, Julie helped Robert find work there, mostly as a stagehand. He wrote songs and poems, and after some coercing from Julie, occasionally had an opportunity to perform in small roles onstage.

In early 1940, he went back to Delaware to get Dorothy.

"I won $2,300 (in a Penny Fair at the 4H Club). I got on a Greyhound bus in an ice cream suit and a Panama hat, and I fell on my nose in Philadelphia in four feet of snow, stoned. Lived in a girl's dormitory where my wife was staying. She was working for the Penn Mutual Life Insurance Company and she quit her job. And I blew the whole stash on her friends. We went down to Delaware and I borrowed $54 from the guy and we got married ... Ignatius Cooper, justice of the peace—at large or something like that— esquire. Licenses, dogs, hunting, marriage: $2."

And so it was, in Dover, Delaware, on March 16, 1940, Robert Mitchum and Dorothy Spence, he twenty-two, she two months shy of her twenty-first birthday, got married in an officer of the court's kitchen "with the odor of burnt cabbage" wafting in the air. Afterward, the newlyweds loaded up and moved to California. Robert had twenty-six bucks to his name with "no job or prospects for one."

The daily grind didn't get off to a good start. He clarified for interviewer David Frost: "My wife was pregnant and I needed $500 ... I was working at Lockheed gluing airplanes together inexpertly.... Finally, one night I threw a clamp across the room and hit the foreman on the head.... In a sort of fit of embarrassed desperation, I became a movie actress."

In a suit he borrowed from a working actor, Mitchum went to see the producer Harry "Pop" Sherman, whose claim to fame was producing the Hopalong Cassidy cowboy pictures starring William Boyd. By the time Mitchum met the two men, they'd already made almost fifty movies together in eight years. Mitchum said they looked him over, along with Pop's assistant, Dick Dickson, and concluded, "Yeah, he looks a little crafty around the eyes. Yeah, he looks a little ugly, a little mean.... They said, don't shave and don't cut your hair until you hear from us. So, I went out and got $100 a week and all the horse manure I could carry home. And I got thrown off every horse—I mean, flat, bam, gone.... A lot of beard, very little dialogue ... June 1942 ... I just never looked back."

Robert Mitchum made his onscreen debut in 1943's *Hoppy Serves a Writ*. Besides his look and his now-sturdy build, one of his main qualifications for getting gigs was his ability to take a fall. He shot nineteen other films that first year in the business, including a supporting role in a Laurel and Hardy feature called *The Dancing Masters* in which he played a gangster. It's the first time audiences would see him wearing the trench coat and fedora that later became part of his noir trademarks. "I got the work because I was good at it. I was reliable," he said about those early days. "Whenever I wasn't doing anything else, I could always do a Hopalong Cassidy."

The next year he appeared in *Thirty Seconds over Tokyo*, starring Spencer Tracy, a groundbreaking action film about the Doolittle Raid, the first American airstrike on Japan after Pearl Harbor. *Tokyo's* director, Mervyn LeRoy (*Little Caesar, Mister Roberts, Gypsy*), was impressed by the young actor and Mitchum was signed to a standard seven-year contract with RKO Pictures, one of the Golden Age of Hollywood's Big Five studios. Mitchum's first starring performance was in the title role of the 1944 western *Nevada* and in 1945 he was cast in *Story of G.I. Joe*. His portrayal of the honorable, no-nonsense platoon leader Lt. Bill Walker earned him a Best Supporting Actor Oscar nomination, and his career took off. He branched out from horse operas and war flicks, appeared in several iconic film noir roles, and smoothly stepped into the shoes of the romantic leading man.

His world-weary, sleepy-eyed, seen-it-all-before swagger, brooding volatility, and unpretentious two-fisted image proved to be attractive to audiences. He was "a man's man and a woman's man at the same time," wrote critic Carrie Rickey. By the 1950s, Mitchum was a heavy-duty star. Even a brief stint in the Los Angeles County Jail on a marijuana charge couldn't take the air out of his popularity. In fact, it cemented his "bad-boy" standing with his fans. Years later, David Frost asked, "Did that affect your career when you came out?" "Oh, enormously, yeah," Mitchum replied. "I got out and went back to work. . . . The only thing is, I had to resign from the local scout troop."

With his cultivated nonchalance, Mitchum downplayed both his status as an actor—"One of the greatest movie stars was Rin Tin Tin—it can't be too much of a trick"—as well as his talents. "Listen," he said of his unclenched acting style, "I've got three expressions: looking left, looking right, and looking straight ahead."

Even if that were true, and it's not, Mitchum must have had something going for him. As an actor, he has 133 acting credits to his name, more than fifty of them in his first decade alone. Highlights of his career, pre-Eastern Shore, include classics like 1947's *Out of the Past* (considered by many as one of the greatest noir films ever made), 1955's *Night of the Hunter* (number thirty-four on the American Film Institute's greatest thrillers) and 1958's *Thunder Road*, the archetype for all the car-chase movies that followed. Mitchum was a *Thunder Road* coproducer and the screenplay was based on his original story idea. He also sang the hit title song. It wasn't his first musical success, either; a year earlier, he'd released an album called *Calypso—Is Like So . . .*

Robert and Dorothy Mitchum had three children, James (1941–), Christopher (1943–) and Petrine Day (1952–), named after her maternal grandmother. Forever a man of contradictions, "a sophisticate and primitive," Mitchum praised his wife in public, while perpetuating his notoriety as a womanizer. He was rumored to have had an affair with almost every leading lady he ever worked with. Tinseltown celebrities he was romantically linked to include Marilyn Monroe, Shirley MacLaine, and Lucille Ball.

Perhaps to curb her husband's access to female company, or as the *Post* article put it, "the frenetic over-stimulation of Hollywood," Dorothy instigated the family's move to a more detached environment.

They ended up on the Eastern Shore.

"I asked this real estater what the natives did in these parts," Mitchum told his biographer, Lee Server. "He said, 'We don't do nothing but go crabbing and drink.' I knew he was telling the truth because right after he said that he fell on his ear. Man, he was stoned. I said, 'This is it! We'll dig in here!'"

Where they dug in was Belmont Farm (c. 1845) in Trappe, a secluded estate located on 280 acres of fields, woods, and prime Choptank River waterfront with a protected cove on Bolingbroke Creek. The house is a stately two-and-a-half story Georgian-style construction with additions on the wings, a widow's walk cupola, and views galore. Today's tax records indicate a living space of 6,256 square feet. Elegant but comfortable, the property sold for $140,000. After the Mitchums moved back to California, subsequent owners subdivided sections of the farm. Now a carved-down twenty-nine-acre parcel with a 900-foot shoreline, Belmont Farm, having undergone significant upgrades and modernizations in recent years, sold in 2017 for a little more than two million dollars.

Throughout its history of titleholders, Belmont has been well cared for, so there wasn't much renovating or repairs required of the Mitchums when they moved in. They did, however, remodel the kitchen and install high-quality cabinetry in several rooms, jobs Robert and Dorothy oversaw themselves. In 1992, Belmont was part of the Annual Maryland House and Garden Tour. Owners Boulton and Lois Irvin told the Easton *Star Democrat* that when they did some updating to one of the rooms, they found Mitchum's name written on a few of the boards of the cabinets.

When the Mitchums hit the Shore, the natives were delighted and for the most part banded together to protect the privacy of their new neighbors the best they could. With a well-publicized preference for hanging out with the crews and misfits working on his movies rather than other stars, Robert Mitchum garnered a local reputation for being both a down-to-earth, hard-working, tractor-driving, hay-baling family man who loved animals and a good-timing, hard-drinking roughneck with a temper.

"In Maryland," he said, "I'm not an actor. I'm just another farmer. I like it that way." In 1961, he remarked to gossip queen Hedda Hopper that "the farm is 12 miles by land and five minutes by water from Easton in Talbot County . . . where the only topics for discussion are hunting, fishing and drinking."

No wonder he fit in around here.

For seven years, the Mitchums lived a generally quiet life on the Eastern Shore, while "Mitch" made a few of his most noteworthy films, including, in 1962, his biggest commercial hit, the star-studded D-Day epic *The Longest Day* and the once-derided, now-classic *Cape Fear*, in which he played the very bad bad-guy Max Cady. *The List of Adrian Messenger* came out in 1963. The mystery thriller teamed up Mitch with Tony Curtis, Burt Lancaster, and his *Out of the Past* co-star Kirk Douglas. In 1967, he released two westerns shot toward the end of his Talbot County residency: *The Way West*, again with Douglas, and *El Dorado*, a John Wayne western where Mitchum displayed some of his best comic work. He insisted that out of all his movies, 1961's army comedy bomb *The Last Time I Saw Archie* was his favorite. "I got paid a hundred grand a week, the first time that ever happened, and I went home Christmas and New Year's. So, I couldn't give less of a fuck who saw it. It's my fay-vo-rite."

Petrine Mitchum was eight years old when the family moved to Belmont. James, eleven years older, stayed in L.A. and came to visit on holidays. Chris went to boarding school and college and stayed on the farm during the summer until he married in 1964.

Petrine attended Country Day School in Easton. She still stays in touch with some of her classmates from those days.

"I was virtually an only child when we lived on the Eastern Shore," Petrine recalled in 2019. "I had no idea of how famous my father was and that's part of why my parents moved to Maryland, to shield me from Hollywood. We loved water sports—my dad loved boating; Chris loved skiing. My fondest memories of Belmont are riding my horse through the woods and along the dirt road from Chancellor Point to the next road over—it was a long sandy road through the forest which we could gallop! I also loved swimming with my horses in the creek. It was so wonderful living right on the waterfront and being able to go crabbing off the pier. It was total freedom in nature. It was a glorious place to be a kid."

While the Belmont years were, by most standards, tranquil, Mitchum was still Mitchum. When asked about celebrity-seeking rubberneckers who dared invade his Eastern Shore privacy, Mitchum quipped to the *Evening Sun* that he didn't mind visitors, "But my children shoot at them." In a 2015 *Star Democrat* newspaper article, Ken Tighe, the seller in the property's most recent transaction, confided, "I heard some wild stories. There's a big crack in the front gate. I heard he and Yul Brynner had bought matching Aston Martin "Goldfinger" cars and were racing them down Chancellor Point Road and Yul didn't quite make it."

It comes as no surprise that a movie star might know how to make a lasting impression. Restaurant sightings of Mitchum occurred everywhere from Kent Island to Ocean City. The people involved never forgot their brush with fame. People tell stories of literally running into him at Easton Hospital, in grocery stores, and on street corners. Some of Mitchum's most legendary local antics occurred at Easton's Tidewater Inn, and they all involve alcohol.

Connie Schutz was twelve and living on the Dupont Estate at Horn's Point in Cambridge, where her father, Philip L. Ozman, worked. The Mitchums "drove up to our house to ask directions to our neighbor's house who had a horse for sale. It was very exciting as our parents had just taken us to the Super 50 Drive-in in Trappe to see *Thunder Road* so we recognized him right away!" Later her dad and the movie star would bond over many late-night conversations at the nearby country club, where Ozman moonlighted as, of course, a bartender.

The reactions Mitchum got in public, especially from women, were notable. His wife said that they'd knock her over to get next to him. Eastern Shore ladies were not immune to his charismatic presence. Sharon Clevenger Cropper remembers the time her mom Betty was backing out of a parking space in Easton when she saw Mitchum cross behind her. "She stopped to let him go by and he touched the trunk of the car. He waved and went on past. Mom was thrilled. I thought she never would wash that car."

Among the best of friends the Mitchums made on the Shore were William "Bill" and Betty Clay McAllister. They met at the Cambridge Yacht Club where Bill, a board member and artist, was painting a mural for the bar. "They told me I could drink for free while I was working on it, so I was in no hurry to finish." The two couples became close, and since Bill's job with Western Publishing Company required a lot of travel, the McAllisters and Mitchums would meet up at various places around the globe.

"It was always fun to hang out with Bob and Dorothy," Bill said in an interview a few months before he died in December 2020. "Dorothy was delightful, she and my wife were friends, and she was a good influence on her husband. She could put the brakes on him when he needed it. Because he was so famous, he attracted people everywhere he went, they clamored around him all the time.

Women in particular were always looking to get close to him. He'd grin and enjoy it most of the time. He had the capabilities to create a situation, particularly if someone were pestering. He could shut that down with a word or two, sometimes just a look. Bob could turn his tough guy image on and off.

"He was smart, but didn't always act smart, he was a movie star but didn't act how you think one would act like. He was fun and funny, very intelligent, and well read. He had a great memory. He could read a script in the morning and know it in the afternoon. Not all movie stars are good actors, but Bob was. He didn't take anybody too seriously including himself."

For the McAllister family, one of the best memories from the Mitchum years was when Bob went off to do a movie and left Bill the keys to that Aston Martin DB5, the sportscar James Bond made famous, the one he'd raced against Yul Brenner. "Our street—Willis Street—was not exactly an exclusive part of town," Bill pointed out. "That car was the talk of the neighborhood."

Despite Mitchum's recorded proclamation that "if I could outlast some of the movies I've made, the rest is easy, that's for sure. . . . [The Maryland farm] is where I'll finally sit on the porch with a shotgun across my knee and aim at anything that looks like it's going to make me work," it was not meant to be.

In 1966 and 1967, at the request of the State Department and carrying the honorary rank of colonel, Mitchum participated in 152 morale-boosting missions to Vietnam as an observer, where he surprised troops by hopping out of a helicopter and spending hours hanging out with frontline soldiers. Upon returning to the States, the celebrated actor made hundreds of phone calls contacting the loved ones of the men and women he met who were serving in Southeast Asia. He was quoted as saying he'd believed "there were no heroes left" until he visited Vietnam.

Perhaps due to the expense and rigors of running the farm, where the Mitchums raised prizewinning quarter horses, or perhaps because no relocation could slow down the actor's aggressive wanderlust, Dorothy Mitchum hung a "For Sale" sign on Belmont and headed back west. Her husband always regretted the move.

"I'd come back from Vietnam and I called my old lady and she told me she'd sold the farm," he complained to the press, but Petrine clarifies: "My dad loved the privacy and peace of the farm. It was his sanctuary. Mother felt at home, having been raised in Delaware. Dad thought his career was winding down, but he made many movies in those years, many overseas. Mom grew weary of being on her own so much with so much to look after. It was not a happy time."

"Well, I had a farm in Maryland," Mitchum would say about the family's return to the West Coast, "and if you have a farm you should have a horse. Right? So I bought a horse. Before I knew it, I had twenty-two horses and was in business. Then I sold the farm and moved back to California, so what was I going to do with the horses? Get them rooms in the Beverly Hills Hotel? So I had to buy a ranch up near San Francisco to house them."

After going back to Cali, Mitchum appeared on TV and in more than two dozen theatrical releases. He revisited his noir roots in *Farewell My Lovely* (1975) and *The Big Sleep* (1978), playing Raymond Chandler's hard-boiled private eye Philip Marlowe in both. In 1983, he was on the cover of *Time* magazine for his starring role as Commander Victor "Pug" Henry in the ABC miniseries *The Winds of War*. In 1984, he was awarded his star on the Hollywood Walk of Fame. As he aged, society's sensitivities changed, and Mitchum was having none of that. He said what was on his mind, even if he picked the wrong side of an argument just to keep it going. Controversy inevitably followed.

In 1988, Mitchum showed up as the network boss, Preston Rhinelander, in Bill Murray's *Scrooged,* and in Martin Scorsese's 1991 *Cape Fear* remake. He and original costar Gregory Peck flipped character types with Mitchum as a cop and Peck playing Max Cady's shady lawyer. He was the offscreen narrator in 1993's *Tombstone.* His last major Hollywood film was Jim Jarmusch's trippy 1995 revisionist western *Dead Man,* starring Johnny Depp.

Mitchum came back to Maryland in 1987 while filming the *Winds* sequel *War and Remembrance* at the Naval Academy in Annapolis, but there's not much evidence he returned to the Shore with any regularity. Nevertheless, sometime in the late seventies, Bill McAllister's son Sandy was working the dock at the Cambridge Yacht Club when who pulled up in the parking lot but Robert and Dorothy Mitchum. "I'll never forget he was wearing a red scarf and a crisp white shirt looking every bit the movie star. He was always very kind to me. Once, because my father told him I liked them, he sent a huge box of undyed pistachios to me at boarding school with a note saying, "Tell everybody in the dorm to eat their fucking hearts out," but this day they seemed a little melancholy. He said, "This is probably the last time we'll see you." I'm sure they had many places in the world that were important to them, but watching the sun go down over the Choptank for what feels like the last time would make anyone a little sad."

Mitchum and Dorothy stayed together until he passed away from complications of lung cancer and emphysema in 1997 at the age of seventy-nine. "Sure, there were rough times," Dorothy conceded to *People* magazine. "But what people overlook is that Bob is a very family-oriented person. Whatever he does, he always comes back to the family." For his part, Robert would explain the relationship between himself and his wife by asserting, "We continued to believe that the other will do better tomorrow."

Dorothy died in 2014 at the age of ninety-four, just short of her birthday. She was known to be steadfast, smart, and funny. She loved not only her husband but "words, roses, and animals—especially dogs." As a storyteller she could go toe-to-toe with her husband, and she would pop his bubble of self-grandeur as she deemed necessary. She was generous. Her obituary asked mourners to donate to any charity that helped animals or "the Salvation Army, who kept Robert alive during his early vagabond years." As her husband's had been, Dorothy's ashes were given to the sea. Years before, she and Robert had made an after-death pact to meet up at Easter Island.

Ever quotable, Mitchum often remarked on how lucky he was, even if he downplayed stardom with such lines as "Fame is like being a talking bar of soap" and compared being a "personage of the cinema" to being "trampled to death by geese." In a 1983 *Rolling Stone* profile, he acknowledged that he "got a great life out of the movies. I've been all over the world and met the most fantastic people. I don't really deserve all I've gotten. It's a privileged life, and I know it."

He also once confessed, "What counts is peace of mind and laughter—especially laughter. I am more than a happy man—I am delighted and astonished at the way things have gone. I don't regret a damn thing. If I had more comfortable shoes on, I'd jump up and down. Had I known acting is as easy as it is, I'd have started sooner."

Regarding the outrageous stories that propagated his public image, his response was always thus: "They're all true—booze, brawls, broads, all true. Make up some more if you want to."

And if that ain't an Eastern Shore answer, then I don't know what would be.

Born and raised in Berlin, Maryland, Linda Harrison landed one of the most iconic movie roles of the 1960s, in *Planet of the Apes*, and married one of Hollywood's most powerful studio heads. (*20ᵗʰ Century Fox/Photofest*)

LINDA
HARRISON

"She could have been the biggest pain in the ass alive . . . but [she was] the most pleasant, most charming, very cooperative, very hard-working . . . A total joy."
—Mort Abrahams, movie producer

Spoiler alert.

It's one of the great endings in movie history.

The camera pans over a body of water. There's a long shot of a man and woman riding a horse on a beach. They approach a colossal structure more than half-buried in the surf, but despite hints, nothing yet identifies this monolith to the audience. The camera's focus zooms in on the bearded, shirtless George Taylor, the marooned astronaut holding the reins. Taylor pauses then moves their steed forward with more purpose. The camera pulls back and the first massive spike comes into view. As the top of the structure begins to dominate the screen, a second spike appears, a third. Taylor, now dismounted, gazes skyward with an increasingly horrific understanding.

"Oh my God," he says. "I'm back. I'm back home." He looks down, aghast and in medium closeup, as he realizes the implications of his discovery. "All this time," he says. He drops to his knees. "We finally did it." He pounds his fist into the sand. "God. Damn. You," he bellows. "God damn you all to hell!" The beautiful but primitive young woman with him doesn't understand at all. There's a quick cut to a panoramic shot from the rear. And then we see it, what remains of the Statue of Liberty, among earth's most recognizable monuments to human freedom, long lost to what we're left to imagine was the ultimate act of a callous civilization, the cataclysmic self-destruction of our very own human race.

The movie is, of course, the original *Planet of the Apes*.

Released in 1968, Taylor was played by Charlton Heston, heretofore most famous for portraying epic Judeo-Christian heroes like Moses, Ben Hur, El Cid, and John the Baptist. Appearing here as the lone human male, a futuristic Adam, one could say that from a casting perspective, Taylor was in Heston's wheelhouse.

The female character in this classic scene, Eve, if you will, is called Nova, and Nova is played by Linda Harrison, whose journey to the *Planet of the Apes*, and beyond, began on the Eastern Shore. "All my life I've always been open to the universe of possibilities," she will tell you with just a hint of an oceanside accent. "Things can happen if you let them."

Linda Melson Harrison was born in her family home in Berlin, Maryland—"population two thousand"—on July 26, 1945. Weighing in at almost ten pounds, with dark curly hair, Linda would be the middle daughter of five sisters—Kay, Gloria, Linda, and twins Jane and Joan—born to Mr. Isaac Burbage Harrison (1907–1989), a nurseryman who "knew everything about every plant" and Mrs. Ida Virginia Melson Harrison (1914–2010), a beautician.

Both sides of the family had long been connected to the Delmarva Peninsula, and by the early twentieth century, the Harrisons were counted among the region's most prominent lineages. Linda's grandfather, Joseph, along with his brother Orlando, co-owned J. G. Harrison and Sons Nurseries, publishers of an immensely popular nursery catalog, and the largest grower of fruit and shade trees in the world. Operating from Berlin, Harrison Nurseries employed more than 500 local workers and were known to pay the highest wages around. Orlando Harrison was mayor of Berlin for nine years and served in the Maryland state senate. Changing times, however, along with a catastrophic peach blight, ended the company's decades-long economic viability. Family members branched out in a number of directions. Many found success in the region's blossoming hospitality field.

Harrison recalls her Eastern Shore youth with nostalgic warmth: "It was wonderful," she said in one of several 2020 phone calls from L.A. back to the Shore. "Our parents were home with us almost every night. They were devoted to us. I would go to other people's houses and see their parents, and I'd like them okay, but I would always say I liked my parents best."

The family home sat back off the street on four fun-filled acres and was shared with cousins. Burbage and Ida and the girls lived on one side, Aunt Kathrine "Katty" Harrison Davis and her children on the other. A dozen or more for dinner was the norm. "We had a big extended family," Harrison says. "There was always so much going on. After the twins were born, and mother and daddy were busy with them, Aunt Katty kind of looked after me."

She and her sisters rarely, if ever, argued. "That's hard to do with a house full of girls, but our parents wouldn't tolerate it." Linda was also close with her cousin, Helen, daughter of G. Hale and Lois Harrison. "Helen was Great-Uncle Orlando's grand-daughter, born four days after me. She lived in the home where Senator Orlando had lived; where they'd hosted wonderful parties back in the early 1900s. Helen and I were together all the time."

She remembered Berlin as a small but busy place, where nobody locked doors and everything a kid might need was within walking distance. Growing into teenagers, the Harrison sisters and their cousins "took over" Stephen Decatur High School. "I guess the Seahawks had a wild reputation in those days, and there were so many of us Harrisons and Melsons, we just usually found ourselves in the middle of things."

In the early sixties, Ocean City was growing into the mega-resort destination it would become. Linda and Helen would walk the boardwalk and flirt with lifeguards. Linda waited tables at Phillips Crab House but "never listened to what the customers ordered." Management moved her to the hostess station, but she couldn't deal with so many "crazy-sounding" last names, so she asked for first names only. Rebellious by nature, she and her cousin would test curfews and speed limits while visiting boyfriends attending the University of Delaware.

Harrison wasn't a great student. She didn't like to get up early, and she could not wrap her head around the need for such arcane disciplines as algebra and chemistry. Plus, by then, she'd decided she was going to be an actress anyway. On occasion, instead of hanging out with her pack, "I used to sit in front of the mirror and pretend I was doing a commercial."

Berlin's Globe was "the" movie theater in young Harrison's life. Though not a film buff, she saw *Gone with the Wind* at the Globe eight times. Sometimes her Uncle Hale, Helen's father, would pile all the kids into his car and take them to the movies. The rides were often more memorable than the movies they saw. Later, when she was eighteen, living with her sister Kay and trying to make it as a model in New York City, she saw *Cleopatra* starring Elizabeth Taylor and thought, "I really could do that. I'll never forget that moment, because as soon as I had that thought, I spilled my popcorn all over the place."

Returning to the Eastern Shore, "I had a lot of opportunities, a lot of marriage proposals even, but I knew I had to be an actress. I wasn't meant to stay in Berlin. Even my high school yearbook predicted Hollywood would be my fate."

How that prophecy came true was part of a plan.

Sort of.

Harrison had been taking ballet, tap, and acrobatics since she was five years old. She trained three days a week at five dollars a session. "We weren't rich like everybody thought. We were basically farmers, we had land, but sometimes we'd have a good crop, sometimes not. Aunt Katty would put five dollars on her desk to pay for my lessons. I was a natural acrobat. I excelled. Never missed a trick at recitals—I did cartwheels and backbends and walked on my hands. Daddy was involved, and mother made my costumes, but they tried to not let it go to my head too much. They supported me but downplayed it for my own good."

When she was ten years old, Harrison performed an acrobatic dance routine and won $100 in the fifteenth-annual Delmarva Chicken Festival's talent show. Five years later, she won the Miss Delmarva contest. "That was the first time I thought I could maybe go on and do something by competing in these pageants as a stepping stone." When she got back to the Eastern Shore from her short-lived New York adventure, her parents supported her plan of attack. She won Miss Berlin and Miss Ocean City in 1963, and Miss Delmarva in 1964.

Then it was on to Miss Maryland.

"Forward and confident," if not more than a little naïve, and a natural-born envelope-pusher with an hourglass figure, Harrison was challenged by her true ambitions and her approach to beauty pageantry. Her dresses were chosen to be as sexy as possible without blowing the conservative minds of promotors. When other contestants said they longed to be nurses, teachers, or secretaries, Harrison admitted she wanted to be a Hollywood actress. The judges would frown. That was not what they were looking to hear. Nevertheless, she was headed to California to represent Maryland in the Miss American pageant, the winner of which would compete to claim the crown of Miss International. It was July 1965, she was twenty years old, and "when they flew me to California and I got off on the tarmac, I knew immediately this is where I belonged."

Harrison didn't win the contest that day in Long Beach. She was a disappointed runner-up, but she was spotted by a scout from the William Morris Agency. In August she was screen-tested and given a sixty-day option, and in November she was signed to a standard seven-year contract.

Soon after arriving in Hollywood, Harrison met Richard Zanuck (1934–2012), son of 20th Century Fox's president Darryl F. Zanuck, one of the last Hollywood moguls. Richard was a member of a fresh generation of moviemakers, the youngest production chief in the town's history, and a wheeler-dealer in his own right. He and Fox were riding a crest of success from *The Sound of Music.* Harrison was asked to accompany a studio lawyer named Harry Sokolov to a movie premiere because they were both from Maryland. The film was *The Agony and the Ecstasy,* starring a favorite actor of hers, Charlton Heston. She accepted the opportunity with excited glee, figuring she'd maybe get a chance to meet Ben-Hur. Instead she met her husband-to-be.

Zanuck was married, but unhappily so, to actress Lili Gentle, a second cousin of Tallulah Bankhead. The girl at the premiere with the long dark hair and sexy style caught his eye. "I thought he was looking at the people dancing," Harrison recalls. "Turned out he was looking at me. We ended up falling madly in love."

To keep Harrison close while she learned the skills required to act onscreen, Zanuck enrolled her in 20th Century Fox's new in-house talent school. Up-and-comers she studied with include James ("so much fun") Brolin and Sam ("such a nice person") Elliot. Jacqueline Bisset and Tom Selleck were also in the program. "The first thing I learned," Harrison says, "was to be quiet and listen for a change. We learned to work with a camera there. We had acting classes, a dance coach, and a voice coach. I had to work on my Eastern Shore accent. It ran deep. Especially when I went home it would come right back. Where you are born sticks with you. It makes an indelible quality to your voice. People still tell me I have an accent."

Harrison, now on the arm of a studio boss, was also hitting the Tinseltown social scene and "flying off all over the world." At one Hollywood party, Zanuck introduced Harrison to Robert Mitchum, nearing the end of his own Eastern Shore residency, as the server who'd waited on his table the year before in Ocean City. He didn't remember her. A lousy waitress, Harrison was relieved.

After appearing as a cheerleader on TV's *Batman* with Adam West and Burt Ward, Harrison was cast in small roles in the comedies *Way . . . Way Out* (1966), starring Jerry Lewis, and *A Guide for the Married Man* (1967), in which Harrison plays the aptly named Miss Stardust. She then did a turn in an ill-conceived Wonder Woman TV comedy dreamed up by *Batman* producer William Dozier. It went nowhere but appearing in a mirror as the heroic potential of star Ellie Wood Walker, Harrison is technically the first actress to wear the Amazon princess's star-spangled garb onscreen.

Next stop? *Planet of the Apes.*

"I remember so vividly sitting in a restaurant, Chez Jay in Santa Monica (known as the world's most glamorous dive bar), and Dick telling me about this movie called *Planet of the Apes* and he said if we get a green light, you'll play Nova." The original "Bond Girl," Ursula Andress, was considered a top contender for the role, but the project's creative team was very much open to casting a newcomer as Nova. The more Harrison heard about the character, the more she felt an intuitive connection to Nova's innocence, silent strength, and good luck.

The screenplay was based on a book by the French author Pierre Boulle, whose third novel, *The Bridge on the River Kwai*, had been made into a successful 1957 film. His eighth, *La Planete des Singes*, first published in 1963, found a Hollywood champion in Arthur P. Jacobs, a PR whiz whose client list of top-tier actors included Jimmy Stewart, Marilyn Monroe, and Marlon Brando. Jacobs, small of physical stature and fragile of health, but blessed with imagination and moxie, started producing movies by developing *What A Way to Go* (1964) with Paul Newman, Robert Mitchum, and Monroe, who died before filming began. (Jacobs was one of the first people called to the scene of the sex symbol's fatal overdose.) She was replaced by Shirley MacLaine. Jacobs's second film was *Doctor Doolittle* (1967), but he was itching to make a great picture along the lines of 1933's *King Kong*, one of his favorite movies.

For years, despite Jacobs's connections and stubborn enthusiasm, Hollywood studios were reluctant to bankroll a movie built around talking space monkeys. Then, after a number of struggles and false starts, a confluence of factors—serious interest from Heston (top-of-the-heap but in need of a hit) and his director friend Franklin J. Schaffner; a treatment and script from Rod Serling, creator of *The Twilight Zone*; and the modest success of 1966's *Fantastic Voyage* with Donald Pleasance and Raquel Welch —aligned. *Planet of the Apes* began shaping up as a potential reality.

Along with the typical challenges of adapting a book to film, everybody involved knew the fundamental hurdle was how the apes looked. If audiences laughed at the characters onscreen because they appeared unrealistic, or worse, cheesy, the movie would have no chance of success. From early on, Jacobs was badgering Richard Zanuck so much about the project, Zanuck finally budgeted $50,000 and ordered a test to see if the theme of Ape vs. Man could be taken seriously onscreen. For the screen test, the makeup was done by the studio's Ben Nye. Heston read as Taylor and the esteemed Edward G. Robinson portrayed the orangutan antagonist Dr. Zaius. The enlightened chimpanzee researchers Cornelius and Zira were played by Talent School classmates James Brolin and Linda Harrison.

"Both Dick and Heston said if they could get the makeup right," Harrison says, "they had a picture. I did the screen test of some of the appliances, and they were very comfortable, and more importantly, convincing." Test results were successful enough to move the project forward at Fox, but they needed a specialist. John Chambers, a prosthetics genius who revolutionized the professionalism of movie makeup artists, was brought on to lead the makeup team. As depicted in Ben Affleck's *Argo* (2012), where Chambers was played by John Goodman, he was also a government contractor who created disguise kits for the CIA. It was publicized that one million dollars had been allocated for *Ape*'s makeup budget, the highest amount ever at the time.

Writer Michael Wilson was called in to redraft Serling's earnest, somber script into a more fun, satirical take on the material. The theatrical actor Maurice Evans was brought in to replace Robinson as Zaius (the makeup was "a bitch," Robinson said), while Roddy McDowell and Kim Hunter were cast as Cornelius and Zira. "They got really good actors," Harrison explains, "because even with the appliances as good as they were, it was hard to even talk past the makeup. They had to be so good their acting could come through." The makeup work was so effective that later, when the studio hosted a screening of the finished film, Heston didn't recognize Hunter, a woman he'd spent weeks working with on set.

Filming began in May 1967, first along the rugged 120-degree Arizona-Utah border, and then at Fox Ranch in the Santa Monica Mountains west of Los Angeles. It's here that the Ape City set was built. After the original *Planet of the Apes*, the ranch showed up in sequels and on television, and was also used for the making of such productions as *Butch Cassidy and the Sundance Kid* (1969), as well as both the film and TV versions of *M*A*S*H*. Though still a popular place to hike, much of the area where the studio filmed was wiped out in 2018 by the Woolsey Fire.

"In the book the apes were much more advanced, so with the budget we were working on, the apes lived in a more primitive ape city that was built in Malibu," Harrison says. "When the apes would be in cars, being taken to the set, and they'd pass people on the highway, the looks they'd get were the funniest thing."

Early in the film, the first time we see the apes in action, they're attacking a group of uncivilized, near-Neanderthal men and women in a brutal, organized hunt. Nova is captured in this ambush, then caged. Later she's paired as a potential mate for Taylor. "I was playing opposite my idol. I told him how incredible it was, and he said thank you. He gave me advice: 'Don't turn your head so far, they'll get a side view. Go three quarters for the camera.' Otherwise, he was very quiet. He spent time in his trailer. He would work out, run. One time he said, "I wasn't very muscular when I was younger. I had to exercise to get a nice body."

"I enjoyed being with Charlton, he looked after me, and our director Frank Schaffner (he'd win an Oscar in 1970 for *Patton*) and I developed a long-lived fondness for each other, but the work could be hard, exhausting. It was always hot. Nobody knew but the director and the cameraman where the next shot would be. A lot of times it felt like we were playing it by ear, moment-to-moment. Nova was mute, so with no lines I had to express myself, act, with my eyes. I had to show surprise, fear, love. It was physical. There was a lot of running, and jumping, and though it wasn't easy, I was limber, my acrobatic background went a long way. I had to pretend I didn't know how to ride a horse." At least the latex costume, traditional cavegirl with fur glued on, was comfy. "Sexy and wild without nudity. I kept putting holes in it to let it breathe more. I liked it, it showed off my figure. The camera was on me and I loved it."

The movie premiered in New York on February 5, 1968 with the primary filmmakers in attendance as well as such luminaries as Barbra Streisand, Henry Fonda, Vincent Price, and Andy Warhol, along with Rod Serling and Edward G. Robinson. Released nationwide on April 3, 1968, the same day as *2001: A Space Odyssey*, *Apes* was an immediate smash. Early reviews were generally positive, and advertising had worked its magic. The film opened at number one and stayed there for three weeks. Audiences young and old, in all demographics, from those sitting in fancy art deco urban theaters to the rural drive-ins, loved it. It was even a critical and financial success overseas. This ambitious little sci-fi movie about those talking space monkeys was quickly growing into a worldwide phenomenon. Lightning in a bottle, as they say. It ended up the fifth-biggest money-maker of the year and is still considered to be one of the most popular sci-fi flicks ever made.

"I remember Richard talking on the phone that whole weekend, getting box office results," says Harrison. "We drank champagne at the dining room table. I was glad it was a hit, but I was only twenty-two years old. I just wanted more acting roles."

There's no denying the cultural impact of *Planet of the Apes*. It came out during a tumultuous time in American history. The day after the picture was released, Martin Luthor King Jr. was assassinated. Robert Kennedy was murdered while *Apes* was still in theaters. The conflict in Vietnam was raging, and Americans were politically at each other's throats. There was violent student protest, ominous talk of a coming race war, and fears of domestic terrorism. There was division all around and, for the first time, the chaos was being shown every night and day—live—on television.

Planet of the Apes struck a societal nerve. Harrison says that even though the public may have believed the movie had a deeper message, her husband and the other filmmakers saw their work as simply providing entertainment. However, Wilson's screenplay gave the politics of the material a subtle but distinct weight.

The movie's legacy is unambiguous. The American Film Institute (AFI) puts it at number fifty-nine on its list of the all-time great thrillers. The lines—"Take your stinking paws off me, you damned dirty ape" is number sixty-six on AFI's list of cinema's greatest quotes—are the kind that live on. That final scene. The great characters. The imagination and creativity that came together to produce an imperfect but enduring work of pop culture. Before *Star Wars*, *Apes* was among the first films to take full advantage of its popularity through merchandising—tie-ins, toys, and collectibles from the original *Planet of the Apes* were sought after then and still are.

Heston considered Zanuck to be first in perceiving the future of sequels, franchises, and spin-offs. Four sequels followed the first *Apes,* including 1970's *Beneath the Planet of the Apes,* where Harrison, once again playing Nova, finally spoke: "Taylor!" There was a TV show. A Saturday morning cartoon. Tim Burton's remake in 2001, featuring both Heston and Harrison in cameos. A whole new series of films took advantage of advances in special effects starting with 2011's *Rise of the Planet of the Apes.* In 2019, a reboot of the franchise was announced to be in development.

Asked if she still thinks of Nova, Harrison says she does. "Two of her biggest emotional traits were the ability to be afraid and the ability to show love. I was directed to portray her as subhuman, but I have always known she had deeper qualities."

Harrison's close friend was *Cosmopolitan* magazine's editor-in-chief Helen Gurley Brown, wife of Zanuck's colleague David. Asked to pose for the popular and controversial publication, Harrison graces the January 1970 cover with an abundance of beauty, style, and cleavage. Unbeknownst to most, it's as a *Cosmopolitan* cover girl that she made one of her first public appearances as a married woman.

After four years of dating, Harrison married Richard Zanuck on October 27, 1969. "On Saturday we were in San Francisco watching *Butch Cassidy and the Sundance Kid* and a preview of *M*A*S*H,* the next day we were in Las Vegas getting married." The ceremony took place on the terrace of the penthouse suite at the famed Sands Hotel. "I cried all through it. I was so happy. I knew I was marrying a wonderful man who meant so much to me, was so important to me, and I knew children were on the way." Their first son, Harrison, was born in 1971, and their second, Dean, a year later.

Linda's family liked Zanuck. "He first came to Ocean City airport in 1966 in a Lear Jet. It was so fast he almost ended up in [a] wheat field when they tried to land. Unmarried people did not stay together when visiting their parents, so Dick stayed at a hotel in Ocean City. We went to The Paddock [one of O.C.'s most popular nightclubs for more than sixty years before closing in 2014] to dance. Even though I wasn't yet twenty-one, and I've never been much of a drinker, mother and father never drank, I *might* have had a few sips that night."

Her parents used to visit L.A. every couple of years and Zanuck would show them around. "They always remembered visiting the *Peyton Place* TV show set; he'd take them to the best restaurants. We went to a celebrity roast and sat with Charlton Heston and his wife." The Harrisons got a chance to see that "the Zanucks were good people," and "Dick saw that my parents loved me, and I loved my family, and that I came from a strong family background. I think that attracted him to me even more."

Richard Zanuck ended up taking his father's place at the head of 20th Century Fox soon after meeting Harrison. Undeserved nepotism was not unheard of in Hollywood, and the results could have proved calamitous, but "Richard had been groomed for the movie business since he was a child." One of his big advantages was that the younger Zanuck was a peer of the up-and-comers in modern Hollywood, but he was also familiar with his father's friends and collaborators. "He had a foot in both worlds. He knew everyone. We'd go out to eat and he'd have to stop at every table to talk to people. If we flew, there'd always be four or five people on the plane he knew."

Along with rubbing elbows, entertaining was part of the family business. "We lived in the house where Dick's parents raised him in Santa Monica. It was built by 20th Century Fox. Each month we'd host a sit-down four course dinner for twelve to fourteen people. There was always a lot of laughter in that house. I always told his mother [Virginia] how happy I was to have been given the opportunity to live in this great house. I always wanted to live on the water. Growing up, everybody was at the ocean except us. Daddy was at the nursery, way back working in the peach orchards. My boys loved it. When they were babies they'd go to sleep to the sounds of the ocean."

After several box-office failures, Zanuck and his vice president, David Brown, parted ways with Fox and started their own production company. Zanuck-Brown would go on to bring such classics as *The Sting* (1973), *Jaws* (1975), *Cocoon* (1985), and *Driving Miss Daisy* (1989) to the screen. Harrison enjoyed an up-close view as to how movies are made. "Dick had a part in everything. He had to okay scripts, and directors, and cast. A lot of people's livelihoods were affected by his decisions. He had a lot of responsibility and took it seriously. David was fantastic. He'd acquire a lot of the material, find these great scripts. He'd talk to people Dick preferred not to. David was interesting to talk with, and I had so many questions about the industry. I believed they were the most creative, hard-working team in Hollywood because they were."

As the wife of one of the most influential men in the movie business, this young woman from the Eastern Shore, still in her twenties, mingled with pop culture icons and persons of historical significance. When *The Prime of Miss Jean Brodie* was released in England, "We had a showing for Queen Elizabeth and other VIPs. I had to quickly learn how to curtsey. When they introduced me to the Queen, I was between Michael Redgrave and Roger Moore. I'm sure she was probably wondering who the heck is *this* girl?"

Despite living the high life of the rich and famous, Harrison made a conscious effort not to change the way she interacted with her Eastern Shore family and friends. "I always wanted them to know that, hey, this is Linda. I was never that materialistic. I never really felt comfortable with overly expensive things. It never set right with me. I'd always [be] thinking about children who didn't have enough to eat, or people on the street. I could have any designer clothes I wanted, but my wardrobe was simple. Daddy used to say I could wear a sack and still be more beautiful than any girl with all the clothes. I'd just go to the closest store on Wilshire Boulevard to buy the dresses and gowns I needed. Sometimes I'd buy something special, but I had no problem wearing outfits more than once. Dick admired that about me. I had a beautiful, but modest wedding ring. He picked out my jewelry, and that was more important than what it might be worth. I could have driven any kind of car I wanted. I wanted a Chevy Nova."

Beneath the Planet of the Apes was released in May 1970 and starred James Franciscus, with Charlton Heston's Taylor making short framing appearances at the beginning and end. Mostly known from a decade of television appearances, Franciscus was of an athletic stature and sported a particularly Hestonesque profile. In the film, his astronaut character, Brent, is on a mission to find Taylor. Director Ted Post, another TV-trained pro, albeit behind the camera, had directed everything from the prototype primetime soap *Peyton Place* to the western series *Rawhide* starring a young Clint Eastwood. Post did not enjoy his time working on *Beneath*. Studio money was tight at the beginning and got tighter at the end but working with Harrison was a bright spot for him: "She gave the role a dimension it didn't have in the writing."

Harrison liked Post too, and though life was exciting, and the work was extraordinarily fun, she began to realize being a mom and raising her boys were the most important aspects of her life. She began stepping back from the spotlight. She'd been featured in a short-lived television series called *Bracken's World*, and popped up in an occasional TV guest appearance, but her most notable role after the *Planet of the Apes* films was *Airport 75* playing the assistant to Gloria Swanson in what would be the illustrious screen star's last movie. Harrison was in every scene Swanson had and says that the Hollywood giant was not only an outspoken health food advocate, but also spiritual and even a little gossipy. "She said I was an old soul because of the shape of my earlobes, and she then went on to tell me all about her long-ago affairs with famous men."

In 1985, Harrison had a small role in Ron Howard's *Cocoon*, co-produced by Zanuck and Brown and Zanuck's third wife, Lili Fini Zanuck. Harrison and Zanuck had divorced in 1978 but stayed close. The two of them, along with Lili, "worked together to raise good boys. We never said an unkind word. I'd go to their Sunday dinners, they included me in family events, and never left me out of important occasions. She'd put me next to him a lot. When he and I were together, he wrote me a love letter every day. Lili found them and made sure I got them. She's a good person."

Richard Zanuck died at the age of seventy-seven. He was born on a Friday the thirteenth and passed away on one too. Steven Spielberg had just premiered a documentary recapping Zanuck's career. Zanuck saw it on a Wednesday. By then he was ill, not going out much. Harrison says he was touched by so many people showing up to toast him. He loved the movie and sent Spielberg a note of thanks. Two days later he had a massive heart attack and left this world.

Today, Harrison, the sole survivor of *Planet of the Apes* primary cast, lives in California near her sons and their families, enjoys yoga and working in her garden, and doesn't count out the possibility of acting again or perhaps writing a book about her life. She's thankful for the opportunities she's enjoyed and remembers those heady days of the 1960s and 1970s as a time of great adventure, great fun, and great friends.

She's also come to understand the impact of *Planet of the Apes.* "A few years ago, I was at a comic book convention in Baltimore and I was so surprised how much the movie still meant to its fans. There were these long lines for my autograph. It was amazing. I never really used to answer fan mail, but since I returned to L.A. ten years ago, after living back on the Eastern Shore for a while, so many people write, I get three or four letters every day and I realize now how important the movie is to its fans, how much people love Nova."

And her Eastern Shore values still run deep. "Always compliment people, find something to praise," Harrison advises. "It changes people when you tell them there's something about them that you like. I try to give other people confidence. That's one of the best things you can do for people. When someone else tells you that you can do something, you're more apt to do it."

A Salisbury, Maryland, native, Linda Hamilton held her own against Arnold Schwarzenegger's "Terminator" in the movie franchise that catapulted her to worldwide stardom. *(Paramount/Photofest)*

LINDA
HAMILTON

"Linda tries to play it down, but the reality was . . . the whole younger team on the set looked at her and saw her performance, and how well she was prepared, and how well she did the stunts, and how many times she did it and never complained about it . . . they had no [choice] but to try and outdo her, which really wasn't possible to do."

—Arnold Schwarzenegger

If actors are remembered by their most famous roles, nobody's going to be forgetting the Eastern Shore's Linda Hamilton any time soon—thanks to a character named Sarah Connor.

Linda Carroll Hamilton and her twin sister Leslie were born in Salisbury, Maryland, on September 26, 1956. Their parents, Dr. Carroll Stanford Hamilton and his wife Barbara, whom everybody called Bobbi, already had a two-year-old daughter named Laura. Two years after the twins came a son they named after his father. Bobbi was a direct descendent of the *Mayflower* passenger and senior elder of the Plymouth Colony, William Brewster. Hamilton was from Lynchburg, Virginia. After college and medical school, and a stint in the Navy, he opened his own practice in Pocomoke City in 1955. When the twins were five, Hamilton, along with two other prominent locals, was killed in a one-car crash outside Salisbury, late on a Sunday night, returning from a Baltimore Colts season-opening win against the Los Angeles Rams. He was pronounced dead at the same hospital where he was a courtesy staff physician. The lower mid-Shore community was stunned. Eleven children were left fatherless by the accident.

Barbara Hamilton remarried a couple years later. Her second husband was Leslie Payne, an officer with the Salisbury Police Department who was made chief in 1965, a position he'd hold until retirement in 1980. Barbara and Chief Payne would have a son together and remained happily married until his death in 2015. Barbara died in 2019.

The family's social stature notwithstanding, the children experienced a typical "boring" upbringing for their era and for the area. All three Hamilton girls studied piano, there were dogs around, reading and academics and extracurriculars were encouraged. In 1981, promoting her first national exposure, *Secrets of Midland Heights,* a steamy nighttime soap opera looking to capitalize on the success of *Dallas* (1978–1991) but aimed at a teenage audience, Hamilton gave a widely reprinted interview to Harry Harris of the Knight-Ridder News Service. Not yet twenty-five, she spoke with the excited openness that is sapped from even the youngest rising stars today. In that early interview she discussed her Eastern Shore upbringing and her relationship with her sister. "Leslie and I were the Hamilton twins," Linda said. "People who knew us for years simply didn't bother to tell us apart."

In 1970 the Wicomico Civic Center hosted a Children's Theatre production of *Rumpelstiltskin* for actors ages thirteen to eighteen. Out of 175 hopefuls who auditioned, both Linda and

Leslie were cast as the princess. Leslie would take the role for one performance, and Linda did the next. "The second year we did *Toad of Toad Hall* from *Wind in the Willows*. I was Badger and she was Toad. I had the better role. It was 'character' work, and I had the greatest time, because I got to scare children to death. I'd burst out of a pile of leaves, screaming. The joy of it! Even then there was that mean streak in me."

In her senior year she was chosen to be the drama teacher's assistant and directed a one-act play featuring younger students, "but I had no sense then of wanting to be a professional actor."

After graduating from Wicomico High School, Linda and Leslie headed to different colleges. Leslie went to school in Western Maryland, while Linda attended Washington College in Chestertown, Maryland. She preferred the community theater group over the one on campus, however, and an acting professor supposedly told her she had no hope of earning a living as an actress. Nevertheless, she scored lead roles there, and after two years acquired "some glamourized idea about my capabilities. I'm so hot in [Chestertown] I thought, I should quit school and go to New York." She was nineteen and not "old enough to be afraid."

For two and a half years, she studied acting, including under noted teacher and coach Lee Strasburg, and waited tables "fifty hours a week in some of the worst restaurants in Soho." She was robbed four times while living in Chelsea, so she moved to 13th Street, "where all I had to contend with were rats."

She said that, like the rest of her family, Leslie was excited for the things that were starting to happen in Linda's career; both envied different parts of each other's lives. In later years, when Linda was working on *Terminator 2: Judgment Day*, Leslie was a stand-in for her sister and performed a few minor stunts. Leslie Hamilton Freas died unexpectedly on August 22, 2020. A longtime

New Jersey resident, Leslie worked in health care as an emergency room and hospice nurse.

Hamilton's professional debut was a bit part in 1979's *Night-flowers*, a drama about a disturbed Vietnam vet filmed in New York and New Jersey. In 1980, a heady year for sure, she was living in Los Angeles and appeared in four productions, each one increasing in prominence.

There was her first appearance on television in January when she was a guest star on the last episode of a fleeting comedy-drama (the term dramedy didn't yet exist) series *Shirley*, starring Shirley Jones from *The Partridge Family* again playing a widow, and featuring Rosanna Arquette (*Desperately Seeking Susan, Pulp Fiction, The Whole Nine Yards*) in one of her early roles. In October she was in two TV movies. In the first, *Reunion*, she played a teenager crushing on her mom's married ex-boyfriend. The second was a ripped-from-the-headline story called *Rape and Marriage: The Rideout Case* about a woman who accused her husband of rape. Hamilton played the wife, Greta Rideout, and her husband John was played by Mickey Rourke (*Diner, Angel Heart, The Wrestler*). *Rape and Marriage* was a ratings winner, and both leads received positive reviews for their performances. Then, on December 6, *Secrets of Midland Heights*, the show she was promoting in the Harris interview, premiered on CBS.

Hamilton was fourth-billed as the sexy junior J. R. Ewing character Lisa Rogers. Broadcast against ABC's *Fantasy Island* in the middle of a seven-year run and NBC's new show *Hill Street Blues*, *Secrets of Midland Heights* lasted eight episodes. One reviewer called it "possibly the worst thing I have ever seen televised." The Harris article included a tacked-on editor's note letting readers know that the show had already been canceled.

Despite the drubbing they took, the *Midland Heights* creators retooled their failure with some of the same actors, including Hamilton, and took another swipe at the genre with *Kings Crossing* two years later. It lasted one less episode than its predecessor.

Harry Harris described the young-looking, twenty-five-year-old Hamilton as being five-foot-five, "a curvaceous 115 pounds, with green eyes, light brown hair, dimples, and sensuous lips." She talked of what it was like becoming a famous actor from a small town. "I'm a total celebrity in Salisbury," she conceded. "There's been no one there in show business except Linda Harrison who was in *Planet of the Apes*. The town still talks about her. Seeing a familiar face on national television delights them."

As fun as the early thrills of celebrity were to Hamilton, she also pointed out that her career path was challenging. She confided that the lack of control, particularly since she'd moved west, was tiring and even traumatizing. "Can I live up to the demands of the work, the constant strain?" she asked herself out loud.

As she was in pursuit of Hollywood roles, Hamilton was concerned about being typecast. She felt producers assumed because she was pretty, she couldn't act. One of her favorite parts up until then had been the *Rideout* TV movie because it was a serious role and she was playing someone closer to her own age. She was already suspicious of any part tinged with bimbo-ism, yet writers couldn't help describing her as someone whose merest head tilt was perceived as a come-on and declaring that she "oozes a sort of lush, full-bodied sensualness."

Between *Midland Heights* and *Kings Crossing*, Hamilton was in a feature film called *TAG: The Assassination Game* and *Country Gold*, a TV movie about a country music star played by Loni Anderson, who is threatened by Hamilton's ambitious "scheming demon" who looks "too sweet for that kind of thing."

Hamilton played college student Susan Swayze in *TAG*, starring Robert Carradine, who in a couple years would score with *Revenge of the Nerds*, which came out just weeks ahead of the first *Terminator*. The plot of this humorous thriller, written and directed by Nick Castle, revolves around a game where players hunt one another with harmless dart guns and what happens when one participant starts playing for real. A first-time director in 1982, Castle's diverse career has included his next directorial project *The Last Starfighter*, another 1984 theatrical hit, and writing credits for *Escape from New York* (1981), *Hook* (1991), and *August Rush* (2007). As an actor he's appeared as *The Shape*, better known as Michael Myers in four *Halloween* horror movies, including the original in 1978 and the three most recent sequels.

TAG also happened to be the first feature film credit for both Oscar winner Forest Whitaker (*The Last King of Scotland*) and Bruce Abbott (*Re-Animator*), who became Hamilton's first husband. The couple were married for seven years and had one son. In 1994, Abbott married Kathleen Quinlan, who'd come to the Eastern Shore in 1987 to make *Clara's Heart*.

A couple more TV movies came next and then a four-episode stint on that groundbreaking cop series *Hill Street Blues* (1981–1987), where she was Sandy Valparaiso, a girlfriend of the popular character Officer Joe Coffey, played by Ed Marinaro.

Based on a short story by Stephen King, *Children of the Corn* starred Hamilton and Peter Horton as a couple named Vicky and Burt who are driving across Nebraska when they have a run-in with a homicidal cult of juvenile religious zealots. Shot in four weeks on a modest $800,000 budget, *Children of the Corn* more than doubled its money in the first weekend of release in March 1984 and grossed more than $14 million. Horror audiences ate it up, even if critics tended to lump the film in with lesser King adaptations.

The original movie's success inspired seven sequels, two remakes, and a prequel that was released in October 2020.

Hamilton's next film role turned out to be the one she'd be most remembered for. A *Salisbury Daily Times* headline announced the occasion with tremendous fanfare:

Area Girl Appears in Movie

To be fair, when it came out on Halloween weekend 1984, nobody imagined *The Terminator* might become a cultural touchstone. In fact, the original film of the expansive and profitable franchise wasn't even a gigantic hit. It did exceed expectations, stay at number one for two weeks, advance Arnold Schwarzenegger's status as an action star, and kickstart the career of director James Cameron. However, in a year that *Ghostbusters*, *Indiana Jones and the Temple of Doom*, and *Gremlins* topped the box office, *The Terminator* came in at number twenty-one. No small shakes but nothing near what the blockbuster 1991 sequel would achieve.

Hamilton plays Sarah Connor (saying it in Schwarzenegger's accent is required), an ordinary young woman, a waitress in a restaurant, targeted by a time-traveling cyborg assassin from 2029. Sarah Connor is in the crosshairs because she's destined to give birth to a son who will grow up to lead a rebel army of human survivors against Skynet, the super-intelligent computer overlords who have conquered earth. To eliminate the threat of John Connor, humankind's potential savior, the merciless technological tyrants send their robotic killer back through time to cut the threat off at the source.

Hamilton was uncertain of *The Terminator*'s prospects and was coaxed by her agents to take the role, a unique one. Conceived as more of a horror film than a sci-fi action thriller, it was unusual to see a woman as the surviving hero in genre films of any type. Cameron has said that, from the beginning, he was aiming for originality. Established and rising actresses alike are rumored to have been considered to play Sarah Connor, including Sharon Stone, Michelle Pfeiffer, Lea Thompson, and Carrie Fisher. Early on, Cameron had Jennifer Jason Leigh in mind, and Debra Winger came the closest to being cast before Hamilton filled the part.

Keeping in mind that every casting report has to be taken with a grain of Tinseltown salt, the list of potential actors it's been asserted were on the list to portray the Cyberdyne Systems Model 101 Terminator reads like a Hollywood who's who of the era. It boggles the cinephile's mind to imagine such diverse performers as Tom Selleck, Harrison Ford, John Travolta, Jack Nicholson, or Robin Williams replacing Schwarzenegger. Supposedly, two other candidates were Ron Perlman, who would become important to Hamilton's career in a few short years, and Schwarzenegger's longtime rival Sylvester Stallone.

Cameron wasn't the only one with doubts about whether Schwarzenegger was the right choice for their villain. "I didn't take Schwarzenegger very seriously as an actor at that time," Hamilton later confessed. "I said, 'Oh, Lord, why cast a man who looks like a machine as a machine? Cast somebody who's very thin to do these superhuman acts.' And I was wrong. He was used tremendously effectively, and he was served very well by that film."

Once filmmakers locked into Schwarzenegger, shooting was postponed for nine months while their bad guy honored his commitment to *Conan the Destroyer* (1984), the sequel to his 1982 breakthrough *Conan the Barbarian*.

Finally, when cameras were almost ready to roll, Hamilton broke her ankle one week before filming began. Her most physical scenes were delayed until the end of the shoot, but she still spent much of the production in pain. She and Cameron didn't get along so well either.

The budget on *The Terminator* was tight. Cameron knew how to shoot on the cheap and on the fly. Creativity was the key to problem solving, and to "get the shot," guerilla tactics were utilized as required. It was a tense but professional set, and when the picture was released there was no doubt audiences and Hollywood alike took notice. Dick Fleming, from the *Salisbury Daily Times'* film column *The Reel World*, declared the local girl's movie might end up being the best action flick of the year.

Turns out it was a classic.

And Schwarzenegger's "I'll be back" is one of the most quoted movie lines of all time.

Linda Hamilton? She went back to work.

These days, television is where some of the best onscreen and offscreen talent find audiences for their work, but for years movie stars considered TV a downgrade from feature films. Throughout her career, Hamilton has never been snobby about TV. She wanted to work, and she wanted to do good work. The medium was the least of her concerns. She was on everything from *Murder, She Wrote* (1984–1996), to *Frasier* (1993–2004), to *Weeds* (2005–2012). After *The Terminator*, she appeared in two TV movies, hardly noteworthy, except that the first, *Secret Weapons*, where she played a sexy Russian spy, was the last work of James Franciscus (1934–1991), who'd co-starred with fellow Eastern Shore native Linda Harrison in 1970's *Beneath the Planet of the Apes*.

Hamilton's next feature film was *Black Moon Rising*. In this action-thriller she plays the elite car thief, Nina. Nina falls in love with another criminal, Quint, played by Tommy Lee Jones, who's working for the federal government. The plot centers on a valuable and coveted high-tech automotive prototype, the Black

Moon. The reviews of *Black Moon Rising* were mixed. Even those who liked it tended to use puns to compare the whole film to a car-chase sequence—fast, good-looking, and consistently in danger of bursting through the guardrails of credibility.

Speaking of credibility, 1986's *King Kong Lives* has little.

A sequel to 1976's clunky but successful *King Kong* remake starring Jeff Bridges and Jessica Lange, *King Kong Lives* came out in December 1986.

Hamilton played Dr. Amy Franklin, a scientist working at the Atlanta Institute in Georgia. Seems Kong hadn't been killed in his fall off New York's World Trade Center ten years earlier but was in fact in a coma with a heart condition. A giant artificial ticker is built, and to provide a blood transfusion during surgery an adventurer played by Brian Kerwin finds a giant lady ape in Borneo and, in the nick of time, saves Kong's life. Kong wakes up, realizes there's a potential mate in the vicinity, and all kinds of rural romantic hell breaks loose.

It was the floppiest of flops. It opened behind films that had been out for weeks and even audience members who'd been looking forward to it the most couldn't give the picture more than a middling grade. Reviews were brutal.

But Hamilton quickly rebounded with a small screen cult classic.

"Once upon a time begins tonight!" the *TV Guide* advertisement announced on September 25, 1987. "Fate brought her to his world . . . love drew him to hers. A love story of a different kind. You'll be enchanted. Preview tonight."

Hamilton played the crusading socialite Assistant District Attorney Catherine Chandler on CBS's fantasy romance crime series *Beauty & the Beast*. Her love interest, played by Ron Perlman, was a leonine man-beast named Vincent who lived in a community of society's outcasts below New York City's subway system. After Sarah Connor, it's probably Hamilton's best known role.

In his review of the series premiere for the *Daily Times*, Dick Fleming noted that the network seemed to have high hopes but "because of the outlandish premise, forecasters have given the series mixed odds of succeeding."

Fleming wasn't wrong. The best *Beauty & the Beast* ever came in the ratings was forty-ninth, but its devotees, in a pre–social media era, were invested and vocal and went out of their way to show their support for the show. There were fan clubs, fanzines, and newsletters. The critics liked it too. In the first year they were eligible, the cast and crew received a total of twelve Emmy nominations, including one for Perlman, and took home three statues, while the show and Hamilton were Golden Globe nominees. In 1989, both she and the show were again nominated for Golden Globes, and Perlman won. At the Emmys, the two leads were each nominated for their second-season performances, and the show won music and costuming awards.

Hamilton left *Beauty & the Beast* at the end of the second season. She was pregnant and wanted to be an involved mom. Her character was killed off and the show was retooled to attract more male viewers, alienating the fans they'd already earned. George R. R. Martin, the creator of *Game of Thrones*, was a *Beauty & the Beast* staff writer and is on record as saying the show was best early on, but that the loss of their leading lady and the subsequent increased network meddling, along with some stiff competition from ABC's TGIF primetime lineup, was more than producers could overcome.

Bruce Abbott and Linda Hamilton split up before the birth of their child. Hamilton, who has used her platform, including a highly publicized appearance on a 2004 episode of Oprah Winfrey's daytime talk show, to talk openly about her depression and bipolar disorder, claims her share of responsibility for the parting, and the two were able to remain friendly, by all accounts.

Perlman didn't seem to have any lasting beef with being left at the subterranean altar. He and Hamilton reunited on stage for a production of *Love Letters* and for 2005's Vietnam vet picture *Missing in America* with Danny Glover. Perlman went on to have a productive post–*Beauty & the Beast* career and is best known for the comic-book-based *Hellboy* and TV's biker gang epic *Sons of Anarchy*.

The call from Cameron came while Hamilton was six months pregnant and still married to Abbott. He wanted to get the band back together for *Terminator 2: Judgement Day (T2)*.

Hamilton affirmed she was up for it but that she wouldn't be needing anyone to save her this time. This time, she wanted to "play crazy" and kick ass on her own. With that directive, Cameron and co-writer William Wisher Jr. sat down to transform a scrappy but naïve and vulnerable Sarah Connor into an icon of high-octane empowerment. To make it happen on her end, the movie was ten times more physically demanding than the first installment. Hamilton worked out with weights and in martial arts classes three hours a day, six days a week, for thirteen weeks. She took extensive weapons training and even learned how to pick a lock with a paper clip.

This time, Schwarzenegger plays a Terminator Series 800 model 101 good guy, sent back in time to aid a Sarah Connor suffering from PTSD and protect her teenage son John. Hamilton's twin, Leslie, plays her sister's double in a couple of scenes where there are two Sarah Connors, one a terminator impersonating the original. In a nightmarish nuclear annihilation scene that begins on a playground, Hamilton's son appears as the infant John Connor.

T2 was a tough shoot. Everything that made the first film work was ratcheted up. It took eight months to film the sequel. *The Terminator* had been shot in six weeks. Almost every actor was injured at some point. Hamilton suffered permanent hearing damage in one ear when she fired a gun inside an elevator without having reinserted her earplugs between scenes. Thanks to Cameron's perfectionism and access to deep pockets, the start budget of $12 million inflated to $102,000,000, the most amount of money ever spent on a movie at the time. Many prognosticators were predicting a misfire that would change Hollywood's attraction to high-cost risk taking.

It did. Just not in the way naysayers anticipated.

T2 opened on July 3, 1991, and with an overall take of $200 million in ticket sales would end the year as the top-grossing film by far. It made more money in its first week than *The Terminator* made in its whole run. Eventually it would gross more than $520 million. The movie's astronomical success was life-altering for everyone involved.

Critics liked it too, some begrudgingly. Only the most crotchety of reviewers found the results flat or undramatic. *T2* is the sole entry in the Terminator canon to be nominated for Academy Awards, and it won four of the six it was up for: makeup, two sound awards, and best visual effects. At the fan-voted 1992 MTV Movie Awards, *T2* snagged wins for Best Movie, Best Action Sequence, Best Breakthrough for Edward Furlong, Best Male Performance for Schwarzenegger, and Best Female Performance for Hamilton in addition to—against fellow nominees Christina Applegate, Kim Bassinger, Tia Carrere, and Julia Roberts—Most Desirable Female.

Not long after *T2* wrapped, Cameron divorced the director Kathryn Bigelow, the first and only woman so far to win an Academy Award for best director (2008's *The Hurt Locker*), and he and Hamilton moved in together. Hamilton was excited about the future and hoped that the extra attention the new Terminator movie brought her would translate into meatier acting opportunities. Cameron suggested she could maybe be the "female Bruce Willis," but that wasn't the acting career she was looking for. She'd always yearned to do more comedy but already could see Hollywood was once again trying to typecast her. She was being offered three kinds of roles, she said: "police officers, military officers, and lesbians."

Hamilton got a chance to exercise her comedy chops when she hosted *Saturday Night Live* on November 16, 1991, and in her opening monologue spoke of growing up in Salisbury.

"I've been looking forward to hosting the show tonight," she started, "because it gives me a chance to let people know I'm not just the gun-toting grenade-launching Sarah Connor from the *Terminator*. As much as I enjoy it, that's not who I am. I'm just an average American girl. I grew up in the suburbs in Salisbury, Maryland. This is my parents' house"—a contemporary style home is shown on screen—"a great place for kids"—the house explodes, gets a big laugh; a church is shown.

"We used to put on plays in this little church, where I first decided to become an actress"—it explodes and a man on fire runs into frame—"Oh look, there's my high school sweetheart, Larry." Hamilton continues to give the audience a look into her "normal" life, which includes blowing up the supermarket where she first worked, blowing up her first car, and blowing up her agent, Ronnie. During the episode she also appeared in such skits as "Baby Talk," where she and a boyfriend used increasingly disgusting childish love chatter while on a double date, and as a party hostess dealing with the disruptive presence of Dana Carvey's memorable one-off character, Massive Headwound Harry.

In February, Hamilton gave birth to her second child, a daughter. In 2020, she remarked to the *New York Times* that her ill-timed response to becoming an 'overnight success' was to "go and get pregnant with Jim Cameron and completely disappear."

Hamilton came back to the Eastern Shore in 1993 to shoot *Silent Fall* in Talbot County. The murder mystery starred Richard Dreyfuss as Dr. Jake Rainer, a therapist treating an autistic boy who witnessed his parents' killing. Hamilton is his wife, Karen. *Silent Fall* was neither a critical nor box office success, but as always, the cast and crew were welcomed to the Shore with open arms. Actors and extras alike described the shoot as relaxed despite noise from planes overhead and boats out on the water. The stars were seen out and about town, and were reported to be friendly, eating at local restaurants and, in Hamilton's case, working out at a public gym and having long interactions with locals. When she left town to shoot scenes in Baltimore, she was quoted as saying she hadn't realized how special the Eastern Shore was when she was growing up and admitted missing the place.

In 1997, Hamilton had two films released a week apart. The first was *Shadow Conspiracy* with Charlie Sheen and Donald Sutherland and it bombed upon release on January 31, while the volcanic disaster picture *Dante's Peak* with Pierce Brosnan, who was the current incarnation of James Bond, came out on February 7. It would land at number twenty-one for the year like the original *Terminator*.

While making *Titanic* in 1997, Cameron fell for actress Suzy Amis but reconciled with Hamilton after a separation. They married and two years later divorced in a highly publicized $50 million settlement. In her typically candid and non-accusatory fashion, Hamilton would say that though Cameron was a genius and an extraordinary director, for seven tumultuous years they'd been terribly mismatched. "He was all brain and work and I was all heart and living," she's explained. "He had guns next to his side of the bed and I had crystals and fertility symbols next to mine. We were really just not meant to be together."

After the divorce, Hamilton appeared in numerous television guest spots and did voice work in animated projects like *Hercules* (1998–1999), *The New Batman Adventures* (1998), and *Buzz Lightyear of Star Command* (2000). From 2010 to 2012, she had a recurring role on NBC's humorous spy series *Chuck* as the hero's long lost mom, Mary Elizabeth Bartowski. When that gig ended, she left L.A. and moved to New Orleans. Wasn't too long after, Cameron once again came calling.

He called three times before she rang him back.

The Terminator legacy was struggling. In a world where superhero movies were squeezing out all but the most fortunate of other features, one attempt after another to revive the faltering creative property failed. Hamilton hadn't been in an installment since *T2*. They killed her character offscreen in 2003's *Terminator 3: Rise of the Machines*. *Terminator: The Sarah Connor Chronicles* was a 2008–2009 series that took place after the events of *T2* and starred a pre–*Game of Thrones* Lena Headey (Cersei Lannister). In 2015, they again recast the part with a *Game of Thrones* star, Emilia Clark (the khaleesi Daenerys Targaryen), but audiences were unresponsive. In the end *Terminator: Dark Fate* didn't work out as the filmmakers hoped, but Cameron and Schwarzenegger figured if the franchise could be saved from future irrelevance, the real Sarah Connor might be the one person who could do it.

She told them she needed some time to think it over.

One consideration was the physical, emotional, and mental toll returning to the role might take on her. "I look at Sarah as a broken woman living in hell," Hamilton told *Total Film* magazine. "That's not someone you want to keep playing. You don't miss those roles. They cost you a bit, y'know."

Eventually, Hamilton decided to sign on to her first big-budget action role in more than twenty years. The script wasn't finished when shooting began, but the structure was there. Everything after *T2* was no longer counted in the storytelling timeline. Sarah is now an angry and aimless lone wolf who must form an alliance with an enhanced female commando named Grace sent from 2042 to protect another young woman targeted by Skynet and their terminators. Schwarzenegger, the cyborg who ultimately killed John Connor, is now autonomous and secretly integrated into human society.

If the training for *T2* had been extensive, this new adventure would need a focus few people in their sixties would be capable of taking on. The physicality required was off the charts. Preparation started with such commitments as working with a nutritionist and eating no carbs for a year. To build muscle, Hamilton was put on a regimen of supplements and bioidentical hormones. She worked with a trainer—among them, a Pilates instructor, a Green Beret military trainer, a stunt coordinator—every day. She took lessons in Spanish and scuba diving and had regular access to both a physical therapist and a chiropractor. When her work on the movie was complete, she spent "three months on the couch eating pie."

With a screenplay being written as the film was shot, Hamilton found she needed to speak up for her character and on occasion confront her ex-husband director. A notoriously demanding boss, Cameron has a distinct aversion to being questioned on his choices. He and Schwarzenegger once battled over "I'll be back." The director told his star that he wouldn't tell him how to act as long as Schwarzenegger didn't try to tell him how to write.

Here, when Hamilton felt pressured to not give Sarah Conner her due, she would make a stand. "Nobody challenges Jim Cameron's dialogue," she told the British online publisher *Independent* in 2019. "I did. I was the only one who had real power of veto, because everyone's terrified of Jim Cameron. But I'm not," she said. "What's the worst he could do? Fire me?"

A lot of weight was put on her shoulders to carry the franchise, but she didn't let that affect her. She does her job and lets the chips fall where they may. The movie didn't do well and perhaps the damage done to the franchise over the years was too much for even Sarah Connor to overcome. In any case, as the *Terminator* saga appears to be coming to a close of some sorts, after almost four decades, it took *Terminator: Dark Fate* to hear Sarah Connor intone that famous line: "I'll be back."

Today, according to published interviews with *The New York Times* and other sources, Hamilton enjoys the city's spirited yet relaxed and authentic atmosphere and being surrounded by regular people who "care less about what you do or have, more about who you are." Dogs have been a part of her joy since her days as a kid on the Shore and still are. Those who know or have met Hamilton describe her as warm and outgoing, with an easy laugh. She's built a life for herself away from the grind of Hollywood. She loves acting, and as a pro, tries to do the best work possible with the least fuss. Her goal is to make her boss, the director, happy. "I never really wanted to produce and be the one in charge," she's said. "I don't think it brings out the best in anybody."

One of cinema's most unforgettable action heroes might call herself "a lazy movie star," as she told looper.com in 2020, but she understands what made her most famous portrayal one for the ages. "A woman who grows and transforms onscreen is always a wonderful thing to play," she told an interviewer in 2019. "Sarah

went from a vulnerable, normal girl to someone who finds all her deep reservoirs of strength and comes through it all."

It's the most any of us can hope for.

Tallulah Bankhead (shown in a 1940 photo while she was starring in the hit play *The Little Foxes*) was catnip to critics and columnists for fifty years, as she blazed a flamboyant career on stage and screen. She retreated in later life to her sister Eugenia's country estate near Chestertown, Maryland. *(Wikimedia Commons)*

TALLULAH BANKHEAD

"We were fascinated by her, but we were scared to death of her, too. . . . She had such authority, as if she ruled the earth, as if she was the first woman on the moon."

—Joan Crawford

She was that rarity—a Groucho, an Elvis, a Beyoncé—a star so bright she only needed a first name. With her brazen larger-than-life attitude and image, deep voice, distinct mannerisms, and fluid sexuality, Tallulah Bankhead was an icon of stage, screen, radio, and television, an unpredictable geyser of personality and wit, and a daring, decadent diva of epic proportions. While most of her contemporaries have long since been forgotten, the untamed and outspoken Bankhead has proven hard to shake.

In her bestselling 1952 autobiography, Tallulah acknowledged her own culpability in having been branded "a harridan, a hussy, a rebel, a calculated troublemaker," and called herself the foe of moderation and the champion of excess. Throughout her career, she was as open as any public figure could be when discussing her outrageous reputation and swashbuckling celebrity lifestyle. She was emotional and impulsive. "I'm not content with boiling,"

she wrote. "I boil over . . . I attract disorder. I provoke controversy," and she admitted that she charged into fights, fracases, and feuds with her "hair on fire."

A histrionic child of the Deep South, Tallulah ran wild as an overripe teenager in New York City, found fame in London, trod the boards from Broadway to Santa Barbara, starred in about a dozen Hollywood films, and was one of the last big stars on radio.

No party was ever in full swing until Tallulah arrived.

So with all that, one might be expected to ask: How did a woman as saucy, as worldly, and as famous as Tallulah Bankhead—a woman whose legend looms so remarkably it sometimes can't be separated from what's real—end up spending eternity in a little country cemetery on Maryland's Eastern Shore?

Tallulah Bankhead was christened next to her mother's coffin.

A southern belle of noted beauty, Adelaide "Ada" Eugenia Sledge married William B. Bankhead on January 31, 1900. His father and brother were U.S. senators, and he would go on to serve eleven terms in Congress, the final two as Speaker of the House. Ada and Will's first child, Ada Eugenia, was born in 1901, Tallulah a year later. Three weeks after the birth of her second daughter, Ada Bankhead died from blood poisoning brought on by an infection. On her deathbed, Ada told her sister-in-law Marie, "Take care of my baby Eugenia. Tallulah will always be able to take care of herself."

The girls were mostly raised by their paternal grandparents, Captain John and Tallulah James Brockman Bankhead. Little Tallulah was a homely and overweight child. Eugenia was the pretty one. "Sister was the top Bankhead girl until I got into the theater," Bankhead was later known to tell people.

A performer and exhibitionist from the get-go, the self-proclaimed ugly duckling did everything she could to garner the attention she craved. Bankhead's early flair for both comedy and the dramatic, her memory for the written words of literature and plays, and her skills as a mimic marked her destiny. "My doom was sealed," she said, "when I saw a girl turn cartwheels at a circus in Birmingham." She claimed that her very first "performance" had been witnessed by Orville and Wilbur Wright when her Aunt Marie hosted a party for the famous brothers. Attendees were asked to perform for the honored guests, and Bankhead won the day with an imitation of her kindergarten teacher.

As the Bankhead sisters matured into world-class showoffs, it got harder and harder to reign them in. Tallulah threw tantrums. Her grandmother would have to douse her with a bucket of water to get her to quit. "To deny me anything," Bankhead would explain as an adult, "is to inflame my desire." When Tallulah was ten, she and her sister were packed off to the first of several boarding schools they would attend during the next few years.

While the sisters were away in New York that first winter, their dad came to visit over Christmas vacation and took them to see their first professionally produced play, *The Whip*. The experience landed hard on Tallulah. "*The Whip* was a blood-and-thunder melodrama in four acts and fourteen scenes imported from London's Drury Lane Theatre," she wrote in her autobiography. "Nothing I had ever seen or heard or read had made such an impact on me."

Tallulah blossomed, and when she was fifteen, she submitted a photograph in a movie-casting contest but forgot to include her name or address. She learned she was a winner while browsing through magazines at a drugstore. Her image was in *Picture-Play* with a caption that read, "Who is She?" The publisher instructed the mystery contestant to contact them ASAP! For not the last time, Bankhead's indulgent grandfather, Captain John, supported her desires and, flexing his clout as a United States senator, wrote to the editors to vouch that out of the fifty respondents they'd heard from, his granddaughter was the girl that they were looking for. Her grandmother advised her father, who'd remarried a younger woman named Florence McGuire, to "let her go on the stage. She's not worth a damn for anything but acting."

Arriving in New York City "under the wing" of her Aunt Louise (who didn't stick around long), Bankhead discovered her contest win didn't amount to what she'd hoped. She did, however, find a home at the Algonquin Hotel, where she charmed the artistic and literary elite who famously gathered at the bar there.

Bankrolled by her grandfather with an always quickly spent allowance, Tallulah made a splash at the Algonquin, and at every opportunity she made a scene. Though she hadn't yet taken to drink, she began using drugs with regularity. Her line was that her father had warned her about men and booze but never mentioned a word about women and cocaine. Jane Cowl, a playwright and actress Bankhead looked up to, marveled at the blooming wannabe but also prophesied disaster to a mutual acquaintance: "[Bankhead's] face is an evil flower," Cowl commented. "She's so intense she vibrates. She's one of the most violently beautiful women I've ever seen, and she seems completely unconscious of it. But she's doomed. She'll come to no good."

After small roles in three silent films, Tallulah made her New York stage debut in 1919 and then performed as a supporting player in a succession of ill-fated productions. Dissatisfied with both her career and a stalled-out love life, she got word from a theatrical impresario named Charles Cochran that the famed British actor Sir Gerald du Maurier had a part for her in his upcoming show, *The Dancers*.

Tallulah told everyone she knew but was soon heartbroken to find out that the offer would not in fact be forthcoming. At the prodding of a fortune teller and her actress friend Estelle Winwood, and after borrowing a $1,000 stake from the wealthy businessman, politician, and family friend T. Coleman DuPont (1863–1930), Bankhead moved to London anyway. She showed up on du Maurier's doorstep pretending she hadn't gotten word to stay home. He didn't believe her, but he apologized anyway, explaining that the role she'd been considered for had been cast and his show was already in rehearsals. Bankhead played down her disappointment and acted as though the celebrated thespian's rejection was no big deal.

It was a big deal. Cochran, feeling somewhat responsible, arranged another meeting with du Maurier. He told Bankhead not to wear a hat this time and to show off her long, golden hair. Sir Gerald's daughter, Daphne, who with *Rebecca* in 1938 would become counted among the most famous romance novelists in the world, was visiting her father at the time. She said, "Daddy, that's the most beautiful girl I've ever seen in my life." The meeting adjourned with du Maurier convinced there was no one else in the world who could fill the part he was writing but Bankhead.

The next morning, there was a contract waiting for her.

Audiences ate her up. A hit from the start, Tallulah was soon the most popular actress working in London, and she appeared in more than a dozen plays during the next eight years. Her success was phenomenal. In England, where she spent the happiest and most exciting years of her life, Tallulah was regarded as America's greatest actress. Night after night, legions of frenzied fans who couldn't get inside, primarily young women, would line up hours in advance to *maybe* get a glimpse of their idol outside the theater. On occasion, there'd be a stampede.

While Tallulah was cutting a dazzling "swath in London," Eugenia, who everybody called Sister, was blazing quite an adventurous trail herself. A lover of travel, her family estimated she crossed the Atlantic Ocean by ship eighty-four times. Steering clear of anything resembling an occupation, Sister was considered by many to be even prettier, smarter, and funnier than her junior sibling. Both had a love life that was robust. For the most part, the Bankhead girls were confident of their place in the world.

Moviemaking, on the other hand, was in a precarious state of flux. The year 1929 marked an end to the Roaring Twenties in every regard. The box office took a thrashing, and the talkies changed everything. Actors who'd been stars before the public heard them speak were losing everything. The studio system, controlled by powerful empire builders, still ran Hollywood, but Tinseltown was fighting an image problem.

A plague of scandals resulting in a public backlash prompted the power players to institute the Motion Picture Production Code, a list of self-imposed, self-censoring rules. A morals code was included in every actor's contract. It wasn't so much that the bigwigs cared what improprieties their employees might be up to, but they wanted a way out if the civilian populace caught wind of any misstep. Big money-making stars were rarely cut loose, but punishments were doled out. With hindsight, 1931 might not have been the most perfect time for Bankhead to return to America to give the talkies a shot.

Nevertheless, Paramount Pictures put her under contract for five pictures at $50,000 each. First, in New York, she made *Tarnished Lady* , directed by a novice George Cukor. Cukor would go on to direct such classics as *The Philadelphia Story* (1940) and the 1951 remake of 1937's *A Star is Born*. In 1965 he won the Academy Award for *My Fair Lady*. He and Tallulah remained close friends the rest of their lives.

But *Tarnished Lady* fizzled. As did *My Sin* and *The Cheat*.

Bankhead headed west. The first picture she shot in California was *Thunder Below*. She called it "a double-jointed dud."

Devil and the Deep (1932) gave Tallulah top billing over Gary Cooper, Chares Laughton, and, in his fourth film appearance, Cary Grant. The movie, an off-center melodrama about the wife of a jealous submarine officer, was met with a who-cares response from moviegoers. Tallulah had the hots for Cooper, the star of 1928's *The First Kiss*—which was filmed in St. Michaels on the Eastern Shore—and at one point during production was supposedly seen chasing the younger actor as he ran from her private trailer. She'd met Cooper a year before in New York when she was set up on a date with him. "I thought Cooper the handsomest man on screen," she wrote. "Strong, silent type! Silent is right. Gary never opened his trap throughout the evening."

Her other *Devil and the Deep* costar, Charles Laughton, presented the show's headliner with problems beyond rejection of her lustful advances. Their personalities and acting styles presented opportunity for a colossal, ego-driven conflict. In several takes of one scene, Laughton slapped Bankhead so hard he knocked her out of camera range, and in close, confrontational dialogue he'd intentionally spray spittle in her face.

That movie was a flop, and the next one was too. Hollywood couldn't quite figure out what to do with Bankhead. As the Great Depression deepened, censorship advocates such as the National League of Decency zeroed in on anything and anyone they deemed vulgar. In 1934, William H. Hays, the man the studios chose to enforce the rules, circulated the "Doom Book," a list of 150 actors considered "unsuitable for the public." Tallulah was on page one, singled out for her "Verbal Moral Turpitude." As for her side of the argument, Tallulah called Hays "a little prick."

Even under close supervision, acting well behaved was always difficult for her.

Tallulah ended up making two more appearances in unsuccessful films before heading back to New York, back to the stage. She took her punches from her inability to score a cinematic winner, but she also made sure her fans knew she carried no regrets about her year in Hollywood. "I bagged a quarter of a million," she wrote. "I lived in splendor, did my share of skylarking between pictures." Her rented house was rumored to be a place where parties with no boundaries lasted for days, but she asserted in her memoir that while residing in Tinseltown she didn't "encounter much hell-raising. Their medium gone vocal, most of its inmates were too busy learning how to talk to engage in shenanigans . . . there was another deterrent to hijinks. If you have to face a camera at seven in the morning you think twice before opening the second quart of Old Grand-Dad."

A run of half a dozen or so East Coast plays went nowhere. She shined, but nothing hit. A few years later, a *Life* magazine cover story looked back at this time in Tallulah's career and recalled that, "Somehow it seemed impossible to find parts for this strange electric woman with the languid eyes, the panther's step, and the siren's husky voice."

While rehearsing a new play called *Jezebel* in summer 1933, Bankhead took ill and collapsed. "What they found in my abdominal cavities and adjacent areas was hair-raising," she wrote. "There's a technical name for the contortions of my innards, but I can't remember it" is the conclusion of her official reporting of events.

What happened was that she almost died during an emergency five-hour hysterectomy needed to combat the advanced development of a sexually transmitted disease. Weighing in at seventy pounds when she left the hospital, in true Bankhead form she told her doctors on her way out, "Don't think this has taught me a lesson!"

A few short years later, Hollywood was in a tizzy to have its way with the literary world's latest bestseller, Margaret Mitchell's 1936 novel *Gone with the Wind*. In a letter to her sister, Eugenia wrote that in her opinion there was one person who could play the book's spunky heroine, Scarlett O'Hara. "Who but you," Sister wrote, "were born and bred in that briar patch."

One person who agreed with Eugenia, at least for a while, was *Gone with the Wind*'s producer David O. Selznick. After seeing Tallulah in a performance of *Reflected Glory*, Selznick reported back to his boss and father-in-law Louis B. Mayer, "I've got our Scarlett." Unfortunately, the mogul nicknamed the King of Hollywood and the outspoken actress had a combative history. Mayer ordered Selznick to "look a little further."

The search for Scarlett would drag on for two years with more than 1,400 actresses, both unknown and famous, auditioning, including Bette Davis, Katharine Hepburn, and Joan Crawford. Tallulah was first to screentest, and she believed she had the chops to win out. "I felt I had qualifications beyond any of the hundreds of candidates . . . the looks, the Southern background and breeding, the proper accent," but with Scarlett being sixteen when the story begins, she was concerned about being too old.

Tallulah, like everybody else, knew the project's creative team was scouring "the continent from the Yukon to the Yazoo" for their star, and though she was thrilled she might have a chance to fill such a coveted role, she wasn't convinced she'd be cast. "For months I was leading in the Scarlett Derby whilst Selznick and his aides kept looking in treetops, under bridges, in the Social Register, and on lists of parolees from reformatories, but my bones told me I wouldn't get the part." A campaign to win Bankhead the job, spearheaded by her Aunt Marie, gathered steam in the Deep South, and the *Gone With the Wind* folks received thousands of letters supporting her as the obvious logical choice to play Scarlett. Even Alabama Governor Bibb Graves sent Selznick a telegram saying they should just go ahead and give her the role and be done with it.

Variety was reporting she had Scarlett clinched, but in those bones of hers Tallulah knew better. In a letter she wrote to Selznick, she made clear she was not content to wait around to see if "no one better comes along." Later, Selznick offered her the character of prostitute Belle Watling instead of Scarlett, a role she may have been great in, but Bankhead declined. Like every blow she ever took, Tallulah laughed it off in public, but her friends knew she was severely wounded by losing Scarlett O'Hara to Vivian Leigh.

Tallulah got married for the first and only time in 1937.

It didn't take.

She and stage actor John Emery, a John Barrymore lookalike, called it quits after her father died in September 1940. Never able to resist an easy shot, Bankhead wrote, "By way of compensation my sister Eugenia has been hitched seven times, three times to the same victim."

In 1939, Tallulah starred in what she and most critics considered the best role of her career, appearing as the callous Regina Gibbons in Lillian Hellman's *The Little Foxes*. The play premiered in Baltimore, and when it opened in New York two weeks later, there were twenty curtain calls. Tallulah had her first American hit, but she and Hellman fell out over politics. "As a playwright I have tremendous respect for her," Tallulah declared.

"As a person, she is not my cup of tea." They didn't speak to each other for twenty-seven years.

It was during this time Tallulah met the actress who would become her protégé and friend, Eugenia Rawls. Rawls was an understudy for the actress playing Bankhead's stepdaughter in the Broadway production of *The Little Foxes*. Tallulah liked Rawls and thought she looked like a young version of herself, so at the first opportunity Eugenia was moved up into first position.

When it came time to make the film version of *The Little Foxes*, Tallulah's role, one she'd made famous, went to one of her biggest rivals, Bette Davis. After *Jezebel* in 1938 and *Dark Victory* in 1939, *Foxes* was the third time in four years Davis starred in a film in a part Bankhead originated on Broadway. She'd been nominated for an Academy Award for *Jezebel*, won for *Dark Victory*, and was once again nominated for *The Little Foxes*. Perhaps Tallulah's antics onstage and off had left a bad taste in the mouths of silver screen decision makers, but by all accounts, except her own —she played it down, as usual—Tallulah was furious over this particular casting snub.

The Little Foxes closed on Broadway after 410 performances, and the cast took off for a national tour that, according to Eugenia Rawls, covered 25,000 miles and included eighty-seven one-night stands. The same year, on September 15, Tallulah got a call right before curtain time in Princeton, New Jersey, notifying her that her father, who had suffered a heart attack, was dying. The show went on. By the time Tallulah arrived at his bedside, her father had passed.

A few weeks later, when *Foxes* played Cleveland, Bette Davis was in the audience. She did not visit backstage.

Meanwhile, John Emery, whom Tallulah had been separated from since Will Bankhead's death, fell in love with the actress, ballerina, and Russian defector, Tamara Geva (1907–1997). The two were living together, and Emery asked Tallulah for a divorce. She agreed under the stipulation he wouldn't remarry for at least one year, to which he obliged, marrying Geva a year later to the day. On reflection, Tallulah described the end of her marriage this way: "It's tough enough to be bogged down in a legend," she confided. "It would be tougher to marry one."

In 1943, Bankhead bought a secluded property in Westchester, New York that she named Windows. Her nephew, William, who still lives on the Eastern Shore, not far from where his mom and aunt are buried, remembers visiting as a boy: "The swimming pool was up on a hill and you could see down into this valley. What was most interesting to me was that there were rocks and boulders coming out of the ground. We don't have that around here. I still remember exactly how the house was laid out, the floorplan. There was a parakeet that would fly around inside and a mynah bird in the kitchen that would always say 'Do you want to go to New York? Do you want to go to New York?' I remember the long winding driveway and her white Cadillac convertible with the red leather upholstery. I can still smell that car."

Soon after purchasing her country estate, Alfred Hitchcock offered Bankhead $75,000 to play journalist Constance Porter in his World War II drama, *Lifeboat*. As she said, "off I dashed to Hollywood."

She gave "Hitch" and *Lifeboat* her all. Every scene was filmed in a tank holding thousands of gallons of water, and after days of working sopping wet, Tallulah caught pneumonia twice. Though on her best behavior, Tallulah's unquenchable thirst to expose herself ensured she kept up her longstanding habit of forgoing underpants. When crew members grumbled about always seeing more of Bankhead than they'd contracted for, Hitchcock is alleged to have answered that he wasn't sure if their complaints were a problem for wardrobe or hairdressing.

Tallulah comes close to stealing the movie. *Lifeboat*, adapted from a John Steinbeck story, is considered her best work on film, and she gave most of the credit to her director. Made during the actual war, *Lifeboat* was controversial at the time of its release. It was accused of being subversive, of making the enemy look good. She called the notion "moronic."

Lifeboat received three Academy Award nominations including Best Director, Best Original Story, and Best Cinematography. When Tallulah won the Best Actress Award from the New York Film Critic's Circle for her work in the film, she accepted by saying, "Dahlings, I was wonderful."

Her next movie was *A Royal Scandal*. Her role as Catherine the Great of Russia would be her last as leading lady.

At every chance, Tallulah ran off to Windows, where she was able to indulge herself in some of her less disreputable passions. She collected pets. She was a great sports fan. She followed boxing, horseracing, and—most of all—baseball. She loved the New York Giants and she worshipped at the altar of Willie Mays. Her favorite TV shows were soap operas. She swam and picnicked by the pool with friends, including Eugenia Rawls, Eugenia's husband and Bankhead's lawyer Donald Seawell, and their children. Rawls remembered how at night "Tallulah would give us a choice of films: *Lifeboat* or *The Royal Scandal*."

The insatiable attention-grabber was becoming a recluse, which was maybe not a bad thing. By the late 1940s, Bankhead's addictions and "I'm pure as the driven slush" behavior began to take a heavy toll. Her proclivity for stripping in public increased with uninhibited regularity. She smoked up to 150 cigarettes every day. She took uppers to get going, and downers to go to sleep, sometimes in gargantuan and/or conflicting dosages. She was drinking more than ever. She'd always suffered from severe insomnia and could easily slide into depression, but now her energy was faltering, her motor giving out. "Nobody can be exactly like me," she once asserted. "Even I have trouble doing it."

But she wasn't quite done doing it yet. In 1950, Tallulah was hired to host *The Big Show* on radio. The medium was feeling the threat of television's increasing gravitational pull and was looking for new programming. *The Big Show* premiered in November to great success. Singers, comedians, actors, and personalities from all walks of life made appearances, and the variety program was a Sunday evening entertainment staple in millions of homes for three years. She was named radio's Woman of the Year.

Tallulah's last turn on Broadway was in Tennessee Williams's *The Milk Train Doesn't Stop Here Anymore*. The show closed after five performances. Her last movie was the 1965 British horror film, *Fanatic*, released in the U.S. as *Die! Die! My Darling!*

Tallulah never thought of television as being for her—"I'd rather go over Niagara in a barrel"—but she was a regular guest on various variety programs and talk shows. One of her biggest TV gigs was playing herself in a 1957 episode of *The Ford Lucille Ball-Desi Arnaz Show* titled *The Celebrity Next Door*. Her last acting role was portraying the villainous Black Widow on *Batman*. In December 1967, she appeared in a sketch on the *Smothers Brothers Comedy Hour*, and the next May she was on the *Tonight Show* with guest host Joe Garagiola. Two of her co-panelists for that "lost" episode were Beatles John Lennon and Paul McCartney.

Tallulah was growing frail. She was prone to accidents. She must have known her final curtain call was looming.

By the mid-1960s, Sister still loved to travel, but her primary residence was on the Eastern Shore. Eugenia was living on a farm between Chestertown and Rock Hall, supported and cared for by her friend, the super-rich and philanthropic du Pont heiress Louisa d'Andelot Carpenter. "I had two people who cared for me growing up," William Bankhead says, "my mom and Mrs. Carpenter, and that was what I knew. Mrs. Carpenter was part of my family. Louisa Carpenter was a generous woman. She did a lot of good for a lot of people. There was massive wealth in her family, but also massive generosity. She moved here to be close to her family in Delaware and bought the farms for the purpose of waterfowl hunting.

"We had cousins in Alabama, but for their own reasons they weren't really on speaking terms. So, our family had our own little enclave up here on the Eastern Shore. These were people who'd had relationships long before I came along. They'd known each other for a long time and cared for and looked after each other. My mother was funny, intellectual, and wanted to enjoy life. She could interact with anyone from world leaders on down, and that's the way I was brought up. Though I had access to a fine education and spent time in places like France and Italy growing up, *this* is where I was raised."

"Before our second daughter was born," William continues, "we asked my aunt if it was okay to name her Tallulah. Our first had been named after my mother and my mother-in-law. She said, 'You know there's a lot of baggage that goes with that.' But it was a family name so that's what we did. We call her Tally.

"When my aunt got older, she came here to visit more than she did when she was busy. I couldn't tell you how often she came, she was just family, I never tracked her time with us. I will say that when she was in town it wasn't a normal visit like when others would come to see us. She was outspoken. Any association with her was not a quiet one. There was staff that came along. The hours she kept were very different. It's like when we lived in Europe and didn't get dressed for dinner until 10 o'clock at night. In the theater, it would be 11 or midnight before everything was over, so life would start in the middle of the night and then the next thing you knew it would be daylight. Also, in the theater, backstage, most dressing rooms were unisex. Only occasionally would a lead actor or actress have their own dressing room. People changed costumes in one common area. There was no shame. So, when everybody was around, there was no shame here either. They'd all be out there in the pool running around naked. One time a local plumber came by to do some work and even though what he saw took him back at first, eventually he said well, if they're not afraid to stand there like that, I'm not afraid to look."

In July 1968, Tallulah visited her Shore family for the last time. The Bankhead sisters spent Tallulah's final summer playing cards, dining with friends, and arguing. After three months, Bankhead went back to New York where she caught the flu, then pneumonia. She died at St. Luke's Hospital in New York on December 12, 1968, at the age of sixty-six.

On December 14, at Eugenia's insistence, a private funeral was held at St. Paul's Episcopal Church near the Kent County village of Fairlee. Her New York friends hosted a memorial service two days later.

Though she held no "formal conviction about religion or life in the hereafter," Tallulah had given the ending of her story much thought over the years. In her autobiography she wrote, "Though I fear many things—my shadow, opening night audiences, the dark—I have no fear of death."

They say her last words were "codeine—bourbon."

St. Paul's was established in 1692. Among the pastors who have served this congregation are the Rev. Dr. William Smith, the founder of Chestertown's prestigious Washington College, and Reverend Sewell S. Hepburn, whose granddaughter Katherine grew up to be a pretty famous actress in her own right.

Tallulah's casket was lined in blue silk, and she was dressed in a favorite nightgown, complete with cigarette burns. Before the lid was closed, Louisa Carpenter slipped in a lucky rabbit's foot that Bankhead's father had given his youngest daughter in February 1937, when *Reflected Glory* opened in Washington, D.C. She'd carried it with her ever since, and thanks to Mrs. Carpenter, she took it with her to the grave.

Eleven years later, Eugenia died at the Kent and Queen Anne Hospital in Chestertown, Maryland on March 11, 1979 after complications from a surgery. She was buried next to her sister.

William Bankhead says,

"Basically, it doesn't bother me that people go to the cemetery to visit my aunt's grave. My aunt set a lot of precedents for today's modern woman. That's one of the reasons I think women in particular are drawn to visit her gravesite. I don't really understand it, but if people have that need, if that's what does it for them, so be it. The only time I ever got mad was when one of the local historical organizations announced they were going to have a party at the site. That was too much for me and I let them know it. I think those kinds of places should be more solemn and aren't places to throw a party."

Tallulah's legacy includes almost 300 film, stage, television, and radio roles. Called Broadway's most original leading lady, she was posthumously inducted into the first class of the American Theater Hall of Fame, and she has a star on the Hollywood Walk of Fame. A dozen books have been written about her. She's inspired countless impressions. Kathleen Turner, Valerie Harper, and musician/actor Suzi Quatro (Leather Tuscadero on TV's *Happy Days*) have played her onstage. She was portrayed by Carrie Nye in the 1980 made-for-television movie *The Scarlett War*, about the making of *Gone with the Wind*, and both she and Eugenia appear as lifelong acquaintances of F. Scott Fitzgerald's wife Zelda in Amazon Prime's 2015 series, *Z: The Beginning of Everything*. Zelda Sayre Fitzgerald, two years older than Tallulah, was also from Alabama, and her renegade antiestablishment mischief rivaled Bankhead's during the age of the flapper. Those 'Bama girls helped turn the post-Victorian world upside down. Most recently, Paget Brewster played Bankhead in Netflix's 2020 miniseries *Hollywood*.

Tallulah's trademark "Hello, Dahling" still resonates, though many would be hard-pressed to provide the catchphrase's origins.

The characters of both Cruella De Vil in Walt Disney's *One Hundred and One Dalmatians* and Ursula from *The Little Mermaid* were at least in part influenced by Bankhead.

In 2014, London's Ritz Hotel introduced "The Tallulah," a limited-availability cocktail named for the time she drank champagne out of her shoe there to celebrate her return to London. It was served in a decanter with a glass version of one of her Louboutins and came with a numbered scroll as a souvenir.

For her nephew, the remembrances are more personal:

"When I was a kid, I would visit my aunt at Windows and there was a planters box filled with pansies at the front door. My favorite flowers to this day are pansies.

"One time when I was little, I went to see her in a play and I asked her, why do you have so much lipstick on? She said, "Well, at plays, some people are sitting way up in the balcony and they can't see, so you have to overdo everything so they can see you. Otherwise, you're just a pale blob."

A pale blob was never something Bankhead aspired to be.

Almost as famous for her generosity as her red-hot reputation, Tallulah was an outspoken supporter of such causes as civil rights and the plight of refugees. There is, however, no argument that she struggled with self-destructive behavior, and though the overt public spectacle of her personal life was the stuff hedonistic mythologies are made of, she did leave damage in her wake. There are also those who might opine that she'd been blessed with abundant talent that was tragically wasted.

Tallulah could not care less.

Which, in the end, brings us not so much as to how Tallulah Bankhead ended up on the Eastern Shore, but why she belongs.

She shared a lot of the character of the Eastern Shore.

Shorefolk speak their own minds in their own voices. They're independent. They're funny. They're storytellers.

They're often unpredictable.

They can never back down from a fight.

They have an abundance of personality.

"Personality?" said Tallulah. "Even the hostiles concede I have it."

In her warm and insightful memoir *Tallulah—A Memory*, Eugenia Rawls concluded with poetry she wrote commemorating the burial of her friend. The untitled poem ended with this stanza:

We followed over muddy, stubbled fields to water's edge,
Heard words intoned and ritual performed,
Then high above, wheeling in the December sky,
The geese came in, exultant,
Their wild cries echoing your name.

On the Eastern Shore, when the wild geese call your name, you're always and forever one of us, no matter how you got here.

ON LOCATION

At the courthouse in downtown Easton, a statue honors Frederick
Douglass, the most famous son of Talbot County, Maryland. Born
into slavery, Douglass escaped captivity as a young man and went
on to become a leading abolitionist and the most-photographed
American of the 19th century. (*grandbrothers/Shutterstock*)

EASTON

Not quite halfway up the Bay, home to a plentiful bounty of flora and fauna and mapped out by some of the first European colonists to set foot in the New World, Talbot County, Maryland is bordered by hundreds of miles of tidal shoreline and is a historic and cultural hub of the mid-Shore. Settled by risk takers, forward thinkers, and colorful characters, overseen by men of commerce and families of clout, harvested by watermen and farmers, and systemically influenced by both the peaceful morality of religion and the cruelty of slavery, Talbot County is, as Dickson J. Preston wrote in his *Talbot County, A History*, where land meets water "in a unique and valuable way."

Easton is the county seat. The historic downtown district spreads east from a courthouse constructed on the site in 1712. The town grew from a tiny colonial village into a significant base of post-Revolutionary political and economic sway. After the division and bloodshed of the Civil War and then the Age of Steam, Easton solidified its standing as a central location to tend to one's Eastern Shore business, be it governmental, commercial, or otherwise.

Easton also has a connection to filmmaking dating back to some of cinema's earliest days.

Most silent movies were shot on flammable film stock. Not only were they treated with complete negligence once any obvious financial benefit was gone, but reels of film would also, on occasion, spontaneously combust and burn down entire storage buildings full of old, one-of-a-kind prints. Thousands of early motion pictures have therefore been categorized as "lost." *I Will Repay*, one such lost movie, was filmed in and around Easton in the autumn of 1917. Based on a short story by O. Henry called "The Municipal Report," the film's plot concerns a post–Civil War publisher who travels to Nashville and gets involved in the personal lives of some of the locals. A one-reeler with the same title had been released in 1916, but that picture had no resemblance to O. Henry's story, nor did it feature as the hero of the piece Talbot County's own acting sensation, George Junkin, working under his stage name of George J. Forth.

I Will Repay, Junkin's fifth movie, was also his fifth released in 1917. He'd auditioned in New York for Vitograph Studios and soon after received a telegram telling him to report for work. His first film was *The Sixteenth Wife*, the story of a newspaper reporter who gets involved with a woman from his past, rescues her from a Turkish strongman with fifteen wives, and convinces her to come back to Kentucky to "wash dishes and make layer lemon cake" instead of joining a harem. It ends with a kiss. A brilliant future was predicted for Junkin in New York movie circles, but despite such journalistic endorsements as "his lovemaking has been pronounced by expert critics as superb," his filmography is a mere seven movies long. In the 1920s, Junkin moved to Missouri where he began, using his given name, a successful career in the upstart radio industry.

Junkin's leading lady, Corrine Griffith, later famous as "The Orchid Lady" of the silent screen, would make almost seventy movies, most between 1916 and 1929. Known as a breathtaking beauty with behind-the-scenes production influence but limited acting chops, the talkies put an end to her onscreen appearances.

She became a successful writer and published eleven books, two of them bestsellers. One of Griffith's husbands was George Preston Marshall, the longtime owner of Washington's pro football team, and she's said to have written the lyrics to *Hail to the Redskins*. In a 1966 divorce from husband number four, she falsely testified she was not actually Corrine Griffith but instead a much younger sister who'd taken the famous woman's place upon her death. Despite this bizarre episode, Corrine Griffith was a successful entrepreneur and a savvy real estate investor and at the time of her actual death in 1979, she's said to have been one of the world's richest women. The *Los Angeles Times* reported her age at time of death as being "79, or perhaps 67, or maybe 61."

Some of the first movie scenes ever shot in Easton were at the train station, the South Harrison Street home of Congressman J. Harry Covington, and at the Hotel Norris, one of several names given to the Hotel Avon (c. 1891). The latter once sat where the Tidewater Inn, opened in 1949, is now located. Ratcliffe Manor on the Tred Avon River was used in the filming of Southern plantation scenes.

Another lost film, *In the Land of Legendary Lore*, released in 1918, was a hyper-fictionalized version of a historic love story between the widowed proprietary governor of Maryland, the third Baron of Baltimore, Charles Calvert (1637–1715), and his future Lady Baltimore, Talbot County's Jane/Betty Lowe (1633–1701). Ratcliffe Manor and the Plimhimmon estate, both dating back to a 1659 survey, were used for background scenery, as was the Religious Society of Friends' Third Haven Meeting House, an Easton landmark that dates back to 1684 and is reputed to be the oldest wooden framed house of worship in America. The third floor of the town music hall served as a studio for indoor sequences. Set decorations and props were "secured from a number of the best homes and leading stores of Easton." Cambridge's *Daily Banner* reported that as many as 600 distinguished citizens and schoolchildren were used as extras.

In the Land of Legendary Lore was based on a romanticized chronicle of Talbot County's early days published in 1898 by the Gazette Publishing House of Easton, Maryland and written by a man named Prentiss Ingraham (1843–1904). Ingraham and his family lived in Talbot County from 1897 to 1902. He'd fought as a Confederate colonel, and after the Civil War traveled the world as a soldier of fortune. In Cuba's war for independence from Spain, Ingraham ran blockades on the *Hornet,* a gunboat built for the Confederacy but captured by the U.S. Navy, which later conducted operations on the Chesapeake Bay.

Colonel Ingraham was captured by the Spanish and condemned to death but escaped. Upon his return to America, he headed west. He met and would eventually write more than 100 stories about Buffalo Bill Cody, helping as much as almost anyone to make Cody famous and to define what would become the American West of myth and legend.

A dime novelist who sacrificed subtlety and style for formatted plots, stereotypical characters, and productivity, Ingraham was one of his day's most prolific writers of mainstream fiction. At the height of his output, he was estimated to have written, in longhand, at least two 35,000-70,0000–word books every month. In his career he published something like 600 novels and 400 shorter works, typically adventure yarns featuring youthful protagonists full of vim, vigor, and patriotic virtue.

The producers of the three-reeler based on Ingraham's Eastern Shore book circulated notices announcing that *In the Land of Legendary Lore* needed ten Talbot County representatives of the "highest type of young womanhood" to appear in the film and that the casting of these embodiments of homegrown feminine purity would be determined by "Popular Selection." At ballot boxes placed around the county, a nickel secured five votes for the aspiring starlet of one's choice. Five bucks bought 500 votes. Voters could cast as many ballots as they were willing to purchase. To make sure potential contestants knew what was at stake, the casting flyer asserted that "some of the greatest movie stars of the day, [had] from obscure private life, quickly attained national prominence, with huge incomes, simply because some silent producer could use their talent and adaptability which he instantly recognized the first time they appeared on screen." The contest winner, Ruth Beauchamp of Easton, was cast as Jane Lowe, and though it was her first experience on camera, the *Star Democrat* reported that her acting, paired with her "dainty and charming personality, has left her work pleasing and has left nothing to be desired."

In the Land of Legendary Lore took three months to produce, six weeks to shoot, and hasn't been seen by anyone in more than a century. It's not even listed on the Internet Movie Database.

As the movies became the most popular form of American entertainment, more theaters opened across the country and the Eastern Shore. The Arcade in Salisbury started selling tickets in 1914. The Arcade in Cambridge, later the Dorset, served audiences from 1920 through the early 1970s. The Prince Theatre in Chestertown operated under one name or another for more than eighty years.

Easton's iconic Avalon Theatre opened in 1922 as the New Theatre, "The Showplace of the Eastern Shore," a 650-seat entertainment palace dedicated to vaudeville and silent movies. Featuring an eighteen-foot lighted dome, player-piano, and a 300-pipe electric-pneumatic organ, the theater was sold early in

1936, renovated in an art deco theme, and then sold again, this time to the Schine brothers' theater chain, the largest in the country.

From John Wayne in *Stagecoach* to the droids and Wookies of *Star Wars*, local movie fans saw everything and everybody at the Avalon. Still, all good things must sooner or later come to "The End." In 1985, after providing more than six decades of moviegoing, the showplace went dark.

But all was not lost. A couple years later, a group of community leaders stepped in to revive the Avalon as a performing arts center. Renovations that began in 1987 were finished in 1989. Hopes were high but construction starts stutter-stepped. In 1992, the property ended up at auction. The sole bidder was the town of Easton. Under the auspices of the Avalon Foundation, the plan to create a preeminent performing arts venue was revived.

The timing was now right. A star was reborn.

Pre-COVID, the Avalon Theatre—with its magnificent acoustics and state-of-the-art sound, lighting, and video capabilities, along with the cabaret-style third-floor space where the ballroom was located—hosted more than 100 shows a year, from national touring acts to the annual Holiday Show and Chesapeake Film Festival events. Though recently renovated again, much of the 1936 art deco style remains, as does almost all the original theater's soul.

In its first go-round, the Avalon Theatre hosted three world premieres, beginning in 1928, with the now long-lost silent picture *The First Kiss*, filmed at Easton's county courthouse and in nearby St. Michaels. *The First Kiss* starred Fay Wray and a wet-behind-the-ears Gary Cooper, and by some reports filled the theater five times a day for three days.

In 1950, the Avalon held a premiere showing of MGM's *Stars in My Crown* starring Joel McCrea, one of the great screen cowboys,

and written by Joe David Brown, who was a resident of Easton at the time.

Tall, tight-lipped, and handsome with an easygoing humor, McCrea was mostly known for his westerns, but he was a versatile actor and a convincing romantic lead. Of all his movies, nearly 100 hundred during a fifty-year career, *Stars in My Crown* was one of McCrea's personal favorites. With an antiracist theme considered bold for its day, the film tells the story of a Civil War cavalryman turned preacher who brought "law and order, love and laughter to a small Southern community" in an "action-filled story of a two-fisted parson whose whisper spoke louder than his six-guns."

The Avalon's newspaper advertisement promoting the Easton premiere also reminded locals that the film was based on the widely read and well-loved novel by a local author.

With "bronze-red hair and mischievous blue eyes," Joe David Brown (1915–1976) was a freelance writer originally from Alabama, a foreign correspondent, a war hero, and—as described by the *Star Democrat*'s Harold Kathman—a beefy, broad-shouldered guy more than six feet tall. Brown had sold his first short story, "The Parson and the Miracle Grindstone," based on remembrances of his minister grandfather, to the *Saturday Evening Post*. The story was a hit, so Brown's next step was to develop the concept into a full-length book. He and his wife Frances happened to be visiting friends in Talbot County when they saw a cottage near the town of Newcomb that appealed to both their sensibilities and their limited budget. The novel *Stars in My Crown*, with a church hymn as inspiration for its title, took the Browns, working together in overnight sessions where he'd write and she'd critique, two months to complete.

Next stop, Hollywood.

Joel McCrea grew up in Hollywood. He attended Hollywood High School with the likes of Carole Lombard, Lon Chaney Jr., and Jacques Tourneur, son of the influential silent movie director Maurice (*The Whip*). Jacques, who three films earlier had directed *Out of the Past*, 1947's film noir standout starring Robert Mitchum, loved Brown's story so much that he worked at scale for the opportunity to helm *Stars in My Crown*. The move backfired in the long run. Taking the upfront financial hit cost him credibility and left him directing less prestigious material from that point.

On Wednesday April 26, 1950, the town of Easton celebrated the premiere of *Stars in My Crown*. Mayor Joseph S. Barnes presented Brown with a key to the city. James Mitchell, who played a doctor in the picture, and later became known for playing Palmer Cortlandt on the soap opera *All My Children* from 1979 until his death in 2010, flew in for the event and was made an honorary Citizen of Easton. Telegrams from Joel McCrea, co-star Ellen Drew, and Jacques Tourneur were read to the audience. Harking back to the lean days in a speech, Brown remarked that the local hospitality was beyond reproach and that he'd "rather be poor in Talbot County than rich anywhere else."

Brown's second novel, *Kings Go Forth*, was made into a 1958 film starring Frank Sinatra, Tony Curtis, and Natalie Wood. His fifth, *Addie Pray*, was turned into 1973's *Paper Moon* starring Ryan O'Neill and his ten-year-old daughter, Tatum. Tatum O'Neill was rewarded for her instinctive performance as the pint-sized con artist protégé Addie by becoming the youngest Academy Award winner in history.

Five years after celebrating *Stars in My Crown* and Joe David Brown, the Avalon hosted its final classic-era movie premiere with *Hit the Deck*, one of MGM's last big cotton candy–infused musicals. Partially filmed in St. Michaels, though you'd never know it, the special guest at the gala Talbot County sneak preview was one of the film's costars, Ann Miller.

Not much more than a story about sailors chasing women, *Hit the Deck* nonetheless came ashore with a pedigree. First there'd been a light comedic play called *Shore Leave* that was made into a 1925 silent picture. Two years later, the play was restructured as a musical featuring tunes by Vincent Youmans and renamed *Hit the Deck*. Turned out to be a winner.

The first cinematic adaptation of *Hit the Deck* came out in 1929. In 1936, Fred Astaire and Ginger Rogers made waves with a remake called *Follow the Fleet*, featuring new music from Irving Berlin. This 1955 version brought back the original title as well as Vincent Youman's songs. The Eastern Shore premiere was part of a fundraising effort to provide music therapy to patients under psychiatric care at the Eastern Shore State Hospital in Cambridge. Mildred Tucker, a resident of Easton and a friend of the event's organizers, happened to be the remarried ex-wife of Vincent Youmans and was able to use her connections to bring the film's premiere to the Avalon.

The movie was the last gasp of a grand musical tradition in cinema. Called contrived, disjointed, and underwhelming by critics and film historians, the picture's highlight is the Navy-themed reprise performance of Youmans's (along with Leo Robin and Clifford Grey) *Hallelujah*. The standout component in the sequence is the seventh-billed Ann Miller's amazing dance performance. She makes this rickety boat float.

Ann Miller, born in Texas, raised in California by a mother who encouraged her to earn her living through dance, was discovered by Lucille Ball in a San Francisco nightclub. At fourteen, she lied about her age to get a movie contract. As a tap dancer, she was a speed demon, claiming to be able to perform 500 taps per minute.

Glamourous and gregarious, Ann Miller made a splash when she rolled into Easton on a chilly February day in 1955.

Local papers praised her friendliness, lack of pretension, and interest in the events of a long day and evening despite fighting a cold. Miller's busy schedule started with a luncheon and key to the city ceremony with Mayor Calvin G. Lomax and the Junior Chamber of Commerce at the Tidewater Inn and continued with a visit to the high school. Then it was over to Cambridge to tour the hospital benefiting from the premiere's fundraising. She went on the air on WCEM, rode in a parade, sat for interviews, and dined with reporters for her evening meal. The movie started at 8:30 p.m. and afterward Miller was the guest of honor at a buffet reception back at the Tidewater.

A self-proclaimed victim of "brassy, good-hearted showgirl" typecasting who never got her breakout star turn, Ann Miller charmed the Shore. Later, she'd tour with Bob Hope and the USO, and gain a whole new wave of fans with Broadway's 1979 smash *Sugar Babies*, a tribute to old-time burlesque. She left this world on January 22, 2004, but Moe and Joe, her gold-painted Mary Jane tap shoes, remain with us as part of the Smithsonian Institution's collection at the National Museum of American History.

After the hoopla subsided, Hollywood and Easton kept their distance for a few decades. When cinematic fame did come back, it was in the form of a location shoot for 1994's *Silent Fall*, about a mute autistic boy who witnesses his parents' murder.

During three weeks in early October 1993, the *Silent Fall* production team filmed around Easton. The town's name on the police station was changed to Waterville, a house on Villa Road overlooking Goldsborough Creek was used for scenes of the Rainers at home, and the historic Ashby House on the Miles River was where the grisly fictional murders took place. For a Halloween

sequence, local children were recruited to go trick-or-treating a couple weeks early, and an important scene takes place at the Crab Claw Restaurant in St. Michaels.

There have been other brushes with cinematic glory for Easton. In 1993, Nicholas Cage buzzed in and out of town while shooting some rural scenes for *Guarding Tess* with Shirley MacLaine that ended up on the cutting room floor, and its most recent cameos came in 2016 with *Jackie*, starring Natalie Portman in an Oscar-nominated portrayal of Jacqueline Kennedy in the days following her husband's assassination. Scenes for this film were taken at the Easton Newman Field Airport and at Tred Avon Manor (c. 1800), a stately manor house located between Easton and St. Michaels that stands in for the Kennedy compound in Hyannis Port, Massachusetts.

Today, Easton is among the Eastern Shore's most dynamic locales, a busy and inviting place that balances commerce and community with its own brand of Land of Pleasant Living hospitality. Hollywood hasn't stopped by in a while, but when the movies do once again come calling, it's a safe bet that Easton will, as always, be ready for its close-up.

BASED ON A TRUE STORY

Cynthia Erivo received an Oscar nomination for Best Actress for her portrayal of Harriet Tubman in the feature film *Harriet*. Tubman, born into slavery on the Eastern Shore of Maryland, became the most celebrated conductor of escaping slaves on the Underground Railroad and is honored today with a National Historical Park and visitor center in Dorchester County. *(Focus Features/Photofest)*

HARRIET
TUBMAN

"The midnight sky and the silent stars have been the witnesses of your devotion to freedom and your heroism."
—*Frederick Douglass*

The history of racial relations on the Eastern Shore is no less complicated than in the rest of the country. Our region's colonial society and economy, a plantation culture with every inhabitant's identity anchored to white supremacy, was built on a foundation of tobacco and slavery. After the Revolutionary War, when the Shore's agricultural trade transitioned to less-labor-intensive crops, many slaves were manumitted by their owners. By the time of the Civil War, half of Maryland's blacks were free. Still, the Southern states were relentless in their use of slave labor. Slave owners here positioned themselves as breeders. Mothers were the determining factor as to who was born into slavery. If the mother was a slave, so were her babies.

As a border state, Maryland, with strong-arm persuasion by President Lincoln, remained in the Union, but on the Eastern Shore the sympathies of many citizens were with the South. The war split families. Brother fought brother on the battlefield.

Post-Reconstruction, lynch mobs and Jim Crow were no strangers to these parts. Many schools, public facilities, and private businesses remained segregated for more than a decade after 1954's *Brown v. Board of Education* Supreme Court decision. In the early 1960s, the Freedom Riders challenged local Shore authorities and there was a protest in the city of Cambridge in 1963 that led to rioting. An even more violent and destructive uprising occurred there during the Long Hot Summer of 1967.

During particularly volatile moments in our nation's ongoing struggle toward a more perfect union, the desire for change can be confrontational and bring violence that scars communities and widens the chasm between neighbors.

But sometimes those efforts to obtain true liberty and justice for all can be stealthy, subversive, and take place under the quiet cover of night, saving not an ideal, but rescuing the lives of actual people a handful at a time.

That's where Harriet Tubman comes in.

In 2019, Martin Chase Productions and Focus Features released *Harriet*, starring Cynthia Erivo and written and directed by Kasi Lemmons. It was the first feature film ever made about Harriet Tubman, although there had been other on-screen portrayals, most notably by Cicely Tyson in the 1978 TV miniseries *A Woman Called Moses*.

Director Lemmon, who is also an actor, opens her Oscar-nominated film with Harriet experiencing one of the seizures that had been part of her real life since she was twelve or thirteen years old, when she was told to accompany a plantation cook to a local store. While they were there, a slave who left work without permission was attacked by his owner. When the slave master ordered young Harriet, then known as Minty, to help restrain the AWOL slave, she refused. The slave broke free and ran. The master threw a two-pound weight that hit Minty in the head.

The assault "broke" her skull. Bleeding and fainting, she was carried to the plantation house of a man she'd been rented out to and was laid across a bench. No medical attention was provided. Two days later, she was sent back to the field despite her severe injuries. Unable to work, she was returned to her master. He tried to sell her, but nobody wanted damaged goods. "They said they wouldn't give a sixpence for me," Tubman later acknowledged.

As a result of her trauma, for the rest of her life Minty suffered from pain, dizziness, intense headaches, and seizures— unpredictable sleeping spells that induced hallucinatory states. Devout in her Christian faith, she believed the profound visons and vivid premonitions she witnessed in this dreamlike condition were direct messages from God.

At the beginning of *Harriet*, Minty's trance is broken by her husband, John Tubman. John has news that a lawyer she'd hired has proven that her mother was supposed to have been freed when she turned forty-five, as Minty is to be when she turns the same age. This is also true to life, and as in both life and cinema, no effort was made by her oppressors to honor this obligation. To dramatize the story for the screen, when Minty and John show her current master their proof, it's ripped up in their faces

In the movie, as in life, she prayed he would die, and he did.

Harriet's owner's son Gideon, played by English actor Joe Alwyn, overhears her prayer. Even though he and Minty have grown up together, he's furious and decides to sell her off. She runs.

Gideon and his men catch her on a bridge. With a proclamation that she will live free or die, she jumps over the side.

Though she did often express those exact sentiments, the onscreen action here is pure storytelling. There was no real Gideon Brodess and no such dramatic first-act exit. Hollywood's flaunting of the phrase "based on a true story" is never a guarantee to any purity of truth. "Story" is always the operative word. *Harriet* captures the spirit and relevance of its subject, and that's often the most essential aspect of what a biographical picture, a biopic, tries to do. It's important to know the facts of Harriet Tubman's life and to recognize her significance to history, but movies must engage through storytelling, as well as convey the essence of a singular life in a reasonable period of time. It's poetic license, and everybody, including the audience, is in on the deal.

Harriet Tubman was born a slave in Dorchester County, Maryland in 1822. Her given name was Araminta Ross.

Because of Dorchester County's central Eastern Shore location and the shape given by its boundaries, residents think of themselves as being from the Heart of the Shore. Captain John Smith explored the region in some of his earliest forays up the Chesapeake. By the time the county was established in 1669, there were hundreds of settlers living along the water's edge, but they were steering clear of the dense upriver forests where dangerous beasts and hostile natives dwelt. The county seat of Cambridge was founded on the Southern bank of the Choptank in 1684. The first black people to arrive came ashore as human cargo.

"Minty" Ross was the fifth of nine children born to Ben Ross and Harriet "Rit" Green, both slaves. Ben was owned by Anthony

Thompson, the master of a large plantation near the Blackwater River. A skilled timber inspector and woodsman, Ben was valued by his master, and Thompson's son kept a promise he'd made to free Ben when he turned forty-five. Rit was owned by a widow, Mary Pattison Brodess, and though Mary's father had stipulated in his will that she be freed at forty-five, none of his heirs paid heed to those wishes. About twenty years before Minty's birth, Thompson became Mary Brodess's second husband and she, along with her slaves, moved to his estate where Ben and Rit fell in love and also married. Linah, Ben and Rit's first child, was born around 1808.

Mary Brodess died and until her son Edward came of age, the assets she left behind were managed by his stepfather. Ben and Rit's second child, Mariah Ritty, was born around 1811, followed by Soph in 1813 and Robert in 1816. In March 1822, sometime around the fifteenth, Minty came along.

A year or so later, when Edward Brodess turned twenty-one, he married and moved to his own plantation ten miles away on Greenbrier Road in Bucktown. He took what was now his property, his slaves, with him. In the years that followed, despite her mother and father living apart, Minty would have four more siblings—Ben, Rachel, Henry, and Moses born in 1832.

Because the Eastern Shore had transitioned from growing tobacco to harvesting corn and grains and stripping the immense forests that grew here, fewer slaves were needed. Whenever markets crumbled, as they did during Harriet Tubman's youth, many slave owners found themselves in great debt. To keep solvent, they often hired out their slaves to other landowners in the area. If worse ever came to worst, they could always straight up sell them. It was illegal to ship new slaves into the country, but cottonfields were blooming across the South, and that brutal business possessed an insatiable appetite for the forced labor of human capital.

When Minty was a toddler, Brodess sold her sister, Mariah Ritty, to a Mississippi slave trader. Her family never saw her again.

Rit worked in the Brodess household. She toiled night and day, as did her older children, leaving Minty at an early age to care for her even younger siblings. Then, as if that weren't responsibility enough for someone so little, her master rented her out as a laborer. She was five or six years old.

The offspring of slaves were not entitled to a childhood.

Minty's first assignment away from home was in the manor of a wealthy planter named James Cook. Here she was expected not only to keep house, and learn the difficult art of weaving; she also was required to check muskrat traps out in the marsh and collect the dead bodies of the large rodents. Muskrat pelts had more value than Minty. The work was wet and muddy and cold, the traps difficult for a child with small hands and limited strength. Everything about it was dangerous. Nevertheless, she was expected to perform these duties even after contracting the measles.

When she couldn't physically go on, Cook sent her back to Brodess, where her mother was allowed to nurse her back to health.

Minty was also hired out as a nursemaid for a woman called Miss Susan. She was required to clean and do chores during the day and at night she had to rock the cradle of Miss Susan's baby so the infant wouldn't awaken her mother with its cries. Minty worked around the clock. At the slightest slackening in her duties or backtalk, Miss Susan, who kept one whip on her mantle and another under her pillow, would crack her across her head, face, and neck. One day Minty was lashed five times before breakfast.

She ran away once and hid for five days.

As she grew older and stronger Minty was assigned to field and forest work, driving oxen, plowing, chopping wood, and hauling logs. It was hard labor, "all the work of a man," with scant food, minimal rest, and constant exposure to the elements. The humidity in summer was merciless; the mosquitos and flies bloodthirsty, but at least she was outside, away from the ever-watchful eye of her worst tormentors. She loved being in nature, and the work made her ever stronger, more resilient.

Before Minty turned twenty, Brodess sold off her sisters Linah and Soph. Linah brought $400 and left her young daughters motherless, while Soph may have been sold with her child. According to Atthow Pattison's will, Rit and her children should have been set free, but instead two more of those children were illegally sold into the living hell of the Southern cotton plantations and no one with any authority cared. Even after hiring that lawyer to look into the intended manumission of her mother and family, their freedom was denied. From the sale of Minty's sisters, Brodess bought a few more acres of land with his profits.

Around the same time, Edward's stepbrother, the son of Anthony Thompson, followed through on his late father's wishes and granted Ben Ross his promised freedom. Ross, with his skills as a woodsman, continued to work for the Thompson family.

Minty wed John Tubman when she was about twenty-two. He was a free black man, she still a slave. It was at this time she took on her mother's first name. Minty Ross was now Harriet Tubman.

After she took ill in her late twenties and was not as productive as she'd been, Edward Brodess again wanted to sell her, but garnered paltry interest in a sick slave. No matter, Harriet was aware her time was nearing. Even after Brodess's death, the one she'd prayed for, Harriet knew his widow Eliza had no qualms over putting her on the block to pay off the family's debts.

Harriet made her decision. "There was one of two things I was entitled to," she later told her biographer Sarah Bradford, "liberty or death, if I could not have one, I would have the other…"

She got her first chance to run in September 1849. She'd made a deal with Brodess before he died that she could hire herself out and pay her owners the lion's share of her fees. She and her brothers Ben and Henry were working on a plantation in nearby Caroline County when the three of them made their escape. Nobody knew they were gone for a couple days, but when they did, Eliza Brodess offered a reward of up to $100 each for the return of her property. "Of chestnut color, fine looking, and about five feet high" is the description given to Harriet in the public notice.

Not long into their flight, Harriet's brothers decided to turn back and forced her to return with them. The next time, and there would be a next time a month later, she left on her own. No man ever dictated her movements or destiny again.

Petite and disabled from her childhood head injury, Harriet was also strong, broad shouldered, and determined. She knew the woods and the marshes like few others. She also knew a little, but far less than she'd come to know, about the Underground Railroad.

The Underground Railroad was a secret system set up by abolitionists, religious activists, free blacks and slaves, and other friends of the cause that provided escaped men, women, and children places to hide, food, and clothing. They set up safe houses and provided guides, conductors, to lead the runaways in their pursuit of freedom along the wilderness, waterways, and old Indian trails of the border states and beyond. The Religious Society of Friends, the Quakers, were numerous in the region and leaders in the antislavery movement. It's likely Harriet's earliest assistance came from members of this devout Christian faction. Guided by these helpers, her faith, and the North Star, Harriet made it to the free state of Pennsylvania after she left the Eastern Shore. "When I found I had crossed that line, I looked at my hands to see if I was the same person. There was such a glory over everything, the sun came like gold through the trees, and over the fields, and I felt like I was in heaven."

Harriet resumes with Tubman reaching Philadelphia. Through the Underground Railroad, she meets the free black man William Still (1821–1902) of Pennsylvania's Anti-Slavery Society. Still, played by the Tony Award–winning actor-singer Leslie Odom Jr., was a real person who dedicated himself not only to helping human beings liberate themselves from slavery but to recording their stories for posterity. Often referred to as the Father of the Underground Railroad, Still was from New Jersey, but his parents had been Eastern Shore slaves. His father was able to buy his own freedom, his mother a runaway who'd witnessed her father being shot and killed by a drunken slaveowner when she was a child.

The film also introduces Tubman and the audience to Marie Buchanon, played by Janelle Monáe, a character created for the movie. Monáe, like Odom Jr., is also known as a singer, and she has been in the cast of such films as *Hidden Figures* (2016) and *Antebellum* (2020). Her character in *Harriet* owns and operates a boarding house for free black persons and the occasional fugitive. She provides Tubman safety, friendship, a roof over her head, a role model of unquestioned self-sufficiency, and a gun.

A year goes by. Though she's been trying, Tubman hasn't heard back from her husband or family. She's been earning money doing various odd jobs and decides to go back to the Eastern Shore to rescue her husband, John. The mission, not her first in real life, but the first in which she did return to the Eastern Shore, does not go as planned. In a rare occurrence, she doubts herself and her purpose. She then gets news that because of Gideon and his mother's dire financial situation, one of her brothers is to be sold. Tubman wants to take more of her family away, but her sister Rachel is too afraid to try to run and Rit won't leave as long as any of her children remain under the thumb of the Brodess family.

After this first cinematic rescue operation, Tubman finds her calling as a conductor. According to the film, by the time the Fugitive Slave Act was passed in 1850, a federal appeasement to the South requiring that even escaped slaves living in free states be returned to their owners, Tubman was an Underground Railroad leader with numerous missions under her belt. In fact, she'd made two at most, both primarily to save family members.

The Fugitive Slave Act erased any safety runaway slaves held in the North and doled out stiff punishment to anybody who helped a person living in servitude break their chains. Many black refugees fled even farther, north into Canada. In the movie, as people are evacuating Philadelphia in fear, Tubman refuses to go until she says goodbye to Marie. She soon realizes Gideon and his henchmen are hot on her trail when she witnesses an act of violence that stokes the fires of her anger and her desire for the end of American enslavement.

In reality, the Slave Act was passed in September, and in December, Harriet Tubman, risks be damned, headed back to Maryland to save Kessiah, the daughter of her long-gone sister Linah, and Kessiah's two children, six-year-old James Alfred and a baby called Araminta after Tubman's given name. Operating from Baltimore with accomplices on the Shore, her mission was successful. She repeated that achievement a few months later using the same tactics to rescue her brother Moses and two other men.

When she really returned to the Eastern Shore for the first time in the fall of 1851, it was with the intention of rescuing John. She'd even brought him a suit—the clothes of a runaway slave were a dead giveaway—but soon discovered that in her absence he'd remarried. John didn't want to leave so she found some other slaves who did and took them with her instead. John Tubman and his second wife, Caroline, went on to raise a family together. Sixteen years later, he was killed in a roadside argument with a white neighbor who shot him in the forehead. The neighbor was charged with murder but was acquitted by an all-white jury.

That December, Harriet led a group north to Ontario and though there's no record of certainty, researchers believe this may be the first time the woman called the "Moses of her People" met Frederick Douglass. Born into slavery thirty miles apart, Tubman and Douglass became two of the most respected figures in American history. He was a couple years older than she, but they admired one another's work and reputation.

Douglass (est.1817–1895) was from Talbot County, outside the town of Cordova on the Tuckahoe River. Of mixed race, Douglass was separated from his mother at infancy and taken from his grandmother as a child. His life journey took him from the Eastern Shore to Baltimore and back again, but in time he became a brilliant and renowned author, orator, and statesman. One of the most extraordinary events in his life occurred when he stood up to a notorious slave-breaker named Edward Covey who prided himself on his barbaric ability to beat and torture away any slave's rebellious nature. Douglass fought back. Covey gave up, and instead of letting word get out that he'd failed at his job, he let the young slave be. Covey's home on Broad Creek, on the outskirts of Saint Michaels, was known as Mount Misery. Given the way normal owners treated their slaves, it's horrific to imagine the monstrous occurrences that took place on the property of a man whose professional calling was to crush the human spirit.

President George W. Bush's Secretary of Defense Donald Rumsfeld bought the four-acre waterfront estate as a weekend getaway in 2003. He owned it for seventeen years until selling in 2020. Not far away, on San Domingo Creek, another member of the Bush administration, Vice President Dick Cheney, also owned a nearby waterfront retreat from 2005 to 2019. This property, known as Ballintober, was once owned by one of Thomas Edison's daughters and her husband, and was named after a medieval castle in Ireland.

Frederick Douglass and Harriet Tubman shared much in common, particularly their connection to the Tidewater region and their hatred for institutionalized slavery, but in crucial ways their lives had been quite different. Douglass was separated from his family as a child. Even in the worst of times during her enslavement, Tubman found comfort in the nearness of her people. Douglass learned to read at a young age while Tubman remained illiterate her entire life. He left his subjugation by train; she ran away on foot. He did his work on the lecture circuit in broad daylight. She did hers under the cover of night.

Tubman had methods she used on those nighttime missions. She usually traveled in winter months, when the nights are long and "people who have homes stay in them." She led her groups out of town on Saturday night because the reward postings wouldn't make it into the newspapers until Monday morning at the earliest. She used her husky singing voice to send coded messages. She wore disguises. She knew her terrain and read the stars and carried drugs to calm crying babies when slavers were on the hunt. She also carried a revolver, not only for the protection of herself and her passengers from external threats but also from dangers presented by a member of her party who might want to turn back.

In 1857, Tubman made a rare springtime trip back to the Shore to rescue her mother and father. She'd gotten word Ben was in trouble. Slaveowners had grown suspicious of him. They thought he might have something to do with so many of their slaves running away. He and Rit were together and in their seventies, ancient by nineteenth-century slave standards. Eliza Brodess had sold Rit to Ben for 20 dollars. To accommodate her parents' physical inability to use her typical routes, Tubman found an old horse and rigged a cart to carry them when they couldn't walk. It was dangerous to break routine, but they made it, and the two elders were able to reunite with their other children who were now living in Canada.

John Brown (1800–1859), like Tubman and Douglass, became one of the major figures in the antislavery movement, but while Douglass employed the power of his language and prestige in the marketplace of ideas, and Tubman used her skills to rescue individual human beings from bondage, John Brown believed violence and armed insurrection were the sole means to ensure the extermination of American slavery. Tubman met Brown the year before his ill-fated raid on Harpers Ferry, West Virginia.

Brown, like Tubman, believed God spoke to him. He foresaw a future that included a free state for former slaves, and he was prepared to wage war to bring his dream to fruition. He'd gone on the attack in Bloody Kansas, which got people's attention, and was once again planning to take aggressive action. He was confident that once he struck the first blow against the establishment, all the oppressed people across the South would revolt against their tyrannical overlords. Tubman never advocated for bloodshed, but she agreed that drastic change could only be accomplished by conflict because the wealth generated by the forced labor of an entire race would not be surrendered without a fight. As Brown worked on his battle plans, Tubman contributed intelligence and helped recruit volunteers to enlist in Brown's army. He called her "General." Brown also met and asked for Frederick Douglass's assistance, but Douglass didn't see his friend's strategy of a nationwide slave revolt as viable.

On October 16, 1859, Brown and twenty-two of his men attacked Harpers Ferry with the intent to raid a government armory and confiscate the 100,000 firearms they believed to be stored at the site. The incursion failed. On the morning of the nineteenth, the armory was taken by US troops led by Colonel Robert E. Lee and Lieutenant J. E. B. Stuart, two men who would play major roles in the war to come. Ten of Brown's soldiers were killed, including two of his sons, and Brown himself was hanged for treason. Six of his raiders followed him to the noose.

Americans saw the open hostilities as a sign of what the future held, and John Brown's death made him a martyr to those dedicated to abolishing slavery. Southerners felt the threat of change in the air. Both sides sensed confrontation on the horizon. The raid brought tensions to a head, and many historians consider the resulting fallout to have been a noteworthy factor in electing Abraham Lincoln president in 1860. An election in which Lincoln received no more than a handful of votes on the whole Eastern Shore, and came in a distant last in the state.

Senator William H. Seward, the former New York governor Lincoln chose for secretary of state, was an ally whom Tubman came to know through the abolitionist community. When he inherited a home and seven-acre piece of land in the fugitive-friendly farming community of Auburn, New York, he offered to sell it to Harriet at a low price on favorable terms. She might not yet be free, but owning land was another step in the right direction.

Tubman went back to the Eastern Shore one last time, and though she did bring a group back north with her, she was unable to pull off her intended goal of rescuing her sister Rachel, along with her two children, Ben and Angerine. These were three more loved ones her family never saw again.

This final mission plays out differently in *Harriet*.

Tubman has a vision that her father is at risk and travels south to extricate her parents before Ben can be arrested for aiding escaped slaves, a charge that one way or another was a death sentence. While there, she discovers Rachel has died and that Rachel's daughter is now assigned, as her mother had been, to work in the Brodess home. This news prompts Tubman to perform a brazen rescue of her niece. A final showdown with Gideon Brodess is now inevitable.

In her life, Harriet Tubman performed at least thirteen journeys into enemy territory to rescue more than seventy living souls from the inhumane yoke of oppression, including many members of her own family. She provided instructions that saved dozens more. Called "Moses" by friend and foe alike, the slavers never knew their adversary's identity until she wanted them to know. Information was a weapon she concealed or wielded on her own terms. Her story was hers alone to tell.

When the Civil War erupted, Tubman joined a group of abolitionists headed to South Carolina to support Union forces. She served as a cook and nurse but also worked undercover as a scout and spy. Despite not ever having been in the Deep South before, the landscape of woods and wetlands were familiar to her. She helped map out the theater of operations and performed surveillance on the local inhabitants and their activities, sometimes working right under their noses while in disguise.

Lincoln's Emancipation Proclamation, issued on January 1, 1863, freed all slaves living in the Confederacy.

In June, Colonel James Montgomery and Harriet Tubman led 300 black Union soldiers on a raid of the plantations located along the swampy, low-country Combahee River. As the first woman to command an armed assault in the war, she guided three steamboats past rebel mines to come ashore and attack. The African American troops seized food and supplies and ransacked the slaveowners' property, burning down houses, outbuildings, and infrastructure. When the enslaved realized what was happening, they came running from every direction carrying babies, rations, animals, tools, weapons, and whatever few personal items they owned and had time to grab. Confederate soldiers and civilians tried to restore order, but the pandemonium was staggering. They turned back or were overwhelmed. When the day was over, the raid freed more than 700 slaves in one fell swoop. Many of the liberated men joined the army of the United States.

Throughout the rest of the war, and for a few months after, Tubman continued to contribute to the effort by scouting and nursing wounded soldiers, as well as providing hope and guidance to the newly freed. On occasion, she returned to her home in New York to check on her people and her real estate.

The Confederacy surrendered in April 1865.

Harriet Tubman was not well compensated for her wartime services. She worked and took in boarders to make ends meet. In 1869 she married Nelson Charles Davis, a veteran and bricklayer from North Carolina who was twenty-two years her junior. They had a baby named Gertie. Nelson died in 1888.

Always an advocate for equal rights for everyone, after her husband's death, Tubman became a more outspoken proponent of women's suffrage. Her faith, always so vital to her and her crusades as an activist, became even more central to her life. With the help of her church, the African Methodist Episcopal Zion Church in Auburn, she lived to see her dream of opening a home and hospital for sick and elderly African Americans. In the late 1890s she underwent brain surgery to ease the pain and headaches from which she continued to suffer. The doctors "sawed open my skull, and raised it up, and now it feels more comfortable."

Tubman never lived much above the poverty level. As she aged, she relied on the kindness of her community and funds raised by the friends she'd made over the years.

Frail and tired, Harriet Tubman died on March 10, 1913. "I go away to prepare a place for you," she said, using her last words to quote the Book of John, "that where I am you may also be."

Dozens of biographies have been written about Tubman, as well as works of fiction, plays, and operas. She's inspired countless works of art. Monuments and memorials commemorating her life and accomplishments have been erected in her honor.

But until *Harriet*, she'd never been given her big-screen due.

As an actor, director Kasi Lemmons made appearances in more than two dozen movies and shows, including Spike Lee's *School Daze* in 1988, *Silence of the Lambs* in 1991, and the horror classic *Candyman* in 1992. Her first directorial effort was the 1996 short film, *Dr. Hugo*, featuring a minor character from her 1997 follow-up *Eve's Bayou*, a family drama with supernatural undercurrents set in 1962 Louisiana. Roger Ebert called it the best film of that year. Lemmons won best-debut directing trophies from the Independent Spirit Awards and the National Board of Review, and *Eve's Bayou* was 1997's highest-grossing independent

picture. Lemmons co-wrote the *Harriet* screenplay with Gregory Allen Howard, whose other credits include *Remember the Titans* from 2000 and 2001's *Ali*.

English-born Cynthia Erivo, who played Harriet, won the 2016 Tony Award for Best Leading Actress in a Musical, as well as an Emmy and a Grammy, for her role as Cecile in the Broadway revival of *The Color Purple*. In 2021, she portrayed Aretha Franklin in the third season of National Geographic Channel's series *Genius*, and she's been cast as the Blue Fairy in the live action version of Disney's *Pinocchio*.

Harriet was shot around Richmond, Virginia, and it is a beautiful film to watch. Much of that credit goes to John Toll, one of only four cinematographers to win back-to-back Oscars. Toll won in 1995 for *Legends of the Fall* and in 1996 for *Braveheart*. He was nominated again in 1999 for *The Thin Red Line*.

Harriet was a financial and critical success, and in 2020, when it was eligible for Oscar consideration, Cynthia Erivo's Best Actress–caliber performance was nominated, as was the song she wrote with composer Joshuah Brian Campbell called "Stand Up." Also nominated for Best Original Song at the Golden Globe Awards and Best Song by Critics' Choice Movie Awards, "Stand Up" was written for the film and was recorded after Erivo completed her work on set. The song's music is "gospel-tinged"—simple then sweeping as it builds to an emotional crescendo. The lyrics speak of crossing the river to freedom and the spirituality of finding salvation in a noble fight.

In 2013, an executive order signed by President Barack Obama created the Harriet Tubman Underground Railroad National

Monument at Blackwater National Wildlife Refuge. Blackwater, which encompasses close to 30,000 acres of timeless and unspoiled tidewater vistas outside Cambridge in the area where Tubman grew up, was created in 1933 as a sanctuary for migrating waterfowl along the Atlantic Flyway. A year after Obama's presidential proclamation, Congress created the Harriet Tubman Underground Railroad National Historical Park, which includes the monument and significant historic sites in Dorchester, Talbot, and Caroline counties. There is a sister park in Auburn that features Tubman's home, her church, and the Harriet Tubman Home for the Aged.

The Harriet Tubman Byway is a self-guided scenic road trip that includes almost fifty sites more than 200 miles north from the Blackwater Refuge, named for the natural color of the waters, across Delaware and to the Pennsylvania state line. Deemed a National Road for its beauty and cultural relevance, the Tubman Byway is considered one of the best driving tours in the country. A good place to start the tour is the Harriet Tubman Underground Railroad Visitors Center at Blackwater. Completed in 2017, the facility offers 10,000 square feet of multimedia exhibits, along with a library, theater, and gift shop. Among other nearby notable stops are the Brodess Farm, the Bucktown Village Store where Tubman was assaulted with the lead weight, and the Harriet Tubman Museum and Educational Center in Cambridge, which since 2019 has been where visitors can see the acclaimed, powerful, and touching mural of Tubman painted by local artist Michael Rosato.

In 2016, the US Treasury under President Obama announced plans to place Tubman on the front of a redesigned $20 bill that was expected to be in circulation by the end of the decade. Though the administration that followed delayed the change, in January 2021 an announcement was made that the initiative was once again on the Treasury's agenda.

In 2020, however, life-size statues of Harriet Tubman and Frederick Douglass were installed inside the very room in Maryland's capital building where slavery was abolished by the state with a new constitution in 1864. The bronze likenesses of the two heroes of the abolitionist movement were made to look as they did at that time, and their inclusion in a place intended to honor the most important aspects of the state's history was approved after the removal of a statue of Supreme Court Justice Roger B. Taney, who authored the 1857 Dred Scott Decision denying citizenship to blacks.

Tubman, all 4' 10" of her, gazes at the front of the room where Maryland's legislation of freedom was ratified.

"America is changing," sculptor Ivan Schwartz of StudioEIS, whose team created the statues, told National Public Radio's WAMU at the unveiling. "Its demand for new symbol-images in our public spaces have become very, very apparent."

Harriet Tubman, a black woman born into the despair of slavery on the Eastern Shore, is now an icon of social activists the world over. The lessons taught by the life she led have never been more meaningful or necessary.

Let's hope we're able to learn them.

The diminutive Annie Oakley became an international sensation as a
quick-shot artist in the touring Wild West Show of "Buffalo Bill" Cody.
For a brief interlude, she and her husband settled down and observed a
slower pace in picturesque Cambridge, Maryland, where she amused herself
by shooting waterfowl from her roof. (*R. K. Fox/Library of Congress*)

ANNIE OAKLEY

"It was heavenly to sit on the porch and look over the bay and dream."

—Annie Fern Swartout, Annie Oakley's niece

More than a century after her 'Most Famous Woman in the World' heyday, Annie Oakley is still recognizable in popular culture. A real-life American folk hero, Oakley is primarily remembered for her legendary sharpshooting and her long association with Buffalo Bill Cody's Wild West show.

What many people might not know about one of the first modern mega-celebrities is that she was also one of the world's earliest movie stars, and she once lived on the Eastern Shore.

Annie Oakley first met Thomas Edison at a breakfast in Paris. It was 1889, and they were in town for the Universal Exposition, a centennial commemoration of the French Revolution. The Eiffel Tower was brand new and the world fair's spectacular main attraction, but the famous inventor's phonograph exhibit drew some of the expo's biggest crowds, and Oakley was part of the Wild West extravaganza that was entertaining thousands of spectators every day.

Oakley didn't care for the local gunpowder. She asked the prestigious Wizard of Menlo Park if he could invent an electric gun. Then, over pastries and coffee and as unpretentious as ever, she probably asked him to sign her autograph book.

Flashback Scenes

August 13, 1860

A log cabin in Ohio, on the edge of the wild western forest

The Moses family welcomes its fifth surviving baby daughter. They name her Phoebe Ann, but her sisters call her Annie. Annie grows into a petite but sturdy child with thick dark hair and large eyes remarkable for their bright, direct gaze. Tragedy strikes when her father dies after getting caught in a blizzard. Then the oldest sister, Mary Jane, dies from tuberculosis. The family goes into a tailspin of poverty and despair. At the age of ten, Annie is sent to the local poorhouse, where she's lent out to a farm family who abuse her with unending servitude and punishment for two years. She escapes. At fifteen, she returns to her remarried mother's home where she earns her keep by shooting and selling small game. She's invited to compete in a shooting match with Frank Butler, a well-known vaudeville marksman who—along with his partner, William Graham—performs as half the act of Graham and Butler. One of the highlights of their act is shooting peanuts off the top of each other's noggins.

Oakley is sixteen. Frank Butler is twenty-four and handsome. He's friendly, funny, and sentimental, and runs a lucrative side hustle squaring off against local marksmen who have more reputation and ego than skill. When he meets Oakley, Butler is thrown by the gender, daintiness, and charm of his opponent. He'd later remember: "The day of the shoot, the slender, shy little girl had her father's Kentucky rifle all polished up for the occasion. She had made a new pink gingham dress to wear with a sunbonnet to match. I can see her now, her blue-grey eyes sparkling with excitement, and her long chestnut hair braided down her back in two pigtails tied at the ends with narrow pink ribbon. I was a beaten man the moment she appeared for I was taken off guard."

Oakley hits the target twenty-five times to Butler's twenty-four.

Butler invites Oakley to join his show. Part of Butler's act involves his faithful dog, George. George doesn't care for most people but takes an immediate liking to Annie.

Oakley and Butler are soon married.

She takes the stage name of Oakley, a village near her birthplace. Though they later share in the financial windfalls from her success, Oakley's family is religious and does not approve of show business. She never liked her last name anyway. William Graham is no longer part of the act, though George has stayed on. The team's called Butler and Oakley now, but on the circuit, with Oakley's oh-shucks image and unmatched sharpshooting skills, there's no doubt she's the star.

While appearing in St. Paul, Minnesota, the couple meet with the distinguished Lakota chief Sitting Bull, the man given most of the blame or credit, depending on one's point of view, for General Custer's brutal defeat at Little Big Horn. Sitting Bull is enchanted with Oakley, and he initiates what becomes a mutual relationship of admiration that lasts until his death at the hands of Indian agency police at Standing Rock Reservation in 1890.

In New Orleans, Mr. and Mrs. Butler introduce themselves to William F. Cody, known far and wide as Buffalo Bill, who's in town with his Wild West show. Cody cuts quite a leading-man profile. He's tall and handsome and carries himself with authority. He sports long dark hair and a fancy goatee. Born in 1846, he was an accomplished plainsman and scout by the time he was in his teens. When he was twenty-one, the Kansas Pacific Railroad hired him to supply its work crews with a dozen buffalo a day for meals, and it was here he earned his nickname by killing 4,280 buffalo in eight months. He entered show business when writer Ned Buntline persuaded him to star in his stage melodrama *Scouts of the Prairie*. In 1883, Cody opened his Wild West show, which in many ways initiated the modern entertainment industry, helped create the culture of fame and celebrity and, in one permutation or another, would perform in public for thirty years.

From its earliest incarnations, Buffalo Bill's Wild West is a dazzling and dramatic production featuring scenarios developed and performed from the mythology of America's recently wrapped western expansion. The forerunner of every film and movie in the Western genre, Buffalo Bill's show offers its enthralled audiences in the grandstands such exciting fare as bronco-busting cowboys and Indians on the warpath, gunfights, and stagecoach robberies.

After months of casual negotiations, it's in 1885 Louisville, Kentucky, where Cody offers Oakley a three-day tryout. She and Butler end up staying for sixteen years. Out of warmth and respect, Cody always calls his little sure-shot star attraction "Missie."

Oakley's act is short. About ten minutes. That's all she needs to wow the congregated. Shirl Kasper, one of Oakley's most reliable biographers, says in her book *Annie Oakley*, "It was an act so skillful and charming that it would endear her in the hearts of a generation, no matter what its length. She didn't just walk into the arena, she tripped in from the grandstand gangway, waving, bowing, and blowing kisses. . . . She stood out, coy and sportive, among the rough characters of the Wild West."

For her ten minutes, Oakley's "a whirl of motion—notably accurate, incredibly fast." After her last trick, which involves one rifle, five shotguns, eleven airborne glass balls, and ten seconds on the clock, she lays her last shotgun on the table, blows more kisses, and takes off across the arena. In one last bit of showmanship, she gives a delighted and adorable kick of her heels before disappearing behind a curtain. The fans roar their approval.

The one tragedy in this era is the death of George.

In 1887, Buffalo Bill's Wild West show tours Europe, starting in London with Queen Victoria's Golden Jubilee. The show is a sensation. The troupe performs for huge crowds and many celebrities, including special exhibitions for various members of royalty, including the queen. Annie Oakley is, of course, everybody's favorite.

In 1889, she meets Edison in Paris.

End of Flashbacks

The story's complicated, the timeline murky, the received credit along the line unfair, but a few years after that meeting between Oakley and Edison, he was in the motion picture business. During the late winter and early spring of 1893, with a desire to make movies regardless of the weather or time of day, Edison employees constructed a 48 x 12–foot wooden structure covered in tar paper that resembled a police paddy wagon, or a "Black Maria." Designed to chase the sun, the entire building pivoted and had a roof that could be opened and closed. Edison's Black Maria is considered to be the world's first movie studio.

On May 9, 1893, at the Brooklyn Institute of Arts and Sciences, Edison premiered the first motion picture ever produced for profit. Shot on a kinetograph, the earliest camera designed to capture images on a moving strip of film, and viewed on a one-person peephole called a kinetoscope, *Blacksmith Scene* shows three men hammering a piece of iron on an anvil and then passing around a bottle of beer.

A few years later, the first kinetoscope parlor, a precursor to the "nickelodeon," opened in New York City. It boasted ten machines in two rows, a different short scene on each machine. For twenty-five cents a patron could view five of the ten available scenes. The venture was a mammoth success. People lined up with coins burning holes in their pockets. Similar parlors soon opened in other cities. To keep audiences coming back, Edison needed to produce more films. Subjects included any action potential customers might find exciting to watch. Vaudevillian performers, cockfights, trained animal acts, historical reenactments, even the illustrious Mr. Edison at work, was fodder for the Black Maria. Also featured, because sex always sells, were moving pictures of dancing ladies, a precedent-setting dorm room pillow fight between nightgown-clad young women called *Seminary Girls*, and the self-explanatory short titled *The Kiss*.

The German bodybuilder Eugene Sandow was the first celebrity Edison filmed. Gentleman Jim Corbett staged a boxing exhibition. In September 1894, during a prolonged engagement in nearby Brooklyn, where the Wild West was playing to 10,000 visitors a day, Buffalo Bill brought fifteen of his Indian actors over to New Jersey for their turn in front of the kinetograph.

Later that fall, Oakley made the trip. Edison wanted to see if his camera could catch the thrilling energy of her marksmanship. The experiment was a success. The resulting footage, *The Little Sure*

Shot of the Wild West, not only captured her gun's smoke but also the plates and glass balls shattering when she hit them. Robyn Asleson, in an article written for the Smithsonian Institution's National Portrait Gallery website, says than in an age obsessed with going ever faster, Oakley was "speed personified." Edison understood that part of her appeal, and it's what helped make Annie Oakley one of our first motion picture stars.

As the nineteenth century turned to the twentieth, the Butlers were touring America with the Wild West and Oakley was a household name pulling down $150 per week when the average worker made under $500 a year. Late one night in November 1901, Cody's entire production was traveling by railroad from Charlotte, North Carolina to Danville, Virginia for their last show of the season. Oakley and Butler were asleep in their stateroom.

Coming in the opposite direction was a freight train whose engineer had misread his orders.

The crash was epic. The two locomotives collided with such force that they were said to have reared up against each other like "two giant beasts in deadly combat." The twenty-one train cars of the Wild West "shattered into thousands of pieces on impact." Five of them, including the Butlers' private coach, ended up in a creek. No people lost their lives but more than a hundred horses were killed outright or had to be put down. Saddles, costumes, and show equipment of all kinds were strewn around the countryside. Oakley was thrown from her bed and left immobile, her spine so injured it took five operations and years for her to recuperate. Though she did later join a different Wild West show for a few years, she never again worked with Buffalo Bill Cody.

Cambridge, Maryland is in Dorchester County on the southern shore of the Choptank River. Settled in 1684, it became the plantation port and center of trade for the area and grew into one of the Eastern Shore's most prosperous towns. Built on tobacco and shipbuilding, by the turn of the century the town's economy was being driven by food canning and packing houses. By 1912, Cambridge was shipping out tons and tons of seafood, fruits, and vegetables daily. It was a town that, as Frank Butler described, offered "four banks, several fine churches, but no saloons."

The Butlers decided to come and stay a while.

They were not unfamiliar with the Eastern Shore, having passed through before, performing and entering shooting competitions. Now that they were thinking about retiring, this "sportsman's paradise" seemed like a pretty nice place to do just that. They bought property facing Hambrooks Bay, a protected body of water off the Choptank, and set about building their Cambridge dreamhouse.

Though to be honest, by all accounts, it was really designed to be Annie Oakley's dreamhouse.

She told North Carolina newspaper reporter Peter Carney that men didn't know how to build a house to suit a woman. She wanted square rooms, no projecting closets, a sink "at a height over which a woman did not have to break her back," and "a hundred and one little things." Local lore has it that one of her architectural innovations were a set of second-floor windows that she could use to step out onto the roof and shoot waterfowl.

Once construction was completed in 1913, the Butlers' lives sound blissful. Kasper writes that Butler talked about the beauty of the area and its people, and the abundance of canvasback ducks, wild geese, quail, herring, perch, crabs, and oysters. One day Butler sat on the porch and watched forty-two oyster boats coming in to sell their day's catch. A friend of the Butlers named Dr. Samuel Fort told a reporter that "out in the cove was a private oyster bed, and a little farther out a ducking blind. A clay pigeon trap, for a little practice now and then, sat on a knoll." Oakley wrote in *American Field* that "while there has been a great deal of game bagged here, I am pleased to say there is plenty left over. When I say there was more than 1,700 game licenses taken out in this county the reader can imagine the amount of hunting that was done."

In 1914, Oakley's niece and namesake, Annie Fern Campbell, came to visit, and in her book, *Missie—The Life and Times of Annie Oakley*, she reminisced about those days. "One thing we enjoyed so much was the open space we had to shoot in. We could shoot at mark(s) out over the water, and in the open field there was a walnut tree with plenty of walnuts to shoot off the limbs."

Butler had always wanted a bird dog, so while living in Cambridge, they welcomed a new member into the family. Dave was a black, white, and tan English setter Frank bought in nearby East New Market. Though the dog's training began pronto, there are those who also might have said Dave was spoiled rotten by his owners. When Oakley decided to retire from retirement, Dave was a crucial part of the act, and even became something of celebrity himself.

Butler and Oakley were generous and popular in their adopted community. They gave shooting exhibitions at the Dorchester County Fair, hosted parties, and entertained local children at their home. Many neighbors remained friends after they moved away, and the Butlers were known to stop in and visit during their travels.

Oakley worked on her autobiography while she lived on the Shore, part of which was published in 1914 by the DuPont Company as the memoir *Powders I Have Used*. DuPont, the country's largest gunpowder manufacturer, was also a sponsor of Oakley and provided her with specially made powders for her shows and demonstrations. The well-known DuPont heir T. Coleman du Pont owned property at nearby Horn Point that was being used as a hunting lodge for his wealthy and connected friends, the Butlers included.

Despite their affection for Dorchester County and their Eastern Shore neighbors, after a lifetime of touring the world, staying in one place wore thin. Annie Fern Swartout wrote, "Those were happy days too we spent in Cambridge, except for the restless spirit Missie displayed and [Frank] and I were always wondering how long she would be satisfied to stay in the cozy place we had there, among such good friends."

Oakley confessed: "I went all to pieces under the care of a home," she said. "We had our own boat, dog, and oyster bed, and settled down to 'live happily ever after.' But I couldn't do it. As Mr. Butler puts it, I am a complete failure as a housekeeper."

In summer 1915 Oakley, Butler, and Annie Fern hit the road on a car trip from Cambridge to San Francisco. When they got to Indiana, they met up with their old friend Buffalo Bill for the last time. William Cody died on January 10, 1917.

The Butlers sold their Cambridge home that year. It's on the National Register of Historic Places and is the lone surviving residence that was either owned or occupied by Annie Oakley as a primary and permanent residence. It's also private property, so the curious are always advised to be respectful.

During the next few years, the Butlers traveled a lot, putting on exhibitions here and there, and became more interested in charity and public service. When two of her sisters died from tuberculosis, Oakley melted down all her medals and contributed the proceeds to a sanitorium. She sent money to poor farms and orphanages, and in her last public appearance performed a show for wounded soldiers in Long Island, New York in 1922.

As the Roaring 20s kicked into high gear, Oakley and Butler spent most of their time in the Carolinas and Florida. In November 1922, the Butlers were visiting friends in Florida when they were in a terrible car accident near Daytona Beach. The two couples were riding in a chauffeured Cadillac when the driver lost control and overturned along an embankment. Pinned under the vehicle, Oakley was the only person with serious injuries—a broken hip and ankle. She spent two months in the hospital and wore a brace on her leg the rest of her life. Butler and Dave provided vigilant bedside love and comfort during these difficult days.

The next February, Dave was hit by a car and killed. The Butlers were grief-stricken.

In ill health, Oakley returned to Ohio to be cared for by her family. Butler was taken in by his wife's younger sister Hulda and her family in Michigan. Knowing her time was running out, Oakley made arrangements for her own burial and left no question as to what she wanted. She picked out her own dress and out of propriety hired a female undertaker to prepare her remains.

Annie Oakley died on November 3, 1926.

Her husband, also unwell, stopped eating and followed her into the afterlife before the month was out

Diminutive, Oakley was about five feet tall and never weighed much more than 100 pounds. She enjoyed a lengthy and strong marriage, was modest in dress and demeanor, and loved her friends and family as much as she was loved by her audiences. She was also the most private of public personalities. In her time, she was as famous as a person could be, but she kept to herself. Much of who Oakley really was is still a mystery to all but those who knew her best, and those folks are also long gone.

It's been noted by many how ironic it is that Annie Oakley was one of the first celebrities to appear in motion pictures and how those pictures replaced the Wild West shows that made her famous. By the time she died, cinema was fast becoming the biggest form of mass entertainment the world had ever seen. The Western was among the most popular of genres and was built on the tropes, stories, and images created and promoted by shows such as Buffalo Bill's, the most famous of its type.

Oakley herself was iffy on the "flickers." In 1915 she said, "I have been offered several positions with the movies, but so far I have turned them down. They don't want to pay enough and until they do, I will not be seen in the movies."

She did, however, do some board trodding in her day. The year before the Paris Exposition, she appeared in an ill-fated play called *Deadwood Dick*, and in 1895, between Buffalo Bill seasons in England, she acted as an orphan in *Miss Rora*. In 1902 and 1903, she had a rewarding run as a sharpshooter in the well-received melodrama *The Western Girl*.

In 1935, not quite a decade after Oakley's death, her fictionalized life story was portrayed on screen for the first time by Barbara Stanwyck, an up-from-nothing underdog success story herself, in *Annie Oakley*. Directed by George Stevens, the movie's tagline was: "Queen of the Roaring 80s . . . Her Name was the Toast of Kings!" Stevens later served in a World War II combat motion picture unit and documented the D-Day invasion and the liberation of both Paris and the Dachau concentration camps. When he got back to Hollywood, he directed many classic films and over the years was nominated for five Best Director Oscars.

He won twice, for *A Place in the Sun* (1951) and *Giant* (1956), the three-hour-plus epic based on Edna Ferber's novel and James Dean's last movie. Robert Mitchum, in his last film, played George Stevens in 1997's *James Dean: Race with Destiny*.

Barbara Stanwyck was an orphaned native New Yorker who worked her way up from Ziegfeld Follies dancer to Broadway star to film actress. She hadn't yet hit her star-making stride of *Stella Dallas*, for which she won her first Best Actress Academy Award nomination. In her long career, she was nominated for three more Oscars—for playing Sugerpuss O'Shea in *Balls of Fire*, the quintessential femme fatale Phyllis Dietrichson in *Double Indemnity*, and the shut-in Leona Stevenson in *Sorry, Wrong Number*. In 1982 she would be awarded an honorary Oscar for her contribution to film. Coincidentally, *Double Indemnity* and *Sorry, Wrong Number*, adapted for the screen from other mediums, were originally penned by James M. Cain and Lucille Fletcher, respectively, both of whom lived at least part of their lives on the Eastern Shore.

Annie Oakley was lighthearted fun constructed on a flimsy historic foundation, though it did capture the excitement of the Wild West show. Stanwyck got positive reviews, as did Preston Foster and Melvyn Douglas the two men who played characters, one a mentor, one a love interest, based on Frank Butler.

Irving Berlin's Broadway musical *Annie Get Your Gun* opened on May 16, 1946 and ran for 147 bulletproof performances. Initially starring Ethel Merman, the show toured the US, England, and Australia, and has been brought back over and over again. The 1999 revival starring Bernadette Peters won Tony Awards for the star and as Best Musical Revival.

In 1950, George Sidney directed a glossy MGM version of the show starring Broadway luminary Betty Hutton as Oakley and Howard Keel as Butler. The next year Sidney directed the same studio's musical version of Ferber's *Show Boat*, which was partially inspired by the Chesapeake Bay's James Adams Floating Theatre.

Gail Davis starred as *Annie Oakley* in the ABC television series that ran from 1953 to 1957. Heavily fictionalized, Oakley and her made-up TV brother named Tagg were assisted in their efforts to keep their town clean of villainy by Brad Johnson's deputy sheriff Lofty Craig.

In 1976, director Robert Altman released the revisionist *Buffalo Bill and the Indians or Sitting Bull's History Lesson* starring Paul Newman as Cody. Oakley is portrayed by Geraldine Chaplin, the daughter of Charlie Chaplin and his fourth wife, Oona O'Neill Chaplin, herself the daughter of the playwright Eugene O'Neill. The movie centers on Sitting Bull joining the Wild West show, as he did in 1885. Scenes involving Oakley include her preparing to leave after what she sees as the mistreatment of her longtime Native American admirer and another where she insists on trying a new trick that leaves her husband with a bullet in the shoulder.

Besides the actresses mentioned, Oakley has been portrayed by such stars as Mary Martin, Jamie Lee Curtis, and Reba McEntire. She's been the subject of biopics, comedies, and dramas. Her story overlaps and intersects with the early years of filmdom and the birth of the modern celebrity. She was a primary influence and symbol in the folklore of America's western frontier as presented to moviegoers around the world for more than 100 years.

As the credits roll and the lights come up, it seems fair to note that Hollywood, along with her own peerless skills and lovable and unique persona, has to be one of the main reasons Annie Oakley endures in our shared national narrative.

Not many celebrated figures get to live in our imaginations past that century mark. Even fewer have the residents of the Eastern Shore been able to call neighbor.

The decades-long patent fight of Dr. Robert Kearns, inventor of the intermittent windshield wiper, was convincingly portrayed by actor Greg Kinnear (pictured above) in *Flash of Genius*. During a few of those years, Kearns lived on a once-baronial estate in Queen Anne's County, Maryland. *(Universal Pictures/Photofest)*

ROBERT KEARNS

"The new device, however useful it may be, must reveal the flash of creative genius, not merely the skill of the calling."
—*Supreme Court of the United States, 1941*

Oxford, Maryland, is a small tidewater town in Talbot County with a long history, a strong sense of community, and a culture that respects both hard work and artistic sensibilities. On this day, the temperature's a humid ninety degrees, but sitting dockside on the Tred Avon River eating a soft crab sandwich and washing it down with a refreshing beverage of choice, there's a breeze coming off the water and life in general feels at least ten degrees cooler. The company's good too. Tim Kearns, a former town commissioner, is talking about what happens when Hollywood decides it wants to make part of your life story into a motion picture.

"The challenge of making a movie based on real events taking place over a long period of time is, how do you tell that story in ninety minutes?" Kearns asks, as some of the neighborhood seagulls reconnoiter the waterfront to see what the lunchtime patrons of Doc's Sunset Grill might be dropping or leaving behind.

"Hollywood needs to knit a story together in a format that allows audiences to relate. The filmmakers have to enhance some of the dramatic aspects of what happened, but it's also romanticized. As a family we had a lot of talks about what repercussions, positive and negative, might come from getting our story out there."

Tim's dad was Robert Kearns. In 1963, Kearns, an engineering professor at Wayne State University in Detroit, invented the intermittent windshield wiper in his basement laboratory. Before Kearns, wipers had one speed for use in conditions from the finest mist to the most torrential downpour. Kearns approached one of the top car companies about going into business together, but no agreement could be reached. Then, a few short years later, that same company was offering his mechanism as a buyer's upgrade on their new models. Other automakers soon followed suit and they all cut Kearns out of any profit or recognition.

He spent decades fighting back.

In 2008, Universal Pictures released *Flash of Genius* based on the trials and tribulations that followed in the wake of those legal battles. The movie stars Greg Kinnear as Robert Kearns, Lauren Graham as his wife Phyllis, and Alan Alda—in a small but vital role—as Kearns's lead attorney. Because the plot of the film takes place over years, different actors were used for any of the Kearns's six children who appeared in scenes where they age.

"The movie begins in 1963 or 1964, so I was six or seven years old," Kearns says. "There's a scene in the basement where I'm bouncing the basketball and being a pain. That came about because the filmmakers needed a character to be a little bit of a troublemaker and I'd told them that as a kid, I hadn't really wanted to be there. It was my duty to help, but whenever I could sneak out of the basement doing whatever I was doing, I'd look longingly out the back door towards where my friends would be. I'd have rather been outside with my friends playing ball."

Detroit was the car-building capital of the world back then. Change was on the horizon for the industry and the city, but there were still a number of well-paying jobs to be had and the affluent hadn't yet fled for the hinterlands. The American Dream was still made of steel and chrome and rode in on four white-walled tires. Motown was playing on AM radio.

"We were just a typical young engineer's family in Detroit," Kearns says with a smile. "Where we lived was still kind of rural and then they built the expressways and things changed. Like in the movie, we really did go for Sunday drives, going for breakfast at that pancake house, sitting around that table. We'd drive around those developing suburbs, it was nothing but farms then, and we'd stop and have giant ice cream cones at end of the day. One of the first modern shopping centers in the world, Northland Center, was built not far away. Diana Ross lived in a high-rise near there. Music was big in Detroit at the time. My sister went to elementary school with Smokey Robinson's daughter. In sixth grade I was in a garage band. Ted Nugent played in the band that practiced in the garage behind the garage where we practiced. Bob Seger was getting big. Brownsville Station played at our parochial school; MC5 played at high school mixers.

"And our father was an inventor."

Growing up outside Detroit, Robert Kearns was a smart, hard-working kid who tried to never miss daily Mass, a practice he continued throughout his life. He was a high school athlete and a violinist. Still in his teens during World War II, he was drafted and served in the Office of Strategic Services, the forerunner of today's CIA. The Kearns kids were never privy to what their father's intelligence agency duties had been, but every Christmas he received a card from General "Wild Bill" Donovan, the agency's founder. After the war, Kearns served in the Marine Corps and earned two engineering degrees. He later received his PhD from Case Western Reserve University.

"An inventor," Tim Kearns repeats. "He invented when he was a kid, invented in high school and college. He taught people how to invent things. I think you have to have a gift for it, but it is a process, and if you follow the process you will come up with an innovation, some new way of thinking." A primary tenet of Kearns' process was elegance, as in using as few components as possible to arrive at the most efficient result.

As depicted in *Flash of Genius*, all the Kearnses were part of their father's ambitious plans from the beginning. "As assistants we were paid employees. That part of the movie is absolutely true. We each had our position." Like their dad, Tim, the second oldest, had a mechanical aptitude so he was slotted into the role of technical engineer. He also possessed an eye for detail, which came in useful. Robert had been injured by a flying champagne cork on his honeymoon with Phyllis and was legally blind in one eye.

In fact, it was this mishap that helped inspire Kearns to solve the problem with standard windshield wipers. He thought about how the human eyelid works. To clean and moisten the eyeball, to allow our vision to work at its peak potential and maximum efficiency, we blink every few seconds as needed. Why couldn't windshield wipers work like that?

Knowing the automobile industry was trying to figure out intermittent wipers, Kearns spent a decade tinkering, conducting experiments with his juvenile management team, and piling everyone into the car for test runs whenever it rained. He used off-the-shelf components to build his device and, when it was ready, he installed it on a 1963 Ford Galaxie.

Through a friend, he arranged a pitch meeting. His simple plan was to impress the Ford executives into bringing him on as an independent manufacturer who would provide the company with a breakthrough feature to which no other manufacturer had access. His vision of starting a family business of significance looked like it could be coming to fruition.

"He was very idealistic," Phyllis Kearns told *Autoweek* when the movie came out. "He thought [Ford] was the Great American Company, and he trusted them. He was very naïve." Their son Dennis in the same article is quoted saying, "Ford said it was interested. They said, 'Show us how they work, and we'll buy it.'"

But they didn't.

They ghosted him. Giant 1960s corporation style.

Kearns's patent for the intermittent windshield wipers was approved in November 1967. Two years later, Ford was offering intermittent wipers to buyers as an add-on to their Mercury brand. Kearns had always seen the automakers as a symbol of principled American resourcefulness. He believed he'd done everything in life the way that was expected of him by God and country. He believed everyone should know the difference between right and wrong and that those who cheated should not be rewarded. He did not yet believe a pillar of American industry would steal from him.

In the early 1970s, Kearns accepted a job with the National Bureau of Standards in Washington, D.C. He and the family moved to Gaithersburg, in suburban Montgomery County, Maryland. In 1976, a device like his showed up on a Mercedes-Benz. It was definitive proof to Kearns that he'd been ripped off. Though the circumstances of the discovery and reaction differ somewhat between real life and cinema, the gist remained the same. Robert Kearns suffered a breakdown.

He disappeared for days. Found delusional at a bus station in Tennessee, his red hair had turned white. He was "never the same."

Tim Kearns says, "One of the hardest parts of living the story of the intermittent windshield wiper is that every day was more important than the day before because you're making an investment and progress, and if you misstep here you sabotage the whole thing and you may not even know it. The pressure becomes exponential."

From then on, all Kearns did was engage in war, even when his family took on collateral damage in the process. The lawsuits, the fight, consumed him. He identified as "litigant." He started with Ford and went on to sue more than two dozen other automakers in the course of thirty years. His basic claim was the same against them all: The corporations who stole his patented invention made money off it and he was owed his share. His argument went deeper too. In his eyes, Kearns was fighting to help protect other inventors from deep-pocketed adversaries who too often find the easiest and cheapest route to obtain intellectual property is to poach it because the entrepreneur can't afford to fight them in court.

Ford denied its intermittent windshield wipers were based on Kearns's device. They alleged they'd been working on something just like it about that same time and any resemblance to his design was coincidental, plus the litigant's system contained no new ideas or concepts anyway. Kearns argued a new combination of existing parts made this a new invention—his.

"He was a great educator," Tim says. "He could educate people. Most importantly, he could educate himself. He understood the nuance and depth of trying to beat patent attorneys at their own game. Lawyers had no emotional attachment. He had to make people understand that it was him against everybody, that he was the guy who could save the world because he was in a position to fight like no other engineer could. He wasn't fighting for himself and he wasn't fighting for money. He never spent a dime on himself. We forced him to buy a suit for court. When a trial was over, he never cashed a check, I had to cash the checks."

Tim graduated from the University of Maryland architectural school in 1986, though his dad never wanted him to be anything but an engineer. "The dream had kind of fallen apart, we weren't going to get a contract, the patents began to expire, it was becoming an all-consuming legal battle." The stress was pulling the family members away from each other and their father in various combinations at different times. Still, for another five years or so after college, he continued to work with his dad on the cases.

Phyllis filed for divorce. She was a peaceful, family-focused woman with a more fine-tuned emotional range. Her husband's crusade was making her sick. She knew he'd never stop battling, and anyone or anything that interfered with the job at hand was a nuisance at best. In many ways, Kearns related better to machines than to human beings. "If somebody cut him open," Phyllis would say with an understanding smile, "he wouldn't bleed, it would be electronics in there." Dennis Kearns told the *Baltimore Sun* in 2014: "My parents were very much in love, but having a war waged in your living room isn't good for the soul." Phyllis later fell in love again and remarried, finding happiness for herself along the way. Tim notes that everyone familiar with the truths of their story knows that without the help of Phyllis and the kids, his father would not have gotten very far in accomplishing his mission. Phyllis passed away in 2013.

In 1990, a jury decided Ford violated Kearns's patents but hadn't intended on doing so. Kearns rejected a $30 million settlement offer. He still wanted either the right to manufacture and contracts to sell the intermittent wipers or hundreds of millions of dollars in compensation. The jury awarded Kearns $6.3 million, which was trimmed by the judge to \$5.2 million. Kearns was astounded he "lost." To get him to drop all future appeals, Ford paid out \$10.2 million. With lawyer bills and loans due, his family estimated he might have broken even. Kearns filed similar lawsuits against General Motors, Daimler-Benz (now Daimler AG), and Toyota.

"Dad fought Ford and made the settlement. He was living in Texas, working on the Chrysler case. I was in Gaithersburg, and the house was being sold in divorce. While dad was working with Bureau of Standards, he used to take a bus from D.C. to Philly and he fell in love with the Maryland countryside. He had the Ford money and didn't have a place to live. He liked the idea of living the life of a 'Maryland gentleman.' I started researching what that meant and landed on the Eastern Shore, where there's a colonial landscape that still exists. I came over here, started talking to the oldest Eastern Shore real estate agent I could find. He drove me around to all these places where my father could live the life that he imagined for himself. Simplicity, history. We looked in Oxford, Centreville, Chestertown, a number of different places. Dad needed to go to the patent office in Alexandra to fight the fight, so when we found Cheston-on-Wye in Queenstown, the easy access to Rt. 50 was a plus. Dad also loved the idea that he'd be the neighbor of Mario Boiardi."

Boiardi was an entrepreneur and businessman who owned a 22,512-square-foot mansion on a forty-three-acre waterfront parcel on the other side of DeCoursey Cove. He was the son of Hector J. Boiardi, the Italian immigrant who created the Chef Boyardee line of food products. "They hit it off and would hang out once in a while."

Cheston-on-Wye had a biography. Patented by William and John DeCoursey, younger brothers of this author's ancestor Henry DeCoursey, the property remained in the family for six generations.

In its heyday the estate was known as an "Emerald Isle" of trees, shrubs, and greenery. The lawn alone stretched for twenty acres. There were stone piers built from blocks of imported granite where much of the business conducted on the Wye River took place. Legend has it there's even a tunnel running under the property from one nearby river branch to the other.

In 1930, a New York stockbroker named Leon Andrus purchased Cheston-on-Wye. By then there was nothing left of the old plantation house but some fire-blackened walls and chimneys, so the new owner had to build. Andrus had made a bundle in the stock market, lost it in the Crash of 1929, and then made a quick rebound. He and his wife were looking for a place where they could retreat in the summer and then retire. They found Cheston-on-Wye and bought what was then almost 100 acres for $50,000. Longtime Centreville-based reporter and columnist Dan Tabler of the Queen Anne's County *Record Observer*, a paper Andrus owned in the 1930s and 1940s, called him the "Boy Wonder of Wall Street," but, as a friend and employee, knew him more simply as Andy. As observed by Tabler, Andrus loved aviation, and Charles Lindbergh gave him flying lessons. However, aeronautics also took something from him that he loved more. His only sons, both pilots, were killed a month apart in World War II.

The transplanted New Yorker was a distinguished environmentalist, an engaged local citizen, and an outspoken proponent of building a Chesapeake Bay Bridge. In 1964, he sold Cheston-on-Wye to Arthur A. Houghton Jr.—an industrialist, philanthropist, patron of the arts, and neighbor—but retained a life estate to the property. Tabler recalled in a 2010 column that in 1947, Andrus, Houghton, and their wives traveled to England aboard the luxury liner *Queen Mary* to present America's wedding gift to the queen-to-be, Princess Elizabeth.

Leon Andrus died at Cheston-on-Wye in November 1989 at the age of 101, almost a quarter-century after his wife passed, and he left no family behind.

Kearns settled on the property in April 1991. The existing improvements weren't "anything special," just a typical Eastern Shore farmhouse built on the foundation of the original homesite. There was a small development nearby that had been subdivided in the 1980s, but otherwise the sprawling and mostly unoccupied Aspen Institute was all that surrounded the quiet, remote-feeling, and whittled-down fifteen and a half acres of Cheston-on-Wye. "My father matched my salary as an architect to be caretaker and live in the house," Tim says. "I lived back there by myself for three years before I moved to Easton and then Oxford. There wasn't much to do, especially in winter. I had a lot of Blockbuster Video late fees, I know that."

Kearns moved in when Tim left. If he was going to be a Maryland gentleman, he was going to be one at war. The house was more like a bunker than a home. Any furniture was there out of necessity. The main living space was his large, open sunroom of an office that was once used for entertaining but was now filled with rows of file cabinets, desks and drawing tables, several computer terminals, and binder after binder of data. Documents and supplies were strewn about the residence. In 1995, Kearns informed Alec Matthew Klein from the *Baltimore Sun* that "I came here to fight lawsuits, not to make friends or have fun."

When Kearns died, nobody in the family wanted the property. It sat as he left it for more than a decade and was sold in 2017.

Soon after he purchased Cheston-on-Wye, Kearns, representing himself, won his argument against Chrysler, which appealed. The case went to the Supreme Court. It would take a few years before Kearns received his $20 million settlement, cents on the dollar as far he was concerned. All future suits against automakers foreign and domestic were dismissed. Much of the money was again gobbled up by debt. Didn't matter. If every penny had gone in his pocket, no one who knew him doubted he'd have continued living his frugal and unassuming lifestyle.

Not that he wasn't savvy in the ways to use the media and his personality to his advantage. In January 1992, while awaiting the final judgment in the Chrysler litigation, Kearns appeared on the NBC talk show *Late Night with David Letterman* to give a demonstration on how his device worked. Letterman's other guests for the show were Kevin Kline and Emmylou Harris, but Kearns was the kind of guest who would fascinate Letterman. Tim and Dennis accompanied their dad to New York for the taping, and they were told they could watch the show from backstage or in the balcony. Tim sat in the balcony near some crusty punk rockers with dyed hair and wearing consignment shop rejected rags. Two nights later, those same guys, the band Nirvana, made their sensational mainstream debut on the same network's *Saturday Night Live*.

The journalist John Seabrook first started talking to the Kearns family when they were still headquartered in Gaithersburg. Tim remembers his spending three days sitting on their front porch and talking to their dad the first time he visited. When Seabrook's article *The Flash of Genius* came out in the *New Yorker* in 1993, it brought more exposure for what Kearns wanted the public to see as a noble David-versus-Goliath fight against bullying and injustice. "*People* magazine came out and interviewed us on that same porch," Tim says.

Through the years, Hollywood sniffed around, but Kearns resisted. It wasn't that he didn't have an interest in doing a movie project; it would help bring attention to his quest, but he was never approached by any filmmakers he felt he could trust to stick to the truth. Long after its publication, Marc Abraham read Seabrook's *New Yorker* piece on Kearns and loved it. He saw that an underlying theme in the story is what it can cost a person to try to live a principled life. It was "the stuff of great American literature."

Beginning as a sportswriter, Abraham's earliest Hollywood credits were writing episodes of *21 Jump Street* and *Moonlighting*. His first work as a producer was 1991's *The Commitments*. Based on a novel by Roddy Doyle, *The Commitments* tells a story about the formation of a Dublin soul band, and though only a modest success upon release, it has since become a cult favorite and is one of Ireland's most beloved films. Abraham's first home run as a producer came with the presidential action hit *Air Force One* starring Harrison Ford, a top five box-office draw of 1997. In 2002, he was a producer on *Tuck Everlasting*, a Disney film that stars Lauren Graham's TV daughter, Alexis Bledel, and among other locations, was shot in the town of Berlin on the Eastern Shore.

None of this mattered much to Kearns. His naivete long obliterated, he was now suspicious of most everyone who crossed his path. It took days for Abraham to convince him he wasn't working with the enemy. In their first talk Kearns asked, "How do I know you're not going to take this and turn it into a story about how Ford and GM were the heroes?" Abraham countered, "Well, with all due respect, Bob, that's not much of a story." Nonetheless, once the producer, who decided this was a story he wanted to direct himself, gained the family's confidence, the Kearns were all in. They provided Abraham and his team everything from documents, photos, and home movies to personal interviews. The Kearnses were allowed to read the screenplay and suggest changes that were often adopted.

Several versions of the script were presented to Universal Pictures during the next few years, but none met with the studio's approval. The execs liked the underdog aspects of the story, but a main worry was that Kearns was never written to be likable enough. Abraham could underplay Kearns's most alienating personality traits—the volatility of his obsessive behavior and the destructive impact his pursuit of vindication had on his family—but the filmmaker wanted, as much as possible, to show the man for who he was. As Kinnear later said, "We decided we weren't going to soften him, we should show him warts and all and let the audience, like his family, forgive the parts of him that were hard."

Robert Kearns died before the film was made. Cancer took him at seventy-seven on February 9, 2005.

Windshield Wiper Man, the screenplay that became *Flash of Genius,* sat on Greg Kinnear's desk for a while, but he loved it as soon as he got past the title and started reading. Tim Kearns says his brother Dennis, who served as a consultant on the film, told him that both Kinnear and Alan Alda had experienced similar situations where someone took an idea of theirs and profited unfairly. They had a connection to Robert Kearns and his story.

Greg Kinnear's big break was as the first host of *Talk Soup,* a humorous cable clip show that launched dozens of knockoffs. The son of a diplomat, Kinnear had less than a dozen minor credits on his acting resume when he was tapped to play against Harrison Ford and Julia Ormand in director Sidney Pollack's 1995 remake of 1954's *Sabrina.* In 1997, he starred in *As Good as It Gets* with Jack Nicholson and Helen Hunt as Nicholson's character's neighbor and eventual best friend. Nicholson and Hunt won Academy Awards for their roles. Kinnear was nominated for Best Supporting Actor but lost to Robin Williams in *Good Will Hunting.*

Before being cast as Robert Kearns, Kinnear embodied real-life characters Major Bruce "Snake" Campbell in *We Were Soldiers;* *Hogan's Heroes* star and murder victim Bob Crane in *Auto Focus;*

and football coach Dick Vermeil in *Invincible*. After *Flash of Genius*, Kinnear would portray the young JFK in the 2011 mini-series *The Kennedys*, for which he earned an Emmy nomination; Joe Biden in *Confirmation* (2016); and Bob Hope in *Misbehavior* (2020).

Lauren Graham was cast as Phyllis, the mom Tim says was "the person who kept the family together, but in giving my father the support he needed while trying to protect us, internalized so much that she developed a traumatic stress syndrome. That scene in the movie where she's at the doctor's office and he tells her she needs to take care of herself, is all true."

Graham had just finished with her career-making role as Lorelai Gilmore in *Gilmore Girls* (2000–2007). The daughter of a lobbyist for the candy industry, Graham grew up in northern Virginia. After *Flash*, she was a costar on NBC's *Parenthood* for five years and in 2016 returned to the fictional town of Stars Hollow in Netflix's *Gilmore Girls: A Year in the Life*. In 2021 she starred with Emilio Estevez in the Disney+ reboot series *The Mighty Ducks: Game Changers*.

Alan Alda (indelibly cast as Hawkeye Pierce on *M*A*S*H*) portrayed an amalgamation of every attorney Tim sat behind in court and listened to as they lectured his father about how "life really works." His dad, however, "could not allow anything that wasn't 100 percent. Black or white, no grays. With lawyers you're getting into all kinds of grays."

"Lawyers are running a business," Kearns would say, "I'm running a cause." During filming, the real Phyllis Kearns, then in her 70s, along with some of the Kearns siblings, visited the set in Toronto for three days. The thrill of watching the proceedings and hanging out with the actors and creative types was offset by the personal stress of seeing their life story, one that wasn't always happy, being reenacted right in front of their eyes. Phyllis found it difficult to hide her emotions. She wasn't alone.

"One of the most remarkable moments," Tim says, is "when she met Lauren Graham." It was a quick hello and a hug, but it meant a lot to them both. While promoting the film, Graham said she felt the weight of portraying a real person. It was her first time doing so, and even though her time with Phyllis was but a brief tearful encounter, they shared a deep bond. "You feel indebted to this family to have shared their story," Graham explained, "so I felt kind of shy and it was just nice to meet her."

Some of the emotion was brought on by the realism of the production. The creative collaboration that needs to come together to pull off a major film project, particularly one set in a different time period, is enormous, and if successful, is so authentic it can be disorienting. "The set designers took all the descriptions my brother could give them to add realism," says Tim. "Everything about that basement was as real as I ever remember it being. The dining room exactly the same as original. The cars were real, the clothes were real, the ambiance was real. My father's idiosyncrasies were real."

Everyone who knew Robert Kearns agreed Kinnear embodied not only the complicated spirit of the man he was portraying but became a physical ringer in every regard. He gained twenty pounds for the movie. He nailed the posture and the tics. Seabrook told National Public Radio that Kinnear captured Kearns's "Midwestern angst." Phyllis Kearns declared "he became Bob." *Los Angeles Times* editor Reed Johnson, however, who'd interviewed the Kearns family in 1993 for the *Detroit News*, wrote that though "Kinnear does a fine job of conveying Kearns' peculiar mix of mental acuity, injured pride, mischievous charm and bemusement," he agreed with one of the film's producers, who conceded that the real Bob Kearns was "ten times as paranoid, ten times as difficult as Greg played him."

In a different NPR interview, Kinnear acknowledged that for him, the main courtroom scenes were the most difficult to shoot, but that in playing them he felt as if his lines "were the culmination of what this guy wanted to say to everybody, and here I was sort of saying the words that Kearns would have, given the opportunity, stood up on top of the mountain and shouted out."

Regarding the Kearns family and their reaction to the film, Kinnear said, "They all watched the movie in kind of a stunned silence. It was very emotional for them, and I think kind of cathartic to see this come to this kind of conclusion. You'd think that the lawsuit would be the conclusion. I don't think that was it as much as having their father's story realized."

The economy was melting down when *Flash of Genius* came out on October 3, 2008. America's automotive industry was in a spiraling crisis and carmakers were looking for financial assistance from the federal government. A hit movie that cast their companies in a bad light—they had not been consulted in the making of the film —was the last thing they needed. Tim doesn't say the release was squashed, but he does note that the timing was unfortunate.

Flash of Genius was in theaters for less than a month. The critical reception was rough, though most reviewers gave the actors, especially Kinnear, low-key props. A few noted its smart but unexciting story arc. *Variety* called the movie "moderately inspiring." Everyone involved thought that if the movie clicked with audiences, Kinnear might get a Best Actor nomination out of his performance, but it opened at #11 while another first-week release, *Beverly Hills Chihuahua*, was numero uno.

Two weeks before opening in theaters nationwide, *Flash of Genius* had an early screening in the Avalon Theatre as the centerpiece of Talbot County's first Chesapeake Film Festival (CFF). Since its inception, the CFF has been an uninterrupted annual celebration of cinematic achievement, following its mandate to "enlighten, inspire, and entertain" through film. Due to the coronavirus pandemic, its entire 2020 slate was conducted virtually and shown free of charge.

The Eastern Shore's own Doug Sadler was the first festival's artistic director. A filmmaker himself, Sadler directed the independent pictures *Riders*, a hard-edged family drama released in 2001, and *Swimmers* in 2005. *Swimmers* is the coming-of-age story of a Chesapeake Bay waterman's daughter, Emma, played by Tara Devon Gallagher. Other members of the cast include two actors now known for their work on television: Shawn Hatosy, who has had important roles on *Southland* and *Animal Kingdom*, and Michael Mosley, who has made memorable multi-episode appearances in shows such as *Scrubs*, *Fear the Walking Dead*, and Netflix's smash crime drama *Ozarks*. Broadway star Cherry Jones plays the matriarch of the family, Julia.

Filmed in Easton, Oxford, Bozman, and other locales, the Avalon Theater appears in the movie, as does the Oxford-Bellevue Ferry and the Chesapeake Bay Bridge. *Swimmers* debuted at the 2005 Sundance Film Festival and won, among other awards, the Grand Jury Prize Best New American Film at the Seattle International Film Festival.

The special guests at the *Flash of Genius* early screening in Easton were Tim Kearns and his youngest brother Bob, along with Marc Abraham. The director enjoyed catching up with the family and kidded Tim about holding high political stature as a town commissioner. Film Festival Director Marie U'Ren told the *Star Democrat* that watching the movie with their guests and having an opportunity to discuss the family's story was a "lasting and memorable experience."

"It's about fatherhood," Abraham proclaimed at the festival's opening event. "It's about being absent. It's about what you leave, what's the legacy."

Part of the legacy of *Flash of Genius* for Tim Kearns is the cinematic reminder of both the good and bad of growing up with Robert Kearns as a dad. Robert's kids always believed whole-heartedly in their dad's vision but could feel hurt by his disengagement in their own lives. They believed in him, yet worried for his state of mind. At times they saw him as the righteous and relentless 5'7" giant slayer who needed them as allies in his virtuous crusade, at other times as a selfish, stubborn, and thin-skinned combination of Captain Ahab and Don Quixote who made his children choose between him and their own well-being. Some of them had been fighting his battles since elementary school, but until his dreams were realized to the fullest, it would never be enough. He wanted things to work out, though his family had a saying that their dad "carried around an umbrella under which it always rained." Kearns was brilliant but preoccupied, intuitive but insensitive, and confident but of a wounded spirit. He was, like all of us to some degree or another, a complex person. Most of us don't have our struggles projected onto the silver screen.

The movie reminds us too of the lessons Kearns taught. For instance, the elegance of thought that is required to innovate. "You need to understand the language of the problem you're trying to solve," Tim says. "He was sensitive to nuance and the characteristics of things. It's like how the technical aspects to movie-making combine with the creative human talent of the cast and crew to build a realized story, down to how Greg Kinnear was able to bring out the nuances in our father's character. When you break things down into the smallest of pieces without predetermined judgments, when you begin to look at problems that way, that's when you'll figure it all out."

Then there's the moral of the story. "My dad believed people shouldn't get away with doing bad things. They shouldn't steal, and if they do, they should get caught." During his life, Kearns sacrificed numerous other important concerns to his convictions, but it was hard not to root for him. Reed Johnson wrote that though he was reminded what "a handful" Kearns had been, for all his angry bluster, there was a basic decency and vulnerability to the inventor of the intermittent windshield wiper that people could tune into.

Finally, there are the family dynamics and how each sibling carved out their own lives beyond their dad's legacy. "My sister Maureen describes the family as a group of closely associated individuals," Tim laughs. "The film created the impression we all had angst.... I think we all just accepted our circumstances and have dealt with the stress differently. We're lucky we got a mix of our father's technical side and our mother's sensitive side. We live in different parts of the country, but out father taught us all to think in the long term and that one person can always make a difference. I understand what a good lifestyle and what a bad lifestyle is. My escape is right here. I like the 'Land of Pleasant Living' lifestyle."

As the last crumbs are wiped away and the seagulls take that as a sign to give up their vigil and move on, Tim recalls one more thing about *Flash of Genius*. The production "flew us all to Detroit to see the movie in what was, at the time, one of these big new cinemas with this huge screen, and I'll never forget it. The flight my wife and daughter and I were on hit a thunderstorm and we missed

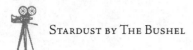

the private screening they held for the family, so the next day they showed it just for the three of us. Here we were, three people in this mega-theatre, all by ourselves, watching a movie about our family. They talk about your life flashing before your eyes. It's supposed to only happen once, but here it was happening and it hit me like a ton of bricks. It was that good. It was that true to life. With the amount of care put into it we were sure that my father would have been satisfied. And that's what was important."

A sculpture on Main Street commemorates a beloved Chincoteague, Virginia, pony whose depiction by author Marguerite Henry spawned a series of bestselling books and a popular 1961 movie. *(Secant)*

MISTY OF CHINCOTEAGUE

"Nothing ever dies as long as there is the memory to enfold it and a heart to love it."

—Ida *"Grandma"* Beebe

From cute little animated mice to giant animatronic man-eating sharks and living, breathing killer whales that need freeing, Hollywood has exploited its audience's emotional reaction to animals since the earliest days of cinema. Unforgettable stories have been built upon the loving connections human characters can make with all kinds of critters: monkeys, pigs, big cats—lions and tigers, rarely those darn housecats—and bears. But for creating cross-species bonds that warm the heart and create long-lasting sentimental impressions, it's hard to top a dog or a horse.

There are more dog stars than you can throw a stick for.

This isn't about them.

This is about a horse.

Misty.

A pint-sized pony from the Eastern Shore of Virginia who became a world-famous celebrity and had a movie made about her.

Misty was born in July 1946 on a Chincoteague Island farm that belonged to Clarence and Ida Beebe. Marguerite Henry's best-selling, award-winning 1947 book *Misty of Chincoteague* is a dramatized account of the pony's origins, but Henry tells so much truth in her work that Misty's tale intertwines fact and fiction.

The legend tells how a herd of ponies—slight of stature, gentle in disposition, and smart—survived the shipwreck of a Spanish galleon and swam to the barrier island of Assateague where their descendants run wild to this day. It's a story dismissed by some, but one that adherents know in their hearts must be true.

Supporters of this theory point to the wreck of the Spanish warship *La Galga*, or *Greyhound*, which was driven thousands of miles off course by a hurricane and ran aground on or near Assateague Island in 1750. The crew and passengers were rescued by members of local tribes, but colonists looted their ship. The way it's told, *La Galga* was completely covered by shifting sand in three days. Many now believe this is the shipwreck that left the ponies stranded on the shores of Assateague.

A 1968 federal report disputes the claim and less mythically says the horses were left there by local settlers. Over the years, various outside bloodlines have been introduced to the stock to stave off disease, so regardless of where the original ponies come from, the herds that live there now are of a different mixed breed than their earliest Eastern Shore ancestors.

Assateague, 37 miles in length, reaches down from the southernmost tip of Ocean City and wraps a protective arm around the much smaller Chincoteague, protecting it from all but the worst conditions the Atlantic Ocean has to offer. The northern two-thirds of the larger island belongs to the state of Maryland, while the lower portion is Virginia's. The two sections are divided by a simple fence. Approximately 150 horses live on either side, and each herd is managed by their respective jurisdictions. They roam in bands, usually consisting of a stallion, several mares, and their foals. They survive on a scarce diet of marsh vegetation and brush, and because of the salt they consume, drink up to twice the amount of water that they would otherwise.

Chincoteague is the name of both the island and the town located there. The island is eight miles long by two miles wide at most. The southwestern inlet between Hammock Point and Gunboat Point on Wallops Island is narrow and has a channel depth of twelve feet. The northern expanse of Chincoteague Bay carries a reputation for calm waters and tranquil boating. When the English arrived here in the seventeenth century, the Chincoteague Indians, named by the white settlers, lived on the mainland and were seminomadic. They came to Chincoteague and Assateague to gather shellfish. It's been said "Chincoteague" means "Beautiful land across the water," but that's disputed by historians. "Large stream" or "inlet" is the most likely translation.

Development was slow here. What progress was made during 150 years or so was wiped out in one "monstrous" tidal wave in 1821. After recovering from that devastation, Chincoteague cashed in on the broadening market for regional oysters, and with new methods of packaging and transporting product, the late 1800s saw an even greater expansion of the industry. "Chincoteague salt oysters" harvested from Tom's Cove were especially well regarded by shellfish connoisseurs. By the turn of the twentieth century, Chincoteaguers were shipping out hundreds of barrels of shucked oysters every day and had built their first post office, retail stores, and hotel.

The first time the annual Pony Penning—the roundup and sale of some of the Assateague ponies on the Virginia side—is mentioned in print is 1835, but the practice had been going on for some years before that. By 1885 it was a community celebration, and in 1909 the custom began of holding the swim on the last Wednesday of July and the penning the day after. Obstinate landowners put a hold on the event for a few years starting in 1920. Participants needed to figure out some workarounds. But it wasn't long before the traditional proceedings were back on the social calendar and bigger than ever before.

With the economic successes of the first decades of the twentieth century, Chincoteague modernized and construction began on a causeway linking motorists to the mainland. There were devastating fires in 1920 and 1924, so a volunteer fire department was formed. To raise money, the firefighters took over the management and sale of the wild ponies that lived on the Virginia side of Assateague.

The year 2025 will be the 100th anniversary of the Chincoteague Volunteer Fire Company (VFC) hosting their annual carnival, pony swim, and penning festivities, which have occurred annually except for two years during World War II and during the COVID-19 pandemic in 2020 and 2021. The most recent of these auctions were still conducted however, albeit online.

Lest anyone think the fire company is in it just for the fund-raising, part of their deal with the state is that they provide care and well-being for their ponies. It's a commitment they take seriously.

The National Park Service maintains the Maryland herd. The ponies are mostly left alone, treated like any other species living on the island. To keep the herd manageable, the service runs a birth-control program, but otherwise it's hands-off. The Chincoteague VFC not only owns and manages the Virginia herd, but they provide their ponies with continual health monitoring and first aid. Limiting human-pony interaction as much as possible, since they don't want the feral horses to become dependent on people, they also vaccinate, deworm, and perform twice-a-year veterinary checks. Since 2017, the Assateague ponies have been besieged by a disease called Swamp Cancer, and though a new vaccination shows promise in fighting the illness, some ponies have died.

The swim from Assateague to Chincoteague is across the narrowest part of the channel, about a quarter mile, and some of it is shallow enough to wade. The healthy fledgling ponies are rounded up, and with assistance from observers and "saltwater cowboys," they're herded together for the five-minute journey from one island to the other. The first foal to make it to shore is named King or Queen Neptune and given away as a raffle prize. The ponies rest before and after the swim, which gives volunteer caregivers an opportunity to evaluate their condition. The next day, colts and yearlings are sold at auction. Though Chincoteague ponies typically adapt to domestic life with relative ease, for worst-case scenarios, the nonprofit Chincoteague Pony Rescue is always looking to step in and provide care for animals bought in haste or without proper consideration of the attention required to raise such good-natured but feisty and clever little horses.

The first year the firemen took over the sale of the ponies, they made enough to make a down payment on a pumper truck. In 2019, with as many as 50,000 people in attendance, 57 ponies were sold at an average price of $4,767 for a sales total of $228,400, the most ever. The highest price paid for a single pony was $25,000 in 2015. On top of the sale, the purchaser of that top-grossing filly gifted the pony back to the fire company to help replenish the herd.

And for the record, no matter the arguments otherwise, most 'Teaguers believe their beloved ponies are descendants of survivors from that Spanish shipwreck.

They aren't the only ones. The author of *Misty of Chincoteague* put her faith in the legend too.

Born in 1902, the youngest of five, and raised in Milwaukee, Wisconsin, Marguerite Breithaupt loved the smell of ink. Her father printed advertising brochures for a living. Marguerite would go to his shop to read proofs and savor the sights, sounds, and smells of the presses he ran. She read books "as fast and furiously" as she could get her hands on them. Libraries were magical locations for her and she never forgot a John Burroughs quote that hung over the door at her nearest temple of collected knowledge: "I come here to find myself, it is so easy to get lost in the world."

As a six-year-old, she contracted rheumatic fever. Upon recovery, because of her susceptibility to other illnesses, she didn't go back to school for six years. Cut off from a formal education and the company of children her own age, she led what she later called a "kind of a quiet existence." When she was 11, she had a piece titled "Hide-and-Seek in Autumn Leaves" published in *Women's Home Companion* magazine and got paid $12 for it. That was when she made the decision that she was going to be an author. At some point, while reading a Zane Grey adventure, she also decided she would someday own horses.

Marguerite attended the University of Wisconsin to become an English teacher and met Sidney Henry while on a fishing camp vacation with her sisters. They married in 1923 when she was a sophomore. Her husband encouraged Marguerite's writing, and after graduating, she worked for McGraw-Hill penning nonfiction articles on assignment. Her work was published in magazines ranging from *Photoplay* to *True Detective* to that bastion of Americana, the *Saturday Evening Post*.

Sid was in the five-and-dime variety-store business. The couple moved into a "Hansel and Gretel" cottage in the country, and she began writing children's books. Marguerite published her first, *Auno and Tauno: A Story of Finland* in 1940. The author, described as vivacious, warm, and sensitive, who because of her ill health had lived a delayed childhood, made a decision about what she wanted to do with her adult life.

Wesley Dennis (1903–1966) was an illustrator with a knack for drawing animals, particularly horses. He published his own popular children's book, *Flip*, about a foal who dreams of jumping a brook, in 1941, and for his illustrated version of *The Red Pony*, John Steinbeck asked Dennis to provide the artwork. In 1946 he did illustrations for a reprint of Anna Sewell's 1877 novel *Black Beauty* which came out the same year as a film version remake of a story Hollywood had been telling since at least 1906. While working on her seventh book, *Justin Morgan Had a Horse* (made into a Disney live-action movie in 1972), Marguerite Henry did not like the art her publisher was offering up, so she went to the library. She started looking through children's books until she discovered *Flip* and the graceful yet fun way the creator captured the movement and personalities of his animal characters. "This artist," Henry later declared, "saw beyond hide and hair and bone. You could see that he loved animals, that he was trying to capture their spirit, personality and expressions."

Dennis lived on a 120-acre farm he'd bought outside Washington, D.C. where he kept horses, ponies, dogs, ducks, and a pet crow named Charlie. Through the years, Henry worked with other notable artists, but together she and Dennis hit a sweet spot. They worked together for more than twenty years and sold millions of books. Dennis would illustrate more than 150 books in his career, fifteen for Henry. His second book with her was *Misty of Chincoteague.*

Misty was born on July 20, 1946, the Saturday before that year's pony swim. In Henry's story, Misty and her parents—the untamable dam Phantom and the imposing stallion Pied Piper—were wild ponies, but in real life they were all three of domestic stock. Misty was a tiny foal, a coppery tan and white pinto with a white tail, mane, and blaze. There was a patch of gold circling her right eye. A pattern on her left side resembled the outline of the United States. Her mother had a similar marking.

Henry arrived in Chincoteague the day after the real Misty's birth and checked into the Main Street inn owned by Miss Molly Rowley, which still operates today as a bed-and-breakfast. Henry had been inspired to visit Chincoteague in search of material for a new book by her editor at Rand McNally, who was aware of the wild ponies and suggested there might be a story waiting for his star author on the Eastern Shore.

Henry spent some time walking around town, checking things out, talking with folks she crossed paths with, but she wasn't sure her editor's instincts were going to pay off. Toward the end of the day, she made her way down to the island's southern end and that's where she encountered a couple kids riding double on what Henry called a shaggy mount. "Cowboy fashion they were pushing and shoving a score of thirsty ponies to take their turn at a water barrel," she said. "I stood at the fence, watching, envying."

She started asking questions.

She asked Paul Beebe and his sister Maureen, aged ten and eight, if they could have any wish granted what would it be. To her surprise, they answered what they wanted most was a pony. Henry was puzzled. Here these children were surrounded by ponies, but that was all they desired. They explained that these ponies belonged to their grandfather and he would be selling them at the upcoming auction. They'd never had a pony of their own.

"I knew I had my story," Henry would later say about that moment in her conversation with the Beebe kids.

On the twenty-fourth, as tradition calls for, the last Wednesday of the month, Henry was joined at the pony swim by Dennis. She got a close view from aboard one of the boats riding herd while Dennis hung from pilings and took pictures. They watched as the horses were marched through Main Street before being inspected and prepared for the next day's auction.

The ponies were kept overnight at Clarence Beebe's ranch, and it was there Henry saw Misty, "new as the morning" for the first time. The foal napped on the ground while her mother stood guard over her and her father pranced around "in attendance." For Henry, it was love at first sight. This fragile baby, this "bathmat of a creature wearing the map of America" was the lone horse that mattered to Henry.

With her illustrator sketching the whole time, Henry approached Clarence "Grandpa" Beebe about buying Misty and taking her back to Illinois to serve as the model of her next book. The writer wanted her muse close. The Eastern Shoreman declined with all the blunt charm possessed by his type. She suggested making the story about Paul and Maureen, about their lives and experiences, the loss of their mom in a car accident and being raised by their grandparents. She felt that Beebe's grandkids could be an important part of Misty's story.

Grandpa Beebe softened.

Henry promised she'd send Misty back when it came her time to foal. That part of the deal was important to Beebe.

She gave him 150 bucks and they shook on it.

Misty, taking her first train ride, was delivered to Mole Meadow, the two-and-a-half-acre residence of Marguerite and Sid Henry, that November. Neighbors in their small town of Wayne had been waiting for weeks to hear news of the pony's arrival. When she got there, she became everybody's pet. Before long, the Henrys decided the best way to avoid spoiling the frisky addition to their family too much would be to provide her with animal companionship. First came a Morgan horse named Friday. Misty was enamored of her new playmate from the start.

After Friday, the Henry menagerie grew to include a cat, a set of twin foxes, and a dachshund named Alex. Most adorable might have been a donkey called Brighty, who'd been named Jiggs when Henry, needing a model for her book about a historic Grand Canyon burro, "rented" him from his owner. Brighty doted on Misty, begged her to be his friend until she had no option but to accept his soulful nuzzles. When Misty left Mole Meadow to make one of her public appearances, Brighty voiced his displeasure from the time she left until she got back. When she did return, he'd grab her by the cheek strap of her halter and not let go. In 1966, Brighty played a very fictionalized onscreen version of his namesake.

Henry wrote in the mornings, and in the afternoons she liked to train and hang out with Misty and her barnyard pals.

Misty of Chincoteague is the story of how siblings Paul and Maureen Beebe, who live in Chincoteague with their grandparents, set their hearts on having a wild pony of their own, specifically the elusive mare Phantom. They work odd jobs all summer to raise enough money to participate in the upcoming auction. Given his first opportunity to participate in the penning, Paul is able to corral Phantom because she's with her baby Misty. During the swim, Misty struggles and Paul saves her. He and his sister buy both mother and foal at auction. They spend a year training Phantom to race and keeping Misty out of trouble. The ending is heartfelt and touching and harkens back to the beginning when Grandpa says she's "not a horse, she's a piece of the wind and the sky."

Dedicated to fourteen Chincoteaguers, the Beebes at the top of the list, and three ponies—Phantom, Pied Piper, and Misty—the book was a hit. As with *Justin Morgan, Misty* was a runner-up for the Newbery Medal, among the most prestigious of honors given to authors of children's books.

Misty was more popular than ever. She received cards and letters from admirers every day. Visitors came alone and by the dozens. If it happened to be raining, the Henrys brought Misty into the house "where she shook hands all around and posed obligingly" for pictures. She was invited to appear at schools, libraries, museums, theaters, and horse shows, and showed up whenever possible. Sometimes she'd be swarmed by fans, or a room would be too warm for her. If she got cranky, Marguerite held a music box to her ears. It soothed her until she and her caregivers were able to make a graceful departure.

The now-famous Chincoteague pony was named an honorary member of the American Library Association and in 1949 attended their convention in Grand Rapids, Michigan. She walked on city streets for the first time, and even rode an elevator to a party thrown in her honor. Gussied up, her mane and tail braided and beribboned, she wore a corsage of roses around her neck. Many VIPs were at the party, and Misty mingled as guests fed her carrot sticks and spoke to her in low cocktail-hour voices.

She lived in Illinois with Marguerite and Sid for close to a decade, and as time passed a realization came to the Henrys that she needed to go back to Chincoteague as promised. The Henrys had thrown her birthday parties since she'd come to live with them, but her farewell party was one of the biggest events the good citizens of Wayne, Illinois could ever remember.

Brighty was heartbroken.

When Misty made it back to the Eastern Shore in 1957, Ida Beebe wrote her friend a letter expressing to her how proud Grandpa was to have the pretty and "unspoilt" pony back. She told Marguerite that she was certain the reason Misty was so beautiful was all the love and happiness she'd been raised on.

But as always with life, we take the bad with the good, and in April of that year, 21-year-old Paul Beebe, home after returning from duty with the United States Marines, was killed in a car crash. Clarence "Grandpa" Beebe died two months later.

In spring 1960, Misty gave birth to Phantom Wings, the first of her three foals, all sired by a stallion named Wings. Phantom Wings would be Misty's solitary son, his name chosen in a write-in contest. Twin girls from South Dakota won the $1,000 prize. *Life* magazine published a story on the occasion.

A studio or two had nibbled at the idea of making a movie from *Misty of Chincoteague*, but nothing had ever come of it. The *Life* article stirred fresh interest. It wasn't long before an agreement was negotiated with 20th Century Fox and a film crew led by producer Robert Radnitz was sent east. James B. Clark was chosen to direct.

Clark, ruddy-faced with a Monopoly-man moustache, wasn't new to working with animals. His first credits were two episodes of TV's *My Friend Flicka*, and he later directed episodes of *Flipper* and *Lassie*. He also was a skilled film editor and had worked on numerous major projects including 1941's *How Green Was My Valley*, for which he was nominated for an Oscar, 1944's *Buffalo Bill* with Joel McCrea, and the 1953 Susan Heyward and Robert Mitchum action-adventure-romance *White Witch Doctor*.

Clark had also been the director on Radnitz's first feature, a tearjerker that came out earlier that year called *A Dog of Flanders*, starring the Mastiff-Lab shelter puppy Spike. Spike was the same canine thespian who, among several other film and TV credits, played the heartbreaking title role in 1957's *Ole Yeller*.

Radnitz liked realism in his films, and as part of his strategy to accomplish his vision, he liked to shoot on location. He thought it was important to get a sense for a place and its people, and to show audiences settings they'd never seen on screen before. He also believed in casting professional actors solely in principal roles and using locals for the rest of his cast. "Mix professional actors with native residents," he explained to reporters, "and something of the natives rubs off on the actors—their talk, their dress, their mannerisms, their accent, it gives you a believable picture."

There are four professional actors in the cast of *Misty*.

David Ladd portrayed Paul Beebe. David was the last of movie star Alan Ladd's three children and had been working in Hollywood since making appearances in several of his dad's films, including the classic Western *Shane* when David was six. *Misty* was his fourth movie as a hired actor. His first was 1959's *The Sad Horse*, his second, *Raymie*, was about a young fisherman and his pursuit of a giant barracuda, and his third was Radnitz and Clark's *Dog of Flanders*. Ladd continued to act after *Misty*, but as he matured, he moved to jobs more behind-the-scenes.

Arthur O'Connell played Grandpa Beebe, and Anne Seymour was Grandma. O'Connell had been making movies since 1938, but for the first decade frequently worked in uncredited roles such as the reporter he played in *Citizen Kane*. He earned Supporting Actor Oscar nominations for 1955's *Picnic* and 1959's *Anatomy of*

191

a Murder. The same year *Misty* was filmed he was in a remake of Edna Ferber's *Cimarron*.

Anne Seymour was from a seventh-generation theatrical family that traced back to eighteenth-century Ireland. Like O'Connell, Seymour also did a lot of TV, and the year she shot *Misty* she appeared in the films *The Subterraneans, All the Fine Young Cannibals, Pollyanna*, and *Home from the Hill*, starring the seemingly ubiquitous Robert Mitchum, who was calling the Eastern Shore home at the time.

Pam Smith played Maureen Beebe. She'd never acted in a movie before but had been in about sixty commercials. She'd have four more professional acting credits after *Misty*.

A couple dozen locals were placed in speaking parts. Lead roundup man Wyle Maddox played himself, as did decoy carver, terrapin farmer, wildlife authority, and "storehouse of island lore" Miles Hancock. A seventh-grader named Wayne Custis was the stand-in for David Ladd. Town barber Wallace Lester was compensated for his scenes and then double-dipped when locals bought haircuts to get the skinny on the visiting Hollywooders. Young Beebe cousins Billy and Denny are in the movie. Maureen, then twenty-two, having lost her brother three years earlier, worked with the ponies in the film, as did her Uncle Paul, the inheritor and operator of Clarence and Ida's ranch. The primary trainer was the esteemed animal handler Les Hilton, who started his work five weeks before the cameras rolled. Hilton was a protégé of Will Rogers and buddies with the war hero-actor-singer Audie Murphy. He'd trained Molly, who appeared as Francis the Talking Mule in seven movies, and the horses used in the 1943 film version of *My Friend Flicka* starring a teenage Roddy McDowell. He was also the trainer who taught TV's *Mr. Ed* to "talk."

Misty, now an easygoing fourteen-year-old mother, couldn't play herself as a high-spirited colt, so as the plot of the picture progressed, three different fillies were stand-ins for her as a foal, a six-month-old weanling, and a yearling.

Filming began Monday, August 22, 1960, on Assateague. A staff correspondent for the *Baltimore Sun* watched a take get ruined by a rubber-necking motorboater. "Boats are like cars around here," muttered producer Radnitz, smoking his long-stemmed pipe, wearing a wide-brimmed hat with one side turned up "Australian soldier style," and slapping at a bloodthirsty greenhead fly "excavating a hole in his chest."

Henry, who was happy Radnitz wanted his film to stick closely to her story, was there wearing "beaded blue jeans with scarlet patches and nail-polish-red cowboy boots." Petite and cordial as ever, Henry could be almost childlike with her grayish blue eyes sparkling excitement. "I'm so thrilled," she told the *Sun* reporter. "Aren't you excited? Isn't this exciting?"

The *Sun* ran a follow-up story on the production a couple months later. The paper informed readers that during the month-long shoot, the actors, executives, make-up artists, wardrobe specialists, and technicians on-set "moved in with the organized confusion of an infantry battalion establishing a beachhead." They took most any problem that cropped up in stride, even when mosquitos "big as blue jays" were attacking them. The costume department bought the actors' wardrobes in local general stores and used stage techniques to make them look worn. The fireman's carnival, during which the penning is always held, was paid to stay more than a month longer than usual. The *Sun* estimated 400 extras were hired to attend the carnival at the rate of eight dollars a day, though another source reported that the children who were there were paid only a dollar. However, they also got a day off from school and were notified they could just go play and eat as many hot dogs as they wanted.

One Saturday night the production crew held a thank-you party for locals at the carnival site. About 3,000 people attended.

Because filmmakers wanted a backdrop closer to the water, Carroll Bull's Farm, on Folly Creek near Accomac, served as a surrogate for the Beebe ranch. To properly dress the set, a porch was added to a tenant house and a forty-foot pine was placed in the front yard. Because the outbuildings were too modern, 600 pine saplings were moved to camouflage them with a "wall of greenery."

In her 1976 memoir *A Pictorial Life Story of Misty*, Henry described how she escaped the masses of people and ponies, the hundreds of actors, stand-ins, and extras, and the technical people scrambling about by going to the Beebes and visiting Misty. "It was as if, long ago, I had mothered a freckle-faced, ordinary little kid, and now, right before my eyes, she was taking on a stature beyond my dreams," she wrote.

The *Sun's* wrap-up ended with the observations that the film crew's headquarters had been at an unnamed hotel in Accomac and that they'd made themselves at home while working on *Misty*. Three things distinguished the movie people from other guests. They went to bed early so first thing every morning they could check the call sheet posted on the lobby bulletin board to see who was due where; they were "a great deal less sophisticated looking than the tourists"; and because most had never eaten them before, "they showed an inordinate enthusiasm for crab cakes."

The moviemaking days were fun for all involved, but the vicissitudes of life continued. Grandma Beebe died in October 1960. Maureen Beebe married a "a Baltimore boy" named Gary Hursh and moved away. Misty gave birth to her second foal, a girl they named Wisp O'Mist, but went by her nickname Little Wisp.

A trailer for *Misty* featured Pat Boone with a group of kids and a copy of Henry's book. The clean-cut pop singer promised "adventure, excitement, and wonderful beauty" in the type of movie "that families the world over have been waiting to see."

There was a Hollywood premiere, but more important to the 'Teaguers there was also a celebration held in the star's hometown. The Eastern Shore opening was on June 14, 1961 at the Island (Roxy) Theatre. It was a beautiful day and Ralph Beebe, Paul and Maureen's uncle and Misty's caretaker, walked the world's most famous Chincoteague pony down Main Street where, as every major star must, she put her hoofprints in wet cement. Henry was in town and signed Misty's name for her. The memento is outside the theater to this day. That evening, inside the theater during the presentation of the finished film, the Shore folk sat in enthralled silence until one of their own came on the screen, then the assembled would erupt into cheers and applause.

Misty, a modest box-office and critical success, is beloved by generations of viewers who appreciate the genre and the nostalgic feel for the era that the picture evokes.

Early in March 1962, one of the worst nor'easters to ever strike the region roared across the Atlantic coastline. Called the Great Atlantic Storm, the Ash Wednesday Storm, or Five-High Storm because it menaced through five high tides, this airborne disaster rolled in with winds measuring more than seventy-five miles per hour and waves up to twenty-five feet. At the mouth of the Chesapeake, the Bay Bridge-Tunnel was under construction and much of the work that had been accomplished was destroyed. Chincoteague and Assateague were completely below the waterline. Some 1,200 island homes were destroyed. Before it subsided, the storm took a total of forty lives and did millions of dollars' worth of damage, in a time when there was nowhere near as many people or structures as there are along today's eastern seaboard.

Misty was pregnant and due to give birth any day.

When the storm hit fever pitch on Ash Wednesday, while boats were thrown inland and homes were getting sucked into the sea, the citizens of Chincoteague were evacuated by helicopter to facilities on Wallops Island. Ralph Beebe and his family weren't able to do much to protect their farm, but through the wind and rain they brought Misty from her stable to the house and left her in the kitchen with plenty of straw and a cat for company. When they were able to return three days later, both she and the cat had not only weathered the storm, Misty had opened the refrigerator and eaten molasses from a container she knocked over.

Meanwhile, kids everywhere were freaking out. Every article about the storm in every newspaper around the country included at least one assurance that Misty was known to be safe.

Across Assateague and Chincoteague, however, the devastation to the wild ponies was extensive and painful. The Beebes lost most of their herd. By one count, sixty-one ponies died on their ranch alone. Fortunately, Misty's first two offspring, Phantom Wings and Little Wisp, remained safe in a barn, by standing on stacks of hay.

Knowing Misty's foal was due anytime, worried, and unable to stay with her due to the damage to the property, Ralph Beebe loaded her up and drove to the Worcester Small Animal Hospital in Pocomoke City. He dropped her off with Dr. Garland E. Finney Jr. on Friday, and on Sunday, March 11, 1962, Misty and Wings once again became parents. Their new daughter was named Stormy.

With all the destruction, the pony herds on Assateague were virtually wiped out. Organizers figured the upcoming penning was a no-go. They needed hope, so Misty clip-clopped in to deliver some. A disaster fund was set up and 20th Century Fox rereleased her movie. Proceeds from this second round of showings were used to bring awareness to Chincoteague's plight and to raise funds to buy back ponies and replenish the herd. Misty and Stormy made appearances across Maryland and Virginia. In Salisbury, crowds were so large a second showing was needed. Attending a screening at Richmond's Byrd Theater, Henry wrote: "Every eye was riveted on the two creatures tittuping down the aisle—one so sure-footed and motherly, one so lithe and wobbly. From a thousand throats came the whispered cry, 'There they are!'"

The efforts were successful, and the 1962 penning went on as scheduled.

Henry published her fictionalized account of *Stormy, Misty's Foal* in 1963. The book was the second sequel to *Misty of Chincoteague*. The first was *Sea Star: Orphan of Chincoteague*, released in 1949, about an orphaned pony and moviemakers coming to the island to film Misty's story. Henry was ninety years old before she wrote the final installment, *Misty's Twilight*, almost thirty years after *Stormy* was published.

Tragedy struck again late in 1964. Phantom Wings and Little Wing ate silage gone bad and died within days of one another. Then in 1970, Maureen Beebe was widowed when her husband was killed in another car accident. She and her two daughters, named for ponies their mom once owned, moved back home. Worst of all, for her fans, Misty herself would soon pass.

In August 1972, Ralph Beebe told longtime *Wilmington Morning News* reporter and columnist Betty Burroughs that at the age of twenty-six, Misty was "like a person near eighty."

Burroughs wrote that when she visited that summer, Misty was surrounded by members of both her human and animal family. Beebe confided to Burroughs that he didn't think the famed pony would be around much longer. "She's slowed down a lot," wrote the reporter, "cataracts are clouding her long-lashed, deep-brown eyes. She's gray where she once was sparkling white and her golden markings now are faded brown."

Two months later, on October 16, 1972, Misty of Chincoteague died peacefully in her sleep. Her body was taxidermied by Charles "Whitey" Oxenham of Glen Burnie, Maryland. The job took the better part of two years. Not everyone supported the decision, Henry among them, but some children appreciated an opportunity to see that she was real even if they didn't meet her when she was alive. "I can't put life back in an animal," Oxenham said, "but Misty is the closest I've come." When Stormy died in 1993 at the age of thirty-one, she too was sent to the taxidermist. Both bodies have been on display in various locations over the years, and they can now be seen at the Museum of Chincoteague.

Ralph Beebe died in 1973. In 1989, the Beebe ranch was sold to residential developers.

Chincoteague was changing.

Misty would have been fifty years old in 1996, and the island acknowledged her importance to their community with a birthday party. The Misty of Chincoteague Foundation, cofounded by Henry, was an important participant in the commemoration. A bronze statue of Misty chasing a duck, sculpted by artist Brian Maughan, was unveiled in July 1997. Based on Wesley Dennis's illustrations from Henry's book, the artist's goal was to capture an image of freedom, joy, and youth. The statue, like the bodies of Misty and Stormy, has been moved a couple times and today is on display at Chincoteague's Waterfront Park. Along with a Misty time capsule scheduled to be opened in 2046, an identical statue was installed at the Kentucky Horse Park in Lexington, Kentucky.

After a series of strokes, Henry died at her home in Rancho Santa Fe, California on November 26, 1997 at the age of ninety-five.

Her husband Sid had died ten years earlier. The Henrys had no offspring of their own but felt close to the millions of children who read her books. The couple kept letters, photos, and drawings that children the world over sent them, telling their stories or asking advice. Henry always responded. She wrote daily until she could no longer do so. Before she died, she completed a manuscript about her poodle Patrick Henry, who was by her side when she left this world.

Henry published almost sixty books in her lifetime. She wrote of birds, foxes, dogs, and mules but always came back to horses. "She never lost that wonderful, exuberant, childlike quality," family friend Susan Foster Ambrose told the *Washington Post*. "She would be fascinated with a sunset or a bird landing in her backyard. She was just so captivated by the small joys in life, and she was able to translate the small joys in life to her readers."

Though fiction, Henry's work was always based on real people, animals, and events. A relentless researcher, the author traveled the world writing her stories. One of those stories, *King of the Wind*, published in 1948 and illustrated by Dennis, won the Newbery Medal. It is about a motherless Arabian colt who is an ancestor of another illustrious Eastern Shore equine, the distinguished racehorse Man o' War.

Maureen Beebe, the last of the original family members from *Misty of Chincoteague*, died on May 25, 2019. She was eighty-one.

Misty's stories—real-life, fictional, and cinematic—are timeless, their legacies endless. Her significance in the history and culture of Chincoteague is immeasurable. A visit to the island provides any number of opportunities for visitors to pay their respects to the celebrated pony's legacy. Her descendants are spread out around the country and she's estimated to have more than a couple hundred of them. There are toys and trinkets of every type made in her image. Breyer Horses, among the most sought after of horse collectibles, sells plastic models of Misty and Stormy. She's been drawn and painted by artists both preschool and professional. Other authors have written more stories about the pony and her offspring, and of this writing a 2019 short film regarding her descendant *Nightmist* is looking to wrap up production as a full-length feature.

Flicka. Black Beauty. National Velvet. The Black Stallion. Hidalgo. Seabiscuit. Secretariat. Joey, the war horse. Misty is part of a cinematic history that chronicles through tales of horses and the people who love them the themes of freedom, trust, and belonging to those with whom you bond.

Upon Misty's passing, in an editorial and a letter sent to the author, Bradford Jones from the *Evening Sun* wrote about the importance of Henry's *Misty of Chincoteague*. "What the story illuminates in its simple and low-key way," Jones wrote, "is the human capacity for warmth and unselfishness, which is a capacity not always predominant and which, to go by the rest of the news, sometimes may not be there at all.

"Misty is dead," he finished, "and that's the least of it. The Misty story lives on, a tiny light in the gritty gloom."

ON LOCATION

The 1879 Hooper Strait Lighthouse presides over the
waterfront at St. Michaels, "The Town that Fooled the British"
in the War of 1812. St. Michaels' lovely harbor on the Miles
River is one of the premier destinations for Chesapeake
Bay sailors. (*Terry Donnelly / Alamy Stock Photos*)

ST. MICHÆLS

Turns out St. Michaels, with its postcard-picture harbor, early colonial architecture, and small-town charm, might be the most Hollywood of all places on the Eastern Shore. Located in Talbot County, bordered on the northeast by the Miles River, with a southwest corner at the head of San Domingo or Back Creek, the village developed around a house of worship, established a reputation as the home port of numerous first-rate shipbuilders, and made a legend of itself in the War of 1812. The film industry's been availing itself of the scenery and hospitality of St. Michaels since before talkies took over, and these days, when walking the town's brick sidewalks or eating steamed crabs on the waterfront, those who care about such things should always keep their eyes peeled for a totally random celebrity sighting.

Be warned though, locals are protective of the privacy of their famous friends. They also enjoy their Eastern Shore-ish reputation for not overpraising prestige and prosperity, so talking *too* much of any celebrity encounter is considered both ill-mannered and fawning.

St. Michael's Parish was established by the Church of England in 1672 and the town's first chapel was completed in 1677 on what is the present site of the Episcopalian Christ Church in the heart of town. From Captain John Smith's earliest explorations of this region, discovering the edges of a vast forest of tall straight trees, shipbuilding as an industry for future settlers was inevitable. By the beginning of the nineteenth century, Marylanders were America's preeminent shipbuilders. The craftsmen of St. Michaels were renowned for producing top-of-the-line log canoes, bugeyes, and, most notably, the fast, sharp-hulled, two- or three-masted ships called the Baltimore Clippers. Popular as commercial vessels, the clipper ships were perfect for transporting high-value freight with remarkable speed and were therefore also prized by pirates and privateers, slave traders, and opium smugglers. Sinking some 1,700 British craft in the War of 1812, they were the scourge of the Royal Navy and merchant ships alike. Because the Chesapeake was known to be home port to so many of these dangerous weapons of the sea, our enemies targeted places like St. Michaels.

On August 5, 1813, more than 2,000 British troops invaded and seized Kent Island in Queen Anne's County. Word spread that an attack on St. Michaels was imminent. Defenses were mounted.

Early in the morning of the tenth, local militia foiled an attempted landing of an enemy detachment. That night, in preparation for an anticipated nocturnal attack, the townspeople are said to have hung lanterns in the trees to fool the Brits into overshooting their targets. Supposedly, it wasn't until the attackers turned to sail away the next morning that they realized they'd been snookered. The lone building to take a direct hit during the bombardment was a house on Mulberry Street where a cannonball crashed through an exterior wall and rolled past a mother walking her baby down a flight of stairs.

Some of this is absolute historic truth.

Some of it maybe not so much.

The Eastern Shore is, and always has been, a place alive with stories and storytellers.

What is certain is that the coming of the steamships and railroads ended St. Michaels' shipbuilding heyday. By the time of World War I, the town had its pockets of wealth, but for most people, making a living was based on how hard they were willing to work and the current market price of crabs and oysters. By the time Hollywood came calling, St. Michaels was more than ready for a little moviemaking excitement.

"Suspense of river piracy. Bold deeds on dark nights. Action! Mystery! Melodrama!"

In 1928, the Paramount Famous Lasky Corporation released *The First Kiss*, starring a young Gary Cooper, number eleven on the American Film Institute's list of the all-time top male stars, and King Kong's future love interest, Fay Wray. Cooper plays Mulligan Talbot, a poor waterman who resorts to crime to pay for his family's rise in status. Wray's his love interest, the richest girl in town.

The film's director was Rowland V. Lee (1891–1975). Born into a showbiz family, Lee had worked behind the scenes in Hollywood since 1915 and as a director since 1920, with a break in between to act some and fight World War I. For *The First Kiss*, he insisted that as versatile as the California landscape was for filmmakers, the true atmosphere and unique beauty of the Chesapeake Bay region could not be faked. If they wanted to shoot a story about an Eastern

Shore waterman, they'd have to go to the Eastern Shore to do it. He said: "Hollywood has been able to reproduce the snowy wastes of Alaska, the deserts of Africa, the strange islands of the Pacific, and Buckingham Palace," but they'd never be able to duplicate "the peculiar beauty and characteristics of the Chesapeake Bay and environs." When Lee's cast and crew arrived in Talbot County on May 25, 1928 one of the first moves the director made was to spread some of that Hollywood bread around. He put the town's entire fleet of workboats under contract as background scenery, set up a casting office in the cabin of a skipjack, and hired eighteen "grizzled watermen" as extras.

Most of the picture was shot in St. Michaels. Along with a fight scene filmed at Mt. Olivet Cemetery—as deduced by James Dawson in his 2013 *Tidewater Times* article "When Hollywood Came to St. Michaels"—and a long-gone mansion known as the Edward Buck House, the primary shooting location was the home of David and Hannah Parkerson, located on property that is now part of the Chesapeake Bay Maritime Museum. Dawson, owner of the landmark Unicorn Bookshop in Trappe, wrote that filmmakers transformed the Parkerson House into the fictional Talbot family's once dignified, now dilapidated estate by adding two rooms and painting the exterior to look weathered and neglected. A wharf was built, and according to a contemporaneous *Star Democrat* report, three tons of oyster shells were placed in the yard, along with an array of boat parts, anchors, and a dozen trees more than thirty feet high.

David Parkerson, St. Michaels born and bred, comes from a long line of watermen and jacks of all trades. David worked as a dock boy at age thirteen, tended bar at one of St. Michaels' most beloved taverns for twenty years, and then captained the town's water taxi for just as long. His grandparents were David and

Hannah Parkerson. David says that, from his point of view, one of the special things about the filming of *The First Kiss* was the place and time in which it was made. "It was a time," he says, "when people like Cooper and Fay Wray didn't need to worry about being bothered, didn't need security. My family ran around on the set with these movie stars, and if anybody approached it was to say hi, how're you doing, maybe shake hands and then they'd go about their business."

In a family lore sidenote, Parkerson's uncle Elmer, who still lived with his parents at the time, was screen-tested to be the next Tarzan but said he didn't get the part because "they liked Johnny Weissmuller's yodel better than they liked my yodel."

During the course of production, some scenes were captured in other locales around the area, including Easton's Third Haven Meeting House (c. 1684) and Wye House plantation, which has been owned by the Lloyd family since the 1660s and was the childhood home of Frederick Douglass. Important sequences were filmed at the Talbot County Courthouse (c. 1712) and jail. When it came time to shoot the climatic courtroom scenes, 200 to 300 locals cast as extras were stationed inside and out. According to Dawson, ten electricians came from New York to light the interior of the courtroom with $30,000 worth of equipment. "Enough power, it was said, to light a small town."

A scene where Cooper's character in disguise robs passengers aboard the Annapolis-Claiborne ferry was filmed on Eastern Bay.

Though filmed at a pace that today's filmmakers would consider breakneck, production still got behind schedule, partly due to weather-related delays. A telegram from the Hollywood home office arrived telling Lee: "You're on location, not vacation. Finish picture and come home."

It was a wrap.

Friendships were made.

Money was spent.

The making of *The First Kiss* remained a fond memory for both the natives and filmmakers for decades to come. Forty years after the fact, Lee wrote in a letter to his Talbot County friends that he recalled St. Michaels as having been "an enchanting village" where his cast and crew had been given "wonderful cooperation and warm hospitality from everyone."

The Eastern Shore is good at hospitality.

We've been doing it a long time.

Calendar pages flip dramatically.

Throughout much of the early to mid-twentieth century, St. Michaels struggled to stay afloat. There were pockets of money, most of it kept within the old families who'd always had it, but otherwise there wasn't much to go around. Then the newcomers started coming. Local folks still bonded through their sense of community and long history together, but even that was slipping. One time a visiting reporter noticed that one of the town characters and sages, Junior Marshall, seemed to know every passerby. "Not anymore," Junior confessed to the correspondent, "but not only was there a time I knew everybody by name, I knew everybody's dog by name."

"It was starting to change," says David Parkerson. He worked behind the bar at the Carpenter Street Saloon and saw the transformation up close. "The working guys would still come in, the watermen, the farmers, the builders, but then we started seeing more wealthy people buying property and more tourists finding the town. It really became an amazing array of people who liked to stop by.

"One time, Mike Ashford was in. Mike owned McGarvey's Saloon and Oyster Bar in Annapolis and was a real character. I wasn't real busy, and he said, Dave, come on over here, I want to introduce you to a friend of mine. I said sure. It was an older guy and when I got close, I said, aw man, that's Walter Cronkite. He and Mike had been best buddies for forty years. They loved sailing. I was surprised to see him, but mainly because he'd been there for an hour and a half and I hadn't noticed who he was."

"Clara's Wisdom, Clara's Warmth, Clara's Secret"

Shot in and around St. Michaels in fall 1987, *Clara's Heart* is a family drama starring Whoopi Goldberg as a Jamaican housekeeper named Clara Mayfield, who forges a strong bond with a troubled young teenage boy. The boy, David, is portrayed by Neil Patrick Harris in his film debut, and Michael Ontkean and Kathleen Quinlan play David's parents. *Clara's Heart* was produced by MTM Enterprises and was directed by Robert Mulligan. MTM was an independent production company founded by Mary Tyler Moore and her then-husband, TV exec Grant Tinker. Robert Mulligan's earlier credits include *To Kill a Mockingbird* (1962) *Summer of '42* (1971) and *Same Time, Next Year* (1978).

The *Clara's Heart* production team assembled professionals from talent pools in Los Angeles and New York but also from the Maryland-Virginia-Washington, D.C. region. About 250 local people were brought in as extras and a few were hired to be stand-ins for the stars. Stand-ins do just that. They stand in while the crew works out all the final details such as lighting, camera angles, and blocking that go into shooting a movie scene before bringing the actual actor onto the set. High school freshman Kevin Colborn was hired as a stand-in for Neil Patrick Harris. He was paid $50 to cut his hair plus $150 a day to be available from 6:30 a.m. through 6:00 p.m. Later, he traveled to Baltimore with the cast and crew, where he ended up with an onscreen appearance as a swim team bully and was given a raise to $380 a day.

On October 24, 1987, a cool and sunny Saturday, the cast, crew, and 177 extras filmed a picnic scene at the Inn at Perry Cabin. Built in the early nineteenth century and named for Commodore Oliver Perry, Perry Cabin was a home and working farm that transferred through various owners until the 1950s when the Hunteman family operated a horse-riding school there. The property was purchased in 1980 by real estate developer Harry Meyerhoff, a passionate horse racing fan. Meyerhoff was a co-owner of the racehorse Spectacular Bid, the winner of the prior year's Kentucky Derby and Preakness. The Meyerhoff family converted the old mansion into a six-room inn. In 1989, Perry Cabin was bought and renovated into a luxury resort by Sir Bernard Ashley, a home-decorating and fashion mogul. Most recently, this twenty-six-acre property on the majestic Miles River sold in 2014 for $39.7 million. Though some scenes for *The First Kiss* may have been filmed there, the picnic scenes of *Clara's Heart* were the first to shoot at Perry Cabin post-original makeover. They wouldn't be the last.

Other parts of *Clara's Heart* shot in Talbot County include the opening funeral scene filmed in the Oxford Cemetery and a private residence on the southern banks of Peachblossom Creek that doubled as the home of the Hart family.

While in town, the cast and crew of *Clara's Heart* stayed at various local hotels and inns. Whoopi Goldberg was often seen shopping or out for a meal. Everyone who crossed her path seems to have enjoyed the experience. Tracey Jones, whose family owns the Crab Claw Restaurant in St. Michaels, remarked to the *Star Democrat* at the time that Goldberg was "real down to earth." Jones said she and the star got to know each other on a first-name basis and that when the rising star won the restaurant's World Series pool, she treated the whole cast to a crab feast with her winnings. "She called and asked us to open the restaurant for her on Monday so she could throw a party. She signed autographs for everybody and went into the kitchen and brought everybody out to dance."

A year later, Warner Brothers granted permission for a premiere showing of *Clara's Heart* at Easton's Tred Avon Movies for the benefit of Sudden Infant Death Syndrome research and the restoration of the Avalon Theatre.

"Life's a Party—Crash It"

Wedding Crashers stars Owen Wilson and Vince Vaughn as jaded DC-based divorce lawyers and life-of-the-party best buddies who crash strangers' weddings to take full advantage of female guests caught up in the passion of the matrimonial festivities. Of the many tasks that needs to be accomplished before a single roll of film is shot on any movie production is deciding where that shooting will take place. Finding and securing those locations is the job of professionals such as locations scout and self-described on-set office manager Carol Flaisher, president of Flaisher Films. Flaisher lives outside D.C. near the Potomac River and specializes in movies made in the Chesapeake region. With over thirty years in business, her resume includes such standouts as *True Lies*, *Philomena*, and *Wonder Woman 1984*. Blessed with personal flair and a knack for knowing what people need and how to provide it, Flaisher's work starts from the time a project is a go. She collaborates with directors or production designers who are creating a film's look and has to match their vision to what's in the script and what real estate is available. Fortunately for Flaisher, who's got a talent for convincing even the most reluctant property owners to join in on the moviemaking fun, she also knows the Chesapeake region better than almost anyone. In 2005 she told the *Star Democrat*'s Christine Neff, "Because I'm a Washington, Maryland, Virginia kind of girl, I can read a script and pretty much say, you know what, Oxford is where you want to be, or St. Michaels might work."

"Like with Perry Cabin," Flaisher said in a 2020 interview, "I had been there as a guest when it first opened. We had friends who lived in St. Michaels, and my husband's a fisherman, so the area wasn't foreign to me. In the case of *Wedding Crashers*, I got a call from the producers, months in advance, looking for that perfect, idyllic place for a fancy wedding on the water, and it flew out of my mouth, 'Perry Cabin.' I said there's no place else that will compare based on the script. They put people out looking all over the Eastern Seaboard, looking for what they wanted. Virginia. There's nothing in Virginia that compares. They looked in Connecticut. There was a place that looked right, but it didn't have the water. There was nothing anywhere like the Inn at Perry Cabin at the time and it is probably still quite unique. And so, six months later they called me and said you were right. It ended up where it had started. At the Inn at Perry Cabin."

And it worked out pretty well for everybody. Those fancy wedding scenes that were filmed at the Inn at Perry Cabin were integral to the movie, and more than 15 years hence, people still show up there wanting to see where *Wedding Crashers* was made.

An open casting call at Easton's Tidewater Inn brought out droves of locals ready for their close-up. Filmmakers were looking for extras to populate the background of an upscale waterfront wedding—guests, waiters, photographers, and yacht crewmen were on the list of types the casting agents desired. Potential extras were told they would need to be available for ten days, that they needed to bring at least two wedding-appropriate outfits for the costumers to choose from, and that they would earn $65 plus overtime for a 12-hour day. Some extras might be needed for up to seven days, while others merely two.

When production commenced, the extras had to be formally dressed and ready to go at 6:00 a.m. They were picked up at the Talbot County Community Center on Rt. 50 and bused into Perry Cabin. At this point, there were as many as 450 extras on set. They'd be put in place, sitting and pretending to talk, or standing and pretending to talk, or dancing and, presumably, pretending to talk. They sipped grape and apple juice from wine glasses and champagne flutes. Set managers moved them around and rotated people in and out of position with a lot of "Sit there, move here, do this, do it again. And again. And again. And again."

After filming at Perry Cabin, the production moved to a waterfront home in Newcomb, near Royal Oak, where a small-scale façade of the inn was constructed as a backdrop for scenes requiring tighter focus on the actors. For sequences taking place at the Cleary Estate, where much of the movie's funniest action occurs, producers chose Ellenborough, a 10,000-square-foot mansion with a long tree-lined drive on Peachblossom Creek. Scenes featuring the interiors of the crashers' law firm were shot in Cambridge at what had once been the headquarters of Nathan's Furniture Store, an Eastern Shore landmark business that once operated eighteen stores on Delmarva. The building now houses the offices of the Dorchester Center for the Arts.

It was estimated that an on-location production the size of *Wedding Crashers* would interact with 150 local businesses and add $5 million to the local economy, but there's always more to it than just the money. Debbi Dodson, Talbot County's award-winning original director of tourism, remembers there was "such a wonderful sense of pride in the community that a major film was being made in Talbot County, that people felt like they could be a part of it, and that the filmmakers were so delighted to be here and enjoy the lifestyle." In many ways, *Wedding Crashers* was the social event of the season.

Not to mention the surprise comedy smash of 2005. The producers' gamble on the screenplay's outrageousness and the chemistry of the leads paid off beyond anyone's ability to predict. The movie made more than $200 million and solidified the careers of most everybody involved. Perhaps that sense of community and the success that followed the filming of *Wedding Crashers* is why in the years since there have been reports of various players revisiting their old Eastern Shore stomping grounds.

But the locals don't say too much. Hanging out with celebrities can be fun, but not everybody has to know about it.

Convenient to the centers of power and influence along the East Coast, boasting what's said to be more miles of waterfront than any other county in the nation, Talbot County offers a relaxed pace, as well as a wide range of choice when it comes to sporting activities, cultural pastimes, and fine establishments at which to eat, drink, and be merry. In the next census, the number of billionaires who own property here is likely to continue to rise. Political insiders, captains of industry, and the masters of the arts and sciences are now part of the scenery. Often they're behind-the-scenes types most passersby wouldn't recognize even after being told their names, while others are stop-you-in-your-tracks famous.

Prominent politicians have always been drawn to St. Michaels. Going back at least to the 1930s and 1940s when the Democratic Party owned a hunting and fishing retreat on Jefferson Island near the mouth of Eastern Bay, historic movers and shakers who have visited the area include Presidents Franklin Roosevelt, Truman, and Eisenhower. President George W. Bush's vice president, Dick Cheney (given his own Hollywood send-up in 2018's *Vice*), owned a nine-acre waterfront estate outside St. Michaels from 2005 to 2019. His colleague, Donald Rumsfeld, Bush 43's secretary of defense, bought nearby Mount Misery in 2003 and sold in July 2020. Mount Misery is where the slave Frederick Douglass was sent to be "broken."

Despite this long tradition of chance celebrity sightings, from back-in-the-day stars such as Jackie Gleason to modern marquee-worthy names such as Eric Clapton and Johnny Depp, residents of this tight-knit little waterfront village are often mum about who they've seen or met. The last thing hospitality and retail workers, real estate agents, and starstruck neighbors want to do is feel like they're violating an unspoken agreement of privacy and anonymity.

Many of their anecdotes go something like this: There's a local guy doing his service job. A lady tourist says to him, "We had breakfast this morning and I swear Julianne Moore (Oscar-winning actress) was sitting beside us." The local guy says yes, that would be correct. Her husband asks, "How do you know?" The local guy says, "A family member passed away. She was here for a funeral." What he doesn't tell the couple is that the funeral was for Moore's mom, or that the acclaimed actress's parents lived in St. Michaels and seeing her around St. Michaels had been a regular occurrence for the past twenty years.

"When you meet these celebrities," says the anonymous source, "the rich and famous, they want to be a regular Joe. Usually they have their sunglasses on, their hat pulled down. They don't want a lot of attention; they're not looking for that. I believe what they're looking for is exactly what we're able to give them."

Looking larger than life in this 1913 photograph, impresario William Aloysius Brady brought colliding railroad cars and big-screen spectacle to the Eastern Shore of Maryland in 1917 with *The Whip*, shot near Queenstown. Brady enhanced his swashbuckling reputation through repeated triumphs as a Broadway producer and heavyweight boxing promoter. (*George Grantham Bain Collection/Library of Congress*)

Coming To The
ARCADE THEATRE
MON.-TUES.-WED.---AUG. 27-28-29

FAY WRAY
GARY COOPER
in
'The First Kiss'

A PARAMOUNT PICTURE

"The First Kiss" should be your first choice for screen entertainment. Brings back tender memories of your first kiss.

From the Saturday Evening Post serial romance, "Four Brothers," by Tristram Tupper.

a
ROWLAND
V. LEE
production

In 1928, *The First Kiss* brought two of the biggest stars of the silent era to St. Michaels, Maryland, for filming on location. In the case of Fay Wray, personal downtime during the movie production included the milestone of getting married to a Hollywood screenwriter named John Monk Saunders in Easton's Calvary Methodist Church. Her co-star Gary Cooper was a witness.

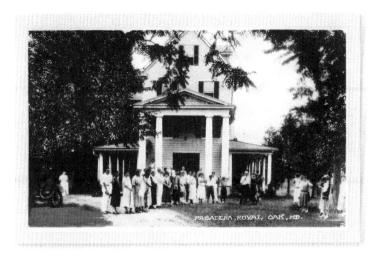

The graciously dimensioned Pasadena Inn in Royal Oak,
Maryland, housed the crew and cast of *The First Kiss* during
their 1928 production. This picture postcard dates to 1924.

A lobby display used to promote the 1928 silent film was printed
in tantalizing color, but like every movie in that era, the celluloid
threading through projectors was strictly black and white.

A 1928 photo kept in a family album depicts the "long-gone" home
of David and Hannah Parkerson of St. Michaels, located on property
now occupied by the Chesapeake Bay Maritime Museum, which was
used as a setting for *The First Kiss*. The original B&W photo has
been colorized by the author. (*Courtesy of the Parkerson family*)

After escaping from slavery in Dorchester County, Maryland, Harriet Tubman (born to the name "Araminta Ross") earned renown with her courageous conducting of many other slaves to freedom in the North. In later life she remarried and settled in Auburn, New York, following intrepid service in the Union Army during the Civil War. Cicely Tyson played Tubman in the 1978 TV miniseries *A Woman Called Moses*, but not until 2019 did she get big-screen treatment in *Harriet*. (*Benjamin F. Powelson/Library of Congress*)

Tallulah Bankhead (second from left) poses with her grandfather, U.S. senator John Hollis Bankhead from Alabama; her uncle John H. Bankhead II, who also became a U.S. senator; and her elder sister, Eugenia. The photo was taken at a Confederate reunion in Washington, D.C. sometime between 1917 and 1920. (*Harris & Ewing; Library of Congress*)

Tallulah Bankhead and Gary Cooper personified Hollywood glamor in the 1932 feature *Devil and the Deep*. (*Paramount Pictures/Photofest*)

This is from Tallulah Bankhead's screen test for the role of Scarlett O'Hara in *Gone with the Wind* (1939). Thousands of devoted fans lobbied hard for her selection, but the coveted role went to Vivien Leigh instead. (*MGM/Photofest*)

Today, the Bankhead sisters, Eugenia and Tallulah, lie side by side in the pastoral St. Paul Cemetery near Chestertown, Maryland. Tallulah's grave is often strewn with flowers and other tokens of remembrance by admirers. (*Secant*)

Linda Harrison, playing Nova, poses with Roddy McDowall ("Cornelius") and other members of the cast of the 1968 science fiction hit, *Planet of the Apes*. The autographed photo is inscribed to the author.

Bea Arthur (center) grew up in Cambridge, Maryland, and enjoyed a headliner's career on Broadway and in television. Here she is with *Golden Girls* co-stars Betty White (left) and Rue McClanahan (right). The lights were dimmed on Broadway at Arthur's passing. (*UPI/Alamy Stock Photo*)

Berlin, Maryland rolled back the calendar when it was transformed into the fictional town of Treegap, the setting for *Tuck Everlasting* (2002), depicting the bittersweet relations between a family of immortals and the normal time-bound people who befriend and love them. Alexis Bledel plays a human girl and Jonathan Jackson her ageless beau. The A-list cast included Sissy Spacek, William Hurt, Ben Kingsley and Amy Irving. (*Walt Disney Pictures/Photofest*)

The Town of Berlin presented director Garry Marshall and the cast of *Runaway* Bride with framed prints by local artist Patrick Henry when Hollywood rolled up for filming. Henry (right) is flanked by Marshall, Julia Roberts, and Richard Gere (far left) in this autographed photo of the presentation. Former mayor Rex Hailey and his wife Shirley Toms complete the first row; deputy town administrator Mary Bohlen is just behind them. (*Courtesy of Patrick Henry*)

Runaway Bride leading man Richard Gere and director Gary Marshall talk things over in front of Berlin's landmark Atlantic Hotel, where pivotal scenes in the 1999 romantic comedy were set. (*Paramount Pictures/Photofest*)

Actor Owen Wilson and director David Dobkin share a relaxed moment during the 2005 shooting of *Wedding Crashers* on location in St. Michaels, Maryland. (*New Line Cinema/Photofest*)

Location manager Carol Flaisher, a veteran of the Maryland filmmaking industry, snapped this night scene during the shooting of *Wedding Crashers* in St. Michaels. (*Courtesy of Carol Flaisher*)

Rapidly fabricating sets that look just like a million bucks is part of the magic of Tinseltown—as in this scene from *Wedding Crashers* production in St. Michaels. (*Courtesy of Carol Flaisher*)

Jack Gerbes is the longtime director of the Maryland Film Office, which promotes the state to movie studios and independent filmmakers. *(Courtesy of Jack Gerbes)*

The Delaware International Speedway makes at least one appearance in the 1990 racing spectacular *Days of Thunder*, directed by Tony Scott (left) and starring Tom Cruise (right). *(Paramount/Photofest)*

Doggone it, the movies have always had a soft spot for canines with personality. American Pitbull Sayuri, owned by Matt and Monique Klosowski of Delaware Red Pitbulls, was a scene-stealer in Quentin Tarantino's 2019 hit, *Once Upon a Time … in Hollywood.* Afterward, she put her best mug forward on the Hollywood Walk of Fame. (*Courtesy of Matt and Monique Klosowski*)

BEHIND THE SCENES

The son of a Washington College president who spent some of his formative years in Chestertown, Maryland, James M. Cain won fame and changed cinematic standards with his *noir* crime fiction. He is pictured here with Hollywood leading lady Lana Turner. *(MGM/Photofest)*

JAMES M.
CAIN AND
FILM NOIR

"In the rancorous universe of James M. Cain's early novels, life's a bitch and she wears lipstick and a skirt."
—Critic-At-Large Hilton Als, *New Yorker*

Eastern Shore folk talk different.

Where on the Shore a person comes from influences their accent, but as a whole, local speech patterns tend to come off as part Southern, part Northern, and part lazy Shakespearean. The historic remoteness of the Eastern Shore has instilled in the locals a cultural identity that includes the nuanced musicality and unique colloquialisms of our shared voice. We sound hardscrabble yet properly raised, like we'd invite you over for a cordial home-cooked meal after punching you in the mouth.

Washington College is located on Maryland's mid-Eastern Shore in the Kent County seat of Chestertown. Founded in 1782, this was the first college named for George Washington and the only one that did so with his blessing. The eleventh-oldest campus in the

United States, the first after the nation declared independence, it was founded with the goal to mold future leaders of the republic. Notable alumni include Maryland Governor Thomas Veazy (Class of 1795), baseball players Homer Smoot (1897) and Bill Nicholson (1936), and actress Linda Hamilton.

When James M. Cain, Annapolis-born and best known as the novelist who wrote *Double Indemnity*, *Mildred Pierce*, and *The Postman Always Rings Twice*, was eleven years old, his father was named president of Washington College. Included among the pillars of "noir" fiction despite his resistance to the "lust and murder" label, Cain is famous for penning stories with boundary-pushing sexual content, cinematic pacing, and characters who display unrefined dialogue. His infatuation with exploring how people talk and his talent for recreating it on paper helped him become known as one of the primary creators of a distinctly American literary genre.

And it was in Chestertown where Cain first picked up his love of the vernacular, the language spoken by ordinary people.

Roman Noir, the black novel, is a subgenre of crime fiction. Noir shares some of the tropes of its pulpy cousin, the hard-boiled detective story, and in the hands of masters, both are capable of transcending cliché. First come the flawed characters—unsavory antiheroes, tough guys in fedoras and dames in slinky dresses, motivated by the basest of emotions and needs, losers looking for trouble and finding it. There's always a femme fatale. Other essential elements include psychological tension and an atmospheric threat of physical violence. These stories exist in a nighttime world without straightforward morals or easy solutions. Every decision is compromised by world-weary angst and skepticism. Right and wrong exist in shades of shadow, hard liquor, and cigarette smoke.

Roman Noir was created by Dashiell Hammett (*The Maltese Falcon, The Thin Man*), a Marylander born in St. Mary's County on the lower western shore, and then transformed by the language and romanticism of Raymond Chandler (*The Big Sleep, The Long Goodbye, Farewell, My Lovely*). Cain is credited with bringing his trademark ear for "real talk" to the party and for focusing on the criminal's point-of-view. The aggressive sex scenes, scalding in their graphic rawness? Those were also Cain's.

When noir slunk off the page and went Hollywood, moviemakers softened its narrative edges. They added mood lighting and stylized photography to the lurid tales of hard people doing rough things to each other. The best actors of the genre delivered their performances with an economy of body language, a dispassionate façade, and a whiskey-smooth, near-lethargic delivery of their lines.

The first of five children belonging to James W. Cain, a college professor and administrator, and Rose, a former opera singer, James Mallahan Cain was born on July 1, 1892, at the Paca-Carroll house (c. 1855) on the campus of historic St. John's College, in the heart of Maryland's capital city. Described by a lifelong friend as quiet, wholesome, and considerate, young "Jamie" was a precocious reader. He loved *The Adventures of Sherlock Holmes* and adventure stories like *The Last of the Mohicans, Treasure Island,* and *The Three Musketeers,* but even as an adult his all-time favorite book was *Alice in Wonderland.* He considered it the "greatest novel in the English language."

Jamie's father, a charismatic, self-involved academic, taught at St. John's and then served as vice president. He was credited for improving the institution's reputation as a small, first-rate school, and when it came time to fill a leadership vacancy at St. John's Eastern Shore counterpart, Washington College, James W. Cain was among the top contenders for the position.

Washington College was struggling to stay afloat. Despite its illustrious history, there were no more than half a dozen professors on staff and enrollment was at a low. Any prestige the institution once claimed was eroding like an unprotected Chesapeake Bay shoreline. James W. Cain enjoyed a reputation as a man who could build academic respectability.

The family waited over the summer of 1903 to find out if James won the job or not, and Jamie was especially anxious. He had earlier convinced his father, chair of the Annapolis Board of Education, to let him skip from third grade to fifth—a mistake from the beginning. Always the runt, nowhere near as attractive as he wished he were, and intimidated by the older girls as much as the older boys, it didn't take long for it to dawn on the ambitious little brainiac that he was now going to forever be playing an unwinnable game of catch-up. He hoped the Eastern Shore might help him get a fresh start.

The Cains were living in Baltimore when James got word the job was his. He loaded the family's possessions aboard a hired bugeye—an indigenous two-masted Chesapeake Bay workboat—and booked passenger tickets on the *Emma Ford*, one of the fanciest and most modern of Chesapeake steamboats, for the ride down the bay and up the Chester River. Upon arrival in Chestertown, they moved into a large home where they were greeted by "neighbors with horses, who came with grins on their faces, and invited us to take a ride; there were farmers with peach orchards, who told us to help ourselves, and apparently meant it.

"But . . ."

An earlier visit troubled Jamie's family. Unlike the trimmed lawns at St. John's, the rustic Washington College campus reminded them of an unmowed field. There wasn't even a brick walkway, just a rickety old boardwalk like some frontier town out west.

For Jamie, Chestertown turned out worse than Annapolis. Thirty miles apart as the crow flies, in customs and influences the two places felt like different worlds. The culture shock stunned him. The church here was a "hick institution." The pride the natives took in their "Southern Blood" was repulsive to his sensibilities. He didn't like swimming in the Chester River. It "was all bottom."

His parents and siblings were specimens of high order. Jamie was not. His mother had presence, grace, and talent. His dad was athletic, handsome, and charming, with a poise and a command of the English language befitting a Yale graduate. His sisters were without fault, and his younger brother was the golden boy. Jamie, pale and pimply, awkward and stocky but not strong, felt like an ugly-duckling outsider among a gaggle of good-looking, overachieving geese. He was an eleven-year-old seventh grader, which on the Shore was considered high school. Boys picked on him and girls ignored him.

Meanwhile, that embarrassing campus boardwalk was really getting on his father's nerves. Something had to be done about it.

To help make the school more presentable, bring its standards closer to those of other esteemed East Coast universities, President Cain hired a local mason named Ike Newton to build a brick walkway. Dressed in dungarees and boots, squatting on the ground laying brick for hours on end, Ike wasn't of the type of athletic build the Cains admired, but he was solid, strong in the way of a laborer. He wasn't an educated man but he was skilled. He was also friendly, and he very much liked to talk.

Bored and lonely, young Jamie Cain listened.

Years later, Cain told the *Paris Review* that "the first man I ever sat at the feet of who enchanted me not only by what he told me but by how he talked was Ike Newton . . . I would sit out there while he worked, listening to him." For the first time, Cain heard how people who were uncultured but not inarticulate spoke. The rhythms, the tempo, the cadence of the language fascinated him, and he took them home with him to share.

His parents were unenthusiastic.

"Horrified" is the word he used.

They'd always insisted on flawless formal English. His mother considered street lingo "low" talk, its dearth of eloquence a type of profanity. His father was obsessed with the way people were "supposed" to speak. But the Eastern Shore bricklayer inspired Cain's taste for authenticity over etiquette. In a 1970 *Baltimore Sun* profile, the writer said, "I was fascinated by the colorful way he talked . . . it opened up a whole new world for me. My style didn't come from Ike Newton, but it came from all the Ike Newtons I listened to after that, and I have him to thank for the fact that I started listening."

Listening. Listening to that rolling, relaxed storytelling simplicity of the language, the depth of thought and imagination, and above all, the way the Eastern Shore bricklayer said what was on his mind without ornamentation. "If a writer owes a debt to what his ears pick up," Cain's biographer Roy Hoopes quotes, "mine would be to Ike."

That Eastern Shore way of talking sticks with you.

Jamie Cain entered college at fourteen. Despite his self-conscious immaturity, by the time he graduated, at an age most boys were beginning their higher education, he'd managed to find himself a girlfriend. Mary Rebekah Clough, from nearby Church Hill, was smart, a year older than Jamie, and said to be related to the author Stephen Crane.

After graduation, Cain was lost. He possessed no understanding of what was supposed to come next, no work ethic, just a vague idea that he was expected to find something to do. During the next four years, he held a variety of jobs, trying to find his niche. He worked for Baltimore's Gas and Light Company, was a state road inspector, and taught school in the Eastern Shore town of Vienna in Dorchester County. He was an insurance man for a short time and didn't sell a single policy. He sold records in a Washington, D.C. store and even toyed with the idea of being a singer, but his mother scoffed at the idea.

Then one day, when he was twenty-two years old, sitting on a park bench in Layfette Park, his back to the White House, James M. Cain heard his own voice say, "You're going to be a writer."

He returned to Chestertown and lived there with his parents for three years. There was a teaching vacancy at the college and Cain stepped in. As an English teacher, he felt it was his duty to become an expert on all elements of writing. He earned his master's degree with a major in history and a minor in drama. He learned to type and submitted short stories to magazines, but no publisher took the bait. In 1918, his father was let go from the college under undisclosed circumstances but bounced back with a high-level job at a Baltimore insurance company.

The younger Cain snagged a writing gig as a crime reporter for the *Baltimore American* newspaper and was then tapped to move up to the *Sun* in 1919. Before the year was out, he enlisted in the army to help fight in World War I. Cain served with the 79th Division in France and saw action in the Meuse-Argonne offensive. He also edited the company newspaper. Right after the armistice, Edward, Cain's brother, was killed in an accidental plane crash.

Cain returned to the *Sun* when he got back to the states, where he became a protégé of H. L. Mencken. In 1920, he married his Eastern Shore sweetheart, Mary. The two of them felt a connection, but they weren't compatible. Nobody could figure out what they saw in each other.

The next decade was eventful. Cain began writing a novel and quit. He quit the *Sun*. He and Mary moved to Annapolis when he took a teaching job at St. John's. In 1924, he wrote his first published article, but then he and Mary separated and he was forced to resign his teaching position after a dispute with the school's president. He contracted tuberculosis and spent that summer writing in a sanitorium. When he was released, his doctor told him to look for a sit-down job. With a recommendation from Mencken, Cain took the train to New York to find writing work. Hired to pen editorials for the *New York World*, he moved in with a non–English speaking Finnish girlfriend named Elina Sjosted Tyszecka and divorced Mary. He wrote his first play and published his first short story in 1928. After a short stint at the *New Yorker*, Cain set his sights on Hollywood.

In 1931, Cain took a job with Paramount Studios. He and Elina, now married, moved to California, where he lived and worked for the next seventeen years. At a salary of $400 a week, he was making twice what he earned in New York, but from the beginning screenwriting did not bode well. His first assignment was to do a rewrite on a remake of the 1923 silent smash *The Ten Commandments* that Cain considered a "masterpiece of hokum."

Turned out, Cain wasn't proficient at the job he was hired for, but he kept failing upward. One studio would fire him and another would pick him up at a higher salary. He'd sit around for weeks, collecting an ever-expanding paycheck and waiting on someone to tell him to write something. Then, early in 1933, the screenwriter Robert Riskin, who would soon earn credits for such classics-to-be as *It Happened One Night* (1934) and *Mr. Deeds Goes to Town* (1936), and later become Fay Wray's second husband, gave Cain some advice. Riskin told Cain that his approach to writing was too mechanical and he'd do better if he could learn to open up and tell stories based on his own knowledge and experience. Cain left the conversation determined to find his voice.

Cain started writing a novel he called *Bar-B-Que*. In a year or so, after changing the title to *The Postman Always Rings Twice*, a random phrase he'd heard someone use once, the book would be his first published full-length fiction and a commercial champ. It would also, however, be a decade before Hollywood would have the guts to touch it.

That same year, 1934, he published an article called "Tribute to a Hero" based on his time growing up on the Eastern Shore. It was not a flattering portrait, and the residents of Chestertown made no bones about their resentment toward Cain and his opinions of their village. The magazine that printed the piece, Mencken and George Jean Nathan's *American Mercury*, also published his short story, "Baby in the Icebox," which became the first movie based on Cain's work. He sold the rights to Paramount Pictures for $1,000. The studio declined to let him write the screenplay.

During the next decade, Cain stayed busy. Still on the Hollywood dole, he published *Double Indemnity*, which was serialized in *Liberty* magazine before being released as a book. He adapted *Postman* for the Broadway stage. He published *Serenade*, a novel about a down-on-his-luck opera singer who falls in love with a beautiful Mexican prostitute, and the serialized novella *Two Can Sing. Serenade* was made into a movie in 1956 while *Sing* was adapted for the screen twice, once in 1939 as *Wife, Husband and Friend* and in 1949 as *Everybody Does It.*

Cain's father died in 1938. *Mildred Pierce* was published in 1941, and in 1942 Cain and Elina divorced. He was then married for two years to the actress Aileen Pringle, a member of the infamous Algonquin Round Table and onetime paramour of Cain's mentor and pal Mencken. Their relationship was volatile, and though not as spectacularly ill-fated as the couples he wrote about, they too were doomed to fail.

Cain and Aileen tied the knot in summer 1944 and honeymooned in San Francisco and Sacramento, returning to L.A. in time for the movie premiere of *Double Indemnity.*

Originally serialized in 1936, there was no way *Double Indemnity* was going to make it to the screen on its first go-round. The story of a sexed-up insurance guy and a seductive vixen who plot to profit from murdering her husband was so steamy and controversial it took eight years and an audience matured by another world war for any studio to consider going to battle with the censors over Cain's most scandalous creations.

As an author, Cain was obsessed with the idea of a man, driven by his lust, "yearning to commit the one crime he is responsible for preventing." He'd worked as a frustrated insurance salesman; his dad had been an insurance supervisor. Insurance fraud was a topic he was familiar with. Cain used those earlier experiences in his working life to build characters and situations that got the details right.

Another major influence in Cain's *Indemnity*, as well as his other most popular works, were the people, places, and things he found while living in Southern California. The locale informed his fiction as no other place could. It was there on the fringes of the dream factory that Cain's irredeemable and unsympathetic characters, sunbaked and thirsty with flop-sweat dreams and tarnished last-stop aspirations, find the unhappy ending to their dead-end travels. "I couldn't seem to write about New York. I couldn't manage the New York idiom," he told the *Paris Review*. "When I got out to California, I found the people there spoke my lingo" and "everything broke for me."

Billy Wilder, one of the most creative and successful directors of Hollywood's golden age, saw the potential of *Double Indemnity* when he found a missing-in-action secretary squirreled away, engrossed in reading proofs Cain's agent was sending around. Wilder, a European Jew who'd fled Hitler's rise, couldn't speak any English when he came to America but was infatuated with his new country's culture. He would eventually win six Oscars, including the prestigious Irving G. Thalberg Award in 1988 for his body of work. Paramount bought *Indemnity* for Wilder to direct and paid $15,000 for the rights.

Wilder wanted to stick to the original story and dialogue as much as possible. Cain was his first choice to write the movie but was under contract elsewhere. Charles Brackett, the director's regular collaborator, called Cain's story disgusting and refused to work on the project. Someone suggested Raymond Chandler. To Wilder's surprise, Chandler was already living in Hollywood, though he'd never written for the screen before despite two of his books having already been made into films. Like Brackett, Chandler hated Cain's work. "Everything he touches smells like Billy Goat," the mercurial crime novelist wrote in a letter to Cain's publisher. He considered Cain to be "Proust in greasy overalls," compared him to "a dirty little boy with a piece of chalk and a board fence and nobody looking."

Cain's dialogue was one sticking point. Wilder wanted to keep as much as they could. Chandler said it wouldn't work. To settle their dispute, they hired a group of actors to read scenes right out of the book. Chandler was right. Cain's words, dialogue included, were written for the way they looked on the page.

When it came time to cast the two main roles, Walter Huff, (changed to Neff for the movie) a gullible wannabe mastermind, and Phyllis Nirdlinger (changed to Dietrichson), the temptress with the "survival instincts of a snake," Barbara Stanwyck was Wilder's first choice, but Fred MacMurray was not. James Cagney, Spencer Tracy, and Gregory Peck were among those who declined the part. Mostly known for lightweight comedy, MacMurray had worked with Stanwyck before in a Christmas romance called *Remember the Night* in 1940. As his contract with Paramount was nearing its end, MacMurray was playing hardball with his studio bosses. He agreed to be in *Double Indemnity* figuring the studio wouldn't let him. Instead, knowing he'd already signed on to do a picture for a different company, the suits said go ahead. They were hoping *Indemnity* would bomb and sink his entire career.

As one of Hollywood's biggest stars, with an income of $400,000, Barbara Stanwyck was the highest-paid woman in America, but her journey began in poverty and despair. Born Ruby Stevens in Brooklyn, New York, in 1907, she was four years old when her pregnant mother was knocked off a streetcar by a drunk and died from her injuries. Ruby and her brother Malcolm, who both witnessed the fatal encounter, were left in the care of their father, who abandoned them in two weeks' time. The children had three adult sisters who would not or could not provide guardianship on a reliable basis, so as she'd later say, "Whoever would take me for five dollars a week, that's where I was."

A hard worker from a young age, she accepted any job offered. One of her sisters was an actress and as she matured, Mildred sometimes let Ruby tour with her. The controlled backstage mayhem appealed to Ruby, as must have the attention that the performers onstage received. By the time she was fifteen, Ruby Stevens was a chorus girl dancing in speakeasies.

It was Barbara Stanwyck who arrived in Hollywood in 1928.

With her husky voice and showgirl's legs, Stanwyck landed her first credited role in a 1929 drama called *The Locked Door*. In 1932, she was the star of *So Big*, based on Edna Ferber's Pulitzer Prize–winning novel. She played the title character in 1938's *Annie Oakley*, and she won her first Oscar nomination for that year's *Stella Dallas*. In her career, she earned more than 100 acting credits and was best known to television viewers as the matriarch in the popular Western *The Big Valley*. The American Film Institute places her at number eleven on their list of the top female stars of all time. When approached by Wilder about *Double Indemnity*, she was reluctant to take on such a shady portrayal, but her director challenged her with a now-legendary question that sealed the deal. "Well," Wilder asked, "are you an actress or a mouse?"

Wilder and Chandler worked together during four tumultuous months, and they changed more than Cain's dialogue. Scenes were added, the ending was changed, and the importance of the third lead, the part of Barton Keyes, Walter's mentor and eventual foe, played by Edward G. Robinson, was bumped up to add emotional resonance to the plot. These tweaks improved the finished project, but if modern critics have a beef with the movie, it's that

Stanwyck's Phyllis lost the motives she held in Cain's version and was "pointlessly" evil in Wilder and Chandler's.

On the other hand, the screenplay could now get past the censors. With good-versus-evil conflict raging across the globe, it was harder for authorities to restrict artistic content. Gable had said he didn't give a damn and celluloid gangsters such as Robinson were shooting up movie screens with profit-making bravado from coast to coast. The more cynical audiences of the 1940s no longer appreciated Hollywood's sanitized version of life. Still, everybody involved with the production of *Double Indemnity* couldn't help but be surprised when they got the green light.

Shot in a little more than 40 days in fall 1943, photographed by the gifted and accomplished cinematographer and inventor John F. Sietz, the look and feel of *Double Indemnity* influenced the future style of the entire noir genre. The story was something new for the screen too: normal-seeming people motivated by their basest desires to commit murder. There'd been crime stories told before, of course, but none as dark as this. Deemed "Not Suitable for General Exhibition," the movie was a moneymaker nonetheless and picked up seven Academy Award nominations including Best Picture, Best Actress, and Best Director. Wilder was so angry when he didn't win (he'd have to wait a year for *The Lost Weekend* to take top honors) that when Leo McCarey was walking up to accept the trophy for *Going My Way*, Wilder stuck a foot out and tripped him.

Cain, never a fan of movies, his own included, sent all three key players autographed copies of his collection *Three of a Kind* and a note telling them how much he'd enjoyed their work. Edward G. Robinson loved the movie and thought it brought him back from the brink of irrelevance. MacMurray, whose other most famous role would be the widower dad on twelve seasons of *My Three Sons*, considered *Double Indemnity* his best film role. Stanwyck's

Phyllis, among the most captivating and enduring of femme fatales, is number eight on the American Film Institute's list of greatest villains, right before the little girl who was possessed by the devil in *The Exorcist.*

As of 2020, *Double Indemnity* is listed as the American Film Institute's eighth greatest love story, twenty-fourth greatest thriller, and number twenty-nine out of America's 100 Greatest Films. In 1992, it was added to the National Film Registry as being "culturally, historically, or aesthetically significant." For Cain's part, he conceded, "It's the only picture I ever saw made from my books that had things in it I wish I had thought of. [The] ending was much better than my ending. . . . I would have done it if I had thought of it."

In 1940, once word got out that *Double Indemnity* had made it past the censors, Cain properties became a hot commodity.

Mildred Pierce, the next film to be made from a published work by Cain, was released as a novel in 1941 to mixed but predominately favorable reviews. The book, which Cain considered his most serious novel, was never a runaway best seller, but for a Cain book it made it to the screen with relative haste.

Influenced by a long affair Cain had conducted with a woman named Kate Cummings, *Mildred Pierce* offered a complex look at a female protagonist trying to make her own way through the world while providing for her daughters. As the close friendship between Cain and Cummings blossomed into something more, Cain witnessed the ways Kate sacrificed to serve her daughter's acting ambitions. He used those experiences as inspiration for a story that, like many of his stories, shows how bad things can get when dreams come true.

Cain's naturalistic, nonviolent tale is about a suburban California housewife who throws her husband out for cheating on her, builds a successful career as a restauranteur, and finds new romance. Then she blows it all up trying to earn the love and respect of her gifted, spoiled, and narcissistic time bomb of an elder daughter, Veda—a character Cain always considered among his best.

For the film adaptation, Michal Curtiz, a Hungarian-born filmmaker responsible for many Hollywood hits, signed on as director. In his career, Curtiz directed seven films nominated for Best Picture, with *Casablanca* his lone winner. He wanted Barbara Stanwyck for Mildred, but she and the other stars at the top of his wish list didn't want to play a character old enough to have a teenage daughter.

Somebody who cared nothing about that was Joan Crawford. She read the script, wanted the part, and like Mildred herself would have done, set out to get it with a tenacious focus.

Crawford came to Hollywood in 1925 at the age of nineteen. A silent-era flapper, she was among those few big names who were able to transition to talkies. Never considered as capable an actor as her rivals, she was still one of the biggest stars in the world for years. In 1937, though, she fell off the list of Hollywood's top moneymakers and within a year went from queen of the movies to box office poison.

Despite the initial reluctance of producer Jerry Wald to hire Crawford, her willingness to fight for the part impressed him, so he hired her even though neither Curtiz nor his cameraman Ernest Haller, who'd won an Oscar for *Gone with the Wind*, wanted to work with someone who was on the outs and rumored to be an unparalleled diva. She won her doubters over, but when the cameras started rolling, *Mildred Pierce* was, in the words of biographer Hoopes, "in the unlikely hands of . . . a washed-up, temperamental glamour girl, and an equally temperamental director, who did not like the star, working with a cameraman who said the star could not be photographed."

When the movie came out in October 1945, it was a critical and box-office triumph and even the bad reviews tended to praise Crawford's performance. Nominated for six Academy Awards, including Best Picture, Best Screenplay, and best Black-and-White Cinematography, *Mildred Pierce* won Crawford her sole Best Actress trophy. Legend has it she didn't think she'd win, so to avoid humiliation she faked pneumonia. When she got word that she'd come out on top, she quickly got out of bed and pulled herself together to talk to the press.

Queen of the comeback, number ten on the American Film Institute's list of Greatest Female Stars, Crawford followed *Mildred Pierce* with a string of successes, and years later, after her star once again faded, made one more dramatic return along with her longtime nemesis Bette Davis in 1962's schlocky horror flick *Whatever Happened to Baby Jane*. The noted English actor Michael Redgrave once credited Crawford's longevity to her ability to outstare everybody else. In a career spanning half a century, *Mildred Pierce* was Crawford's favorite film. Cain never liked it, though he did send Crawford a signed copy of the book. The film was added to the National Film Registry in 1996.

In 2011, director Todd Haynes and HBO produced a five-episode miniseries based on Cain's novel with Kate Winslet in the title role. A tribute to the author's work, using almost every scene in the book and word-for-word dialogue, the production featured gorgeous photography and outstanding performances—Winslet and Guy Pierce won Emmys—but there were negatives. The direct translation of the source material exposed the holes in Cain's plot and in a column for *Newsweek*, Stephen King praised the hard work that went into the project but deemed it "too damn long."

Near the end of his review, King also called Winslet's performance a "genuine star turn. Joan Crawford," he observed, "would have loathed her."

"Stealing a man's wife, that's nothing, but stealing his car, that's larceny" is one of the few lines from Cain's big three that made it from his books to their movie adaptations.

The Postman Always Rings Twice was Cain's first published book of fiction, and it came out in 1934 when he was forty-two. Inspired by the infamous 1920s Snyder-Grey case where a New York woman and her lover killed her husband for the insurance money (and were sent to the electric chair for it), Cain's 35,000-word novella was short, unvarnished, and with its visceral sex and violence, had his fingerprints all over it.

Written with poetic skill and drive but without ornamentation or conventional exposition, much of the tale of Frank, Cora, and "The Greek" is told in snappy, rhythmic dialogue. To the bluenoses and authorities of public morality, Cain's work was crass, if not profane, relying on shock value to sell books and corrupt the innocent masses. As always, the ire of the watchdogs could help sales as much as hurt. The book's blistering reputation earned it a second printing before it was even released. "Banned in Boston" was a slogan worth promoting. Canada would not let such filth cross its border. Even Cain's Eastern Shore alma mater wouldn't put *Postman* on its shelves, but that may have had as much to do with sore feelings for Cain's high-profile disrespect for Chestertown as it did the content of his book.

Cain's tale begins with what is now considered to be one of modern literature's great opening lines: "They threw me off the hay truck at noon." After being given the unceremonious boot, the drifter Frank goes into a nearby tavern to bum a lunch, catches sight of the owner's hot wife, and finagles himself into a job as a handyman. Cain's not playing around. Ten pages in and Frank and Cora are tearing into one another like rutting wildcats. Four pages later, they're plotting murder. Of course, in Cain's world, be careful what you wish for. Soon as Frank and Cora do the deed and get what they want, they turn on each other. There are no happy endings in store for anybody.

The book's success, critically and commercially, established Cain's credentials and opened markets for his stories, articles, and other projects, all while he was still working for the studios on rewrites and original material. Impressing even some of the reviewers who wanted to hate it, *The Postman Always Rings Twice* was a hit and Tinseltown wanted their piece of the action. MGM paid $25,000 for the movie rights.

Of course, due to the story's bleak themes, noxious characters, aggressive sex, and "essential immorality," MGM paid big bucks for something that was too bold for its times.

It took twelve years and the success of *Double Indemnity* for anybody in Hollywood to even consider making *The Postman Always Rings Twice*, and then it passed the censors with relative ease. Director Tay Garnett, who had been shooting movies with mediocre results since 1924, asserted that changes he and his team made to Cain's story were what the script needed to get the go-ahead. "The thing the Hays Office objected to in the original was the sort of low-level quality of the people in it," Garnett said. "We've raised the tone of the story. I guess you could say we've lifted it from the gutter up to, well, the sidewalk."

Lana Turner was signed to play Cora. Born Julia Jean Turner in Idaho in 1921, her family moved to San Francisco when she was six. When her father was murdered after a card game, she and her mother traveled to Los Angeles to find work. The legend is she was discovered at the soda foundation of a Hollywood drugstore. Never thought of as a particularly adept actress, Turner was a Depression-era "Sweater Girl" and a top pin-up model during World War II. Glamor and curves were her primary claim to fame.

Cain liked her. When he asked her why she wanted to play Cora, she told him it was because of the character's honesty. Turner said Cora knew what she was and that what she was going to do was wrong, but she wanted something out of life and was going to do what was necessary to get it. "It's what made Cora so human," Turner reasoned. "She'd kill a man so she could have a little piece of property away out in the hills, a lunchroom, some cabins, and a filling station. You can't help feeling sorry for her."

Postman gave Lana Turner's career a second wind, as *Double Indemnity* did for Stanwyck and *Mildred Pierce* for Crawford. She did a couple dozen more movies and won a Best Actress nomination for 1957's *Peyton Place*. Her private life was one of constant turmoil. She was married seven times. In 1958, her daughter was charged with murdering Turner's boyfriend, an abusive mobster, but was acquitted in the "Hollywood Trial of the Century." This was, of course, after the Fatty Arbuckle Trial of the Century and before the O. J. Simpson Trial of the Century.

John Garfield, nee Jacob Garfinkle, played Frank. Born in the slums of Manhattan's Lower East Side, Garfield was a serious actor who worked his way up from supporting roles on Broadway to a Hollywood contract, often playing the guy most likely to kill or be killed. Rebellious onscreen and off, Garfield was a precursor to the Marlon Brando style of naturalistic actor. He made an impression in his first credited role in Michal Curtiz's *Four Daughters* (1938), even got a Best Supporting Actor nomination out of it. He was nominated in 1948 as Best Actor for his role as a boxer in *Body and Soul*, but in 1951 got caught up in the Red Scare congressional investigations. He wouldn't name names and was blacklisted. In 1952, he died of a heart attack at the age of thirty-nine.

Number forty-nine on the American Film Institute's greatest love stories list, the original film version of *The Postman Always Rings Twice* is considered a consummate example of cinematic noir. In his telling, Cain created a template for crime stories depicted from the criminal's point of view and creating ill-intentioned characters that his readers care about despite their offenses. "Murder has always been written from its least interesting angle," Cain explained, "which is whether the police will catch the murderer." His take was that when audiences live among those who commit the crime, they care for them more. In some ways, it's more honest for us to relate to bad decision makers than those who always do the right thing.

In 1982, director Bob Rafelson released a remake of *The Postman Always Rings Twice* starring Jack Nicholson and Jessica Lange. This new version wasn't a hit, though it did make its money back. Overall, critics were not impressed, but it was among the first in a trend of erotic thrillers that came out during the next few years.

Cain married his fourth wife, an opera singer named Florence Macbeth, in 1947. The couple moved back to Maryland, bought a modest house in Hyattsville, twenty minutes from downtown Washington, D.C., and remained together until she died eighteen years later. "It wasn't supposed to be permanent," Cain said. "Television had just come in and was killing the movies. So we stayed."

During the next 25 years or so, Cain published ten books, including *The Butterfly*, which was made into a bonkers 1982 film with Stacey Keach and Pia Zadora—who as a six-year-old debuted on Broadway in *Midgie Purvis* with Tallulah Bankhead—and was the last onscreen theatrical film of both Orson Welles and James Franciscus. Three of his novels were published posthumously. Cain sometimes talked about why he loved California but felt inept in Hollywood. "I just didn't like the movies. I never liked them. I didn't even go to see the last three or four movies that were made of my books." He remembered his first trip to see a moving picture. It was in 1906 in a Chestertown nickelodeon and he found it simpleminded. "There are some foods some people just don't like," he concluded. "I just don't like movies."

Cain died at home from a heart attack at the age of 85. He left instructions to be memorialized with a cocktail party. A hundred friends gathered to pay tribute to a man many of them remembered as being kind and thoughtful. It wasn't too shabby a sendoff for a self-proclaimed ugly Irish Catholic mama's boy.

Through the decades, Cain's work has fallen in and out of vogue, with a popular resurgence every few years. He's out when literary trends are going big and fantastical and in when pared-to-the-bone storytelling is more in fashion. Certain times, times of struggle and worry, call for that style of writing more than others. His biographer David Madden says picking up a Cain story is "like looking at a loaded gun on a table." Most critics consider his cinematic pacing and get-to-the-point technique his chief attributes, and his approach to storytelling has influenced everything from 1981's *Body Heat* and *The Big Lebowski* in 1988 to 1997's *Jackie Brown* and 2014's *Inherent Vice*.

Cain lived a complex and turbulent personal life, and he left few friends behind when he left the Eastern Shore. In his writing career, he was a police blotter journalist, wrote editorials, plays, screenplays, and nineteen novels, including some considered among the greatest books of crime or any other genre. He wrote love stories but never romanticized anything. As a young man trying to find his place in the world, he spent years trying to figure out what he was supposed to do, and those life experiences, those failures gave him context for his stories and an understanding of life's losers.

In a letter to Fred MacMurray, he wrote in part: "If I have a gift it is to take such people and show that they can suffer as profoundly as anyone else." In the preface of his *Three of a Kind* collection, he declared: "I merely try to write as the character would write, and I never forget that the average man, from the fields, the streets, the bars, the offices, and even the gutters of his country, has acquired a vividness of speech that goes beyond anything I could invent, and that if I stick to this heritage, this logos of the American countryside, I shall attain a maximum of effectiveness with very little effort. In general, my style is rural rather than urban. My ear seems to like the fields better than the streets. I am glad of this, for I think language loses a bit of its bounce the moment its heels touch concrete."

James Cain, wrote his biographer Hoopes, can "say more in fewer words than perhaps any writer ever achieved."

It's kind of like talking to an Eastern Shoreman.

After long conversations with the acting troupe on board the *James Adams Floating Theatre*, which cruised the Chesapeake Bay in the early 20th century, bestselling novelist Edna Ferber applied her novelist's imagination and divested herself of the immortal *Show Boat*. (*Theatre Magazine/Wikimedia Commons*)

EDNA FERBER AND THE JAMES ADAMS FLOATING THEATRE

"What's a showboat?" —Edna Ferber

The story goes something like this: It was 1924. Edna Ferber, a prolific and well-paid newspaperwoman turned fiction writer and playwright, a member of New York's Algonquin Round Table, was in Connecticut with the cast and crew of her new show *Minick*, co-written by the Broadway ace George S. Kaufmann. Ferber had enjoyed the rehearsal process, and now the cast and crew were staging tryout performances, first in New Haven and Hartford, where things had not gone well. On opening night in New London, at an old, rarely used theater, the author watched the houselights dim for a half-filled auditorium. The actors took their places. As the first scene opened, the colony of bats living in the upper gallery, dome, and chandeliers decided to make their theatrical debut. Dive-bombing patrons and players alike, the bats soon found themselves performing to an empty house, their star turn short lived.

After the hysterics of the situation subsided, the reality of the play's complete potential failure weighed heavily on everyone involved except maybe the producer, Winthrop Ames, a wealthy supporter of the arts. Ames, as per his generous character and reputation, was hosting a sandwiches-and-highballs postmortem in his hotel suite for the troupe. To cheer them up he announced, "Never mind boys and girls! Next time I'll tell you what we'll do. We won't bother with tryouts. We'll all charter a showboat and just drift down the rivers, playing the towns as we come to them, and we'll never get off the boat. It'll be wonderful."

Ferber, slumped on a floor cushion, bummed out and half-listening, sat upright. "What's a showboat?" she asked.

They didn't call them the Roaring 20s for nothing. America's Jazz Age was awash in post-war prosperity and upward mobility. The War to End All Wars changed the way people looked at life. The Nineteenth Amendment was passed at the beginning of the decade, and women were breaking some of their cultural shackles. Booze was prohibited, but nobody paid much attention to those rules. Political scandal in Washington, D.C. was front-page news, and Adolf Hitler was rising to power overseas. Gangsters, athletes, and flappers were the most recognizable characters of their times. As our modern celebrity culture took firm root, Hollywood was growing into the world's filmmaking capital, populated by the framers of America's new myths.

The Eastern Shore was transitioning too. After generations of back-breaking, hands-on toil geared to the seasons of the year, nineteenth-century steam engines and other mechanical advances of the first industrial revolution made life a bit easier. Steam trains chugged up and down and all around the Chesapeake Bay region, and iron rails crisscrossed even the smallest of burgs and boros. Folks found they even had a little extra time and money to spend on life's more frivolous pastimes. They were ready for some entertainment. By 1924, the James Adams Floating Theatre had been in business for about a decade.

In his scholarly yet thoroughly entertaining book *The James Adams Floating Theatre*, C. Richard Gillespie, professor emeritus and founder of Towson University's theater program, quotes a 1916 reporter describing Jim Adams as a good-looking short chap with blue eyes, clean-cut features, and wavy dark hair touched by gray. Dressed "conservatively sporty" with a "dazzling" diamond pinkie ring, Adams, born in Ohio in 1873, the fourth of eight, a showman to the core, impressed the newspaperwoman as being handsome enough to be a star if he desired. She called him "built to scale and in first rate condition."

Adams and his wife, Gertrude Powlson Adams—short and curvy with blue eyes, a charming smile, and a welcoming demeanor—wed in 1885 and started their showbiz life together as an aerialist act. In 1902, they founded a small traveling circus and performed a series of one-day stands around central Michigan. Following the long tradition of nomadic American entertainment, Adams caught the wave of each trend that came along. He invested in circuses, carnivals, and vaudeville shows, and by 1911 had made enough money that he and Gertie could retire.

Two years later, in another time-honored tradition in the entertainment industry, Adams unretired.

Traveling with his vaudeville shows, it seems Adams first entertained the idea of building a showboat while visiting one in West Virginia. He was aware of the many floating theaters entertaining the towns along the rivers of the Midwest, and he also knew that no operations like that were working the East Coast. If he went into the showboat business in these parts, he'd have no competition. Not many possessed the know-how or could afford to do what he was about to do.

Adams did his research. He visited dockside ports and talked to the seamen he met about the feasibility and requirements of building a salt-water showboat. In the end, he decided to have his dream project constructed by W. M. Chauncy Marine Railway in Washington, North Carolina. Adams himself picked the wood for the two-story theater structure he designed to outfit the 128' x 34' barge built by Chauncey.

When completed, the theater's 30' x 80' auditorium sat 500, with another 350 in a balcony that ran all the way around the room, and two boxes that sat five each. There was an orchestra pit in front of the stage. The room was stately, painted white with blue and gold trim. There was an electric chandelier and matching wall lights. Backstage were eight humble staterooms for the troupe, four on each deck, and under the stage a galley and dining room for the company of twenty-five that included performers, musicians, and crew. There was an electric generator, a water plant, and an inhouse telephone system. The ticket office and auditorium entrance were on the bow, as was Adams's office. On the upper deck sat the Adamses' private suite. Once again, in the conventions of showbiz then and now, cost reports vary, depending on who was asking.

Launched on January 27, 1914, the showboat, a 436-ton vessel with a scow's fourteen-inch draft, was registered with the Coast Guard as the *Playhouse*. The opening performances in Washington,

North Carolina, were successful with regard to both reviews and box office receipts. The James Adams Floating Theatre was up and running.

In that inaugural forty-week tour of 1914, after performances in North Carolina and on the lower western shore of Virginia, the floating theater made its first and only visit to Tangier Island. The *Playhouse* presented its first mainland Eastern Shore shows in Onancock, Virginia. Records for that first year are sketchy, but in his book, Gillespie pieces together the itinerary. After the showboat left Tangier, it looks like she went on to Saxis, Virginia, and then bounced her way around the Shore with stops in Snow Hill, Pocomoke City, Crisfield, Deal Island, and Salisbury. After probable stops along the Nanticoke River and over to Solomon's Island, then an engagement in Annapolis, followed by Port Deposit near the mouth of the upper Chesapeake's Susquehanna River, the *Playhouse* docked in Elkton. Then it came down the bay to Georgetown, Chestertown, Centreville, Queenstown, and Rock Hall. The boat called on St. Michaels, the lone venue the tour never skipped in twenty-seven seasons, over the first week of November, and probably finished up that maiden season along the Choptank River at such stops as Cambridge, Denton, and Greensboro.

It's estimated that in that first tour the theater visited fifteen communities in Virginia and twenty-one in Maryland. Over time, the schedule would include visits in such places as Chesapeake City, home of the Chesapeake and Delaware Canal; Stevensville on Kent Island; and Oxford, in Talbot County. During the next three decades or so, every April to November, the *Playhouse* would deliver entertainment to communities who were among the hungriest for it.

When the showboat folks pulled into a town, they'd typically stay a week and play six nights with six different shows—comedies, mysteries, westerns, etc.—Monday through Saturday. They left early if ticket sales were slow. Their show consisted of plays and vaudeville acts, with emphasis on the plays. The vaudevillians performed during set changes. The subjects and types of stories varied, but as was the melodramatic style of the day, the scripts leaned into happy endings. Actors played more to type than character. In the early days, tickets cost a quarter, kids a dime, and for another ten or fifteen cents audience members could stick around after the show for a concert given by the orchestra.

By 1924, while Adams was off managing his many Philadelphia real estate investments and cruising around on his yachts, his affable brother Selba and Selba's wife, Clara, ran the day-to-day business of the showboat. Adams's actress sister Beulah and her jack-of-all-theatrical-trades husband, Charles Hunter, joined the cast of the Floating Theatre in 1915, and though they left after a short time, they returned in 1920 and stayed on for the best part of the next twenty years. Beulah, with her long dark curls, dimpled smile, expressive blue eyes, melodious voice, and petite build, was known as "the Mary Pickford of the Chesapeake Bay," and she played the ingenue right up until she retired at age forty-eight. By the mid-1920s, her husband Charlie—a well-read musician and actor with failing eyesight, a taste for alcohol, and a strong imagination— oversaw the troupe's repertoire, writing plays, adapting existing works, and directing the actors. In time, tall, thin, and sensitive Charlie Hunter would become the primary fountainhead from which Edna Ferber's *Show Boat* would spring.

Ferber's friends and family knew not to mess with her when she was writing. There were standing orders not even to phone her "unless someone in the family had been murdered." She called writing a combination of "ditch-digging, mountain-climbing, treadmill and childbirth," yet in dedication to her craft, she aimed to write "three pages a day if possible—a thousand words a day, day after day, week after week, month after month."

Among Ferber's many talents as a writer, she cultivated an ability to see the world through the eyes of characters unlike herself. She could disconnect from living life to observe it, which she measured as being a blessing and a curse. Other strengths included a sharp imagination, an ear for stories, and the ability to write about ordinary people in the popular style of her time.

Ferber was born on August 15, 1885. Her Hungarian-born father Jacob was unhealthy, and her family moved several times during her youth. Jacob went blind young and then died at an early age. Her mother Julia took up her husband's shopkeeping business and was the breadwinner for the family. From ages five to twelve, Ferber lived with her parents and older sister Fannie in an Iowa coal-mining town called Ottumwa, where she was subject to brutal antisemitic treatment that affected the way she looked at her life and the world around her for the rest of her days. She felt herself to be a tougher person than she would have been without those battle scars and believed that her steadfast Jewish identity gave her the "priceless gift of creative self-expression."

One long-appreciated part of her miserable Ottumwa experience was access to the spirit-lifting possibilities of entertainment, particularly those of the theater. She and her family attended vaudeville, minstrel shows, and plays put on by traveling theater companies. She described herself as stage-struck from her earliest memories. At seventeen, partly to help support the family and partly because her mother wasn't going to let her pursue a theatrical career, Ferber gave up her plans to become an actress and instead went to work as a reporter for a local newspaper. A year later, she was hired by a larger-circulation paper in Milwaukee. At the age of twenty-four, burned out and depressed, a broken "basket-case," she decided to give writing fiction a try.

She sold her first short story, "The Homely Heroine," in 1910, and in 1911 published her first novel, *Dawn O'Hara, the Girl Who Laughed*, an unexpected success. By 1912 she was an emerging author and living in New York. In 1920, she was thirty-five and a success. She contributed to top-selling periodicals, published two novels and a half-dozen short-story collections, and a play based on one of her stories was made into a movie starring the very famous Ethel Barrymore. In summer of that same year, Ferber's somewhat autobiographical novel *Fanny Herself* was being filmed in California by the prestigious director Tod Browning (1880–1962) and she visited the set. Browning would go on to helm two films, *Dracula* (1931) and *Freaks* (1932), that were selected by the Library of Congress's National Film Registry as being "culturally, historically, or aesthetically significant."

In the spring of 1924 her novel *So Big* was hitting bookstores to enthusiastic response. It would be the best-selling book of the year, win the Pulitzer Prize, and be adapted for film in 1924, 1932, and 1953. Ferber, however, always one to look forward to the next challenge, was preparing for the production of *Minick*.

Minick proved to have a short shelf life.

Ferber turned to her idea of writing something about a showboat.

By 1924, a visit from the *Playhouse* and the James Adams Floating Theater was a highlight of the year for citizens of the Eastern Shore's small, isolated farm towns and waterside watermen's enclaves. A couple days before the showboat's arrival, the newspaper ads would run and the promotional posters hung in every corner of the community. With no engine of its own, the *Playhouse* was guided from town to town by two tugboats, *Trouper* and *Elk*. When she'd make her entrance along the nearest waterway, with her flags a-flying and horns a-blowing, you know those sights and sounds brought color to what could otherwise perhaps be an uneventful if not dreary day-to-day.

Free parades and concerts roiled the excitement for the week's scheduled evening productions. By the time the actors of the company hit the stage, their audiences were often more than primed to be entertained. Life onboard the *Playhouse* for those actors and the crew was a mix of pleasant living and struggle. They worked hard and needed to be versatile in their abilities, but they spent their in-season traveling the Bay and its tributaries, playing for folks who couldn't wait to see them. For the most part, the actors, as long as they were rehearsed and ready to go, could spend their day doing what they liked— sometimes they read books and wrote letters, sometimes played horseshoes and pinochle, sometimes swam and went fishing. After shows at night, there were concerts, parties, and fish-fries.

Everybody was always well fed.

The view was often spectacular.

Behind the scenes, times could be hard. Wages were low. The showboat's patrons were being siphoned away by movies, records, and radio. Religious citizens from the more conservative villages the showboat visited did not hesitate to express their concerns when the featured fare crossed the lines of their communities' moral codes. There were public images to maintain and trouble to stay out of, so strict rules of programming and behavior were imposed on the troupe. Tensions over how to deal with racial issues were always part of the equation. So, all in all, decline might have been in the air by the time Ferber walked up the gangplank for the first time.

There's some dispute as to where that happened.

Ferber writes in her autobiography, *A Peculiar Treasure*, that she first visited the *Playhouse* while in North Carolina during the fall of 1924, but Gillespie shows in his book that the Floating Theatre was on the upper Eastern Shore at that time in a little town near the head of the Chester River called Crumpton. Several sources support Gillespie's timetable, including a 1937 newspaper article about Selba Adams where he confirms it was in Maryland where Ferber began her *Show Boat* research when she came there to see a show and introduce herself.

Ferber's second visit to the *Playhouse* was in Bath, North Carolina, in spring 1925. By her account, she stayed four days, ingratiating herself with the management, troupe, and crew. She "lived, played, worked, rehearsed, ate with the company . . . sold tickets at the box office window." She soaked up the atmosphere around her. When she was finally able to corner Charlie Hunter, he shared stories of life onboard the Floating Theatre and of the "incidents, characters, absurdities, dramas, tragedies, river lore, [and] theatrical wisdom" in a "stream of pure gold," a "treasure-trove" of material. For these hours he spent with her, Ferber acknowledged being in Hunter's everlasting debt. The *Playhouse* would be the only actual showboat she would visit during her research. She gave Hunter his due more than once, including in a 1926 *Woman's Home Companion* interview. She said he fascinated her that day with his tales of romance and adventure, and his stories of showboat life. He talked for hours, almost right up until showtime. "Oh, Lord," she remembered repeating to herself in silent prayer, "don't let him stop talking."

Show Boat, the novel, written in France and New York, with a setting moved from the *Playhouse*'s East Coast to the *Cotton*

Blossom's Mississippi River, was released as a serial in *Woman's Home Companion* beginning in April 1926 and was published in book form by Doubleday in August of that year. It spent twelve weeks on the bestseller list. Screen rights were purchased by Universal Pictures two months after publication.

In November, composer Jerome Kern and lyricist Oscar Hammerstein II visited the Floating Theatre while it was moored along the Chesapeake and Delaware Canal in Chesapeake City, Maryland. As noted in his special correspondent role for the *Baltimore Sun*, writer, critic, and another member of that infamous Algonquin Round Table, Alexander Woollcott described how the two men got off the train at Elkton and were taken by "panting motor to Chesapeake City which suggests an imposing metropolis, [but] is used to designate a small town on the edge of that tortuous bay." The two famed New Yorkers shared an early dinner with the troupe and watched preparations for the evening performance. They counted the automobiles and horse-drawn wagons full of excited locals lined up to see the show. After the performance, they hung out with the players—"all of whom regard Edna Ferber's book as perhaps the most important book written since the Bible"—and the "amazing" leading man Charles Hunter.

Woollcott razzed the success of Ferber's book, saying the sales figures "infuriate me. I cannot go into a house without seeing *Show Boat* on the table. When I see it[,] I swear." He maintained his distaste wasn't because he didn't like the book, he did, nor was it because of the antagonistic critic character that shares his last name showing up toward the story's end. He swore his animosity toward *Show Boat* was because an earlier work of Ferber, *The Girls*, was overlooked and, in his opinion, far superior.

For her part, however, Ferber said, "It doesn't seem possible that anyone ever had so much sheer fun, gaiety, novelty, satisfaction and money out of the writing of any one piece of work as I have had out of *Show Boat.*"

Show Boat, the two-act musical, opened at celebrated impresario Flo Ziegfeld's new theater on December 27, 1927. Mixing the spectacle of Broadway with serious themes and storyline, in these regards the production was a game-changer for American theater. It was also a big hit.

The plot of *Show Boat*, the novel and musical, follows three generations of the Hawks family—Captain Andy and his wife Parthy, their actress daughter Magnolia and her romance with the handsome and unreliable gambler Gaylord Ravenal, and their daughter Kim, named after Kentucky, Illinois, and Missouri. These were all characters who could easily have been based, at least in part, on the management, performers, cooks, and crew of the James Adams Floating Theater Ferber met during her visit.

And who knows how much of what Hunter told her on that spring day in 1925 made its way into her writing.

In January 1927, Hunter traveled to California to work as an advisor to Universal's chosen production team for *Show Boat*'s first film adaptation.

Before the year was out, on Thanksgiving in fact, after ending the touring season in Queenstown, the showboat hit a submerged object outside the entrance to the harbor in Norfolk, Virginia, and sank, losing "every scrap of scenery, costumes, papers, [and] furnishings." It was the second time the boat had gone down, the first being in a 1920 Independence Day storm. This time weather hindered the boat's salvage and it took two days to raise the hull. Hardly anything was left of the superstructure. The remains were towed to Elizabeth City, North Carolina and the *Playhouse* was rebuilt in time for the 1928 season. Hunter cashed a check in an undisclosed amount that Ferber once gave him. He'd said he'd never use it unless it was absolutely necessary. Hollywood's first swipe at Ferber's story, starring Laura La Plante as Magnolia, Joseph Schildkraut as Ravenal, and Otis Harlan as Captain Andy, with Stepin Fetchit as Jo and Gertrude Howard as Queenie, was a modest hit, but this part-silent, part-sound version is considered a creative misfire. The writers tried to cover too much of the story and the director was not well matched to the material. Released in March 1929, the year did not begin well for the makers of *Show Boat*, the movie.

It didn't end well for anybody. Those Roaring 20s ground to a stunning halt.

The Great Depression was followed by World War II and then the Atomic Age, and Ferber kept right on writing. Her novel after *Show Boat* was *Cimarron*, which was adapted twice into films (1931 and 1960) and was the sole Western to win the Best Picture Oscar until 1990's *Dances with Wolves*. Despite her disappointing experience with *Minick*, from 1926 to 1949 she and George Kaufman coauthored five more plays together. These works include *Stage Door*, *The Royal Family* (a parody of the high-profile Barrymore acting clan), and *Dinner at Eight*, which became a 1933 George Cukor–directed comedy with a cast of stars that included Marie Dressler, Jean Harlow, and two members of the aforementioned Barrymore family, John and Lionel. The 1956 adaptation of her bestseller *Giant*, another sprawling multi-generational story, this time about a Texas rancher who falls in love with the daughter of a champion Maryland horse breeder, was actor James Dean's third and last movie before dying in a head-on collision in his Porsche 550 Spyder.

Before she died on April 16, 1968, Ferber published twelve novels, twelve short-story collections, two autobiographies, and nine plays. She was world-famous but unabashedly American. With her natural empathy and ability to translate what she absorbed into the written word, she was celebrated for telling tales of her fellow citizens fairly and well while still addressing our country's imperfections. She believed she understood America in "its naiveté, its strength, its childishness, its beauty, its reality." Her work and career have stood the test of time, and as her earliest output edges toward the century mark, a milestone for any cultural signifier, it maintains relevance as a look into a specific time and character in our nation's journey.

Things ended less glamorously for the James Adams Floating Theatre. Though there was a boost of publicity and attendance following the cultural impact of the book, the play, and the 1936 movie remake, and many Shore folk still looked upon the showboat's arrival as the nostalgic return of an old friend, the entertainment business was passing it by. Its audience had more choices and the traveling repertory troupes, both on land and water, faded into the wings of history. Money was almost always a problem.

The *Playhouse* sank and was salvaged twice again, once in 1929 and then in 1938, her glory days in her wake. Adams sold the operation to Nina B. Howard of St. Michaels in 1933, who purchased it for her adopted son Milford Seymoure to manage. Howard, the daughter of a German military man and twice the widow of wealthy men, painted the boat red and changed the company's name to the Original Show Boat. Hunter and his leading lady Beulah stayed on after transfer of ownership and until 1937, but many of the other family members, stars, and crew who hadn't already retired or moved on took this opportunity to do so.

Selba Adams died in 1943 and his wife Clara passed in 1951, the same year Hunter succumbed to throat cancer. Of the four primary onboard characters of the company's heyday, Beulah Adams Hunter was the last to go in 1975 at the age of 83.

The Depression took much more of a toll on the showboat's popularity than on Ferber's, and the floating stage made her last appearance on the Eastern Shore in Rock Hall in October 1940. In 1941, Howard sold the *Playhouse* to a businessman from Savannah, Georgia who converted the vessel into a cargo barge. On November 14, less than a month before the Japanese attack on Pearl Harbor, the *Playhouse* caught fire and burned to her last timbers while grounded in the mud of a Savannah River low tide.

The old girl was gone, but her legacy has not been forgotten. Gillespie's book and museums from the Mariners Museum in Newport News, Virginia, to the C&D Canal Museum in Chesapeake City (where Jim and Gertie Adams owned a house and primarily lived from 1928 until their deaths in 1946 and 1952, respectively) feature exhibits from the James Adams Floating Theatre.

And, of course, there's *Show Boat*, the musical. It's sure to be running somewhere as you read this. There are the three films made from it: the 1929 version, the 1936 remake directed by James Whale and featuring the definitive performance of *Ol' Man River* by Paul Robeson's Joe, and the glittery and expensive 1951 technicolor adaptation with Kathryn Grayson and Howard Keel as Magnolia and Gaylord, featuring Ava Gardner as the singer Julie LaVerne.

The James Adams Floating Theatre, that one-of-a-kind "rambling house that had taken perversely to nautical life," full of stories and high spirits, entertained the people of the Chesapeake Bay and the North Carolina coast for almost three decades. Thanks to Ferber, among others, its existence will be remembered as long as there's a spark of romance and nostalgia in an Eastern Shore heart.

Lucille Fletcher and Douglass Wallop spent many happy years as a married couple in bucolic Oxford, Maryland, writing and serving as first reader for each other's manuscripts. She penned *Sorry, Wrong Number,* being performed on network radio by Agnes Moorehead *(Photofest).* Wallop wrote the bestselling book The Year the Yankees Lost the Pennant, which became the evergreen stage favorite Damn Yankees. Jean Stapleton is pictured on the right in this Broadway cast *(Photofest/Warner Brothers).*

LUCILLE FLETCHER AND DOUGLASS WALLOP

"Wham! One long ball hitter, that's what we need! Honest to God, I'd sell my soul for one long ball hitter!"

—*Joe Boyd*

"Operator! Operator! Operator!"   —*Leona Stevenson*

The literary tradition along the Chesapeake is deep and enduring, especially when you include the western and southern reaches of this vast estuary.

Frederick Douglass, the most photographed American of the nineteenth century, was Eastern Shore–born—albeit, infamously, as a slave. As of 2020, he is the only Eastern Shore author to have been paid the honor of publication in the Library of America. On the other side of the Bay, Edgar Allen Poe grew up in Richmond and died a mysterious death in Baltimore on a dreary October day in 1849.

James M. Cain and Cain's friend H. L. Mencken, along with Dashiell Hammett, one of Cain's cofounders of noir fiction, were all from Maryland. Upton Sinclair and Ta-Nehisi Coates hail from Baltimore. Though not born there, poet Ogden Nash called Baltimore home, married an Eastern Shore native, and often summered in Salisbury. F. Scott and Zelda Fitzgerald lived and wrote in Baltimore for five years in the 1930s, and socialized with Mencken and his wife Sara Haardt, a childhood friend of Zelda.

Pulitzer Prize–winning author William Styron (*The Confessions of Nat Turner*) was from Newport News, in the southern reaches of the Bay, while New Journalism founder Tom Wolfe (*The Right Stuff*) hailed from Richmond, at the falls of the history-steeped James River. Best-selling suspense novelist Laura Lippman and her husband, David Simon, producer of *Homicide: Life on the Streets* and the acclaimed HBO series *The Wire*, began their careers as journalists at the *Baltimore Sun*, historically an incubator of notable writing talent. In 2006, they were married by Baltimore's one-of-a-kind impresario (and *Pink Flamingo*es and *Hairspray* filmmaker) John Waters. Technothriller master Tom Clancy (*The Hunt for Red October*), whose CIA action-hero Jack Ryan is still electrifying audiences in a popular Amazon Prime series, was born in Baltimore and lived in a baronial estate overlooking the Chesapeake Bay south of Washington in Calvert County.

You ask about writers from around this part of the country?

Man, Francis Scott Key, the guy who wrote our national anthem, is a homeboy.

But as far as D.C. goes, don't get us started. Some days we're proud to claim a piece of our nation's capital, whose Potomac River tides slosh in and out of the Chesapeake twice a day, but most of the time we would just as soon wash our hands of it.

Here on the Eastern Shore, we honor native authors George Alfred Townsend (*Chesapeake Tales, The Entailed Hat*), Gilbert Byron (*The Lord's Oysters, Done Crabbin'*), and John Barth (*The Sotweed Factor, The Floating Opera*) as being among our finest.

Barth's second novel, 1958's *The End of the Road*, was loosely adapted to film in 1970 with James Earl Jones and Stacy Keach in his first feature film starring role.

The Pulitzer Prize–winning *Beautiful Swimmers: Watermen, Crabs, and the Chesapeake Bay* by William W. Warner is a must-have for any complete Eastern Shore bookshelf. Christopher Tilghman of Charlottesville and Centreville has explored his ancestral roots in *New York Times* Notable Books such as *Mason's Retreat* and *The Right-Hand Shore*, and Pulitzer Prize–winning novelist Ann Tyler of Baltimore set one of her signature heroines adrift on the Shore in *Ladder of Years*.

Now lesser-known than many of these writers, Sophie Kerr (1880–1965) was born on the Eastern Shore in Denton, Maryland and went on to publish more than twenty novels and hundreds of articles and short stories in a prolific New York–based writing career. *Big Hearted Herbert*, a play she wrote with a colleague, was made into a movie in 1934 and remade in 1940 as *Father Is a Prince*. When Kerr died, she bequeathed much of her estate to Chestertown's Washington College. Half of the fund's annual interest is used to provide a cash prize to a graduating senior showing literary promise. Through the years, her endowment has bestowed almost a million and a half dollars, supporting the country's largest literary prize for undergraduates. In 2021, the award was worth $65,000.

James Michener (1907–1987) lived in St. Michaels while he researched and wrote the mega bestseller *Chesapeake*. Hollywood hasn't yet tackled that hefty work of historical fiction but has filmed other adaptations of Michener's writing, including the thirteen-hour TV miniseries *Space*. Partly filmed in Kent County in 1984, *Space* featured several scenes shot around Chestertown. One of those was an extended summer barbecue sequence staged at the home of longtime *Kent County News* writer, editor, and publisher H. Hurtt Deringer, where filmmakers also faked a Chester River plane crash.

Jacob Have I Loved by Newbery Medal–winning novelist Katherine Paterson takes place on a fictitious Chesapeake Bay island that is an amalgam of Smith and Tangier. This coming-of-age young adult (YA) novel was made into a 1989 movie starring Bridget Fonda and was shot in Crisfield, which is also the location for the award-winning YA series *The Tillerman Cycle* by Cynthia Voigt. Helen Chappell's funny and charming *Oysterback Tales* are a long-running but timeless chronicle of the happenings in an eccentric bayside village in the made-up Eastern Shore county of Devanau, where the adventures of her comedic paranormal detective duo Sam and Hollis also materialize. Chadwick the Crab and his friends, as written by children's author and novelist Priscilla Cummings, live in the waters of the bay. As noted earlier, the real-life but fictionalized Misty of Chincoteague series of beloved children's novels is set along the scenic Virginia coastline.

So, yeah, we're proud of our literary resume.

And it doesn't surprise us in the least that two writers who hit the heights of showbiz success, one with an enduring thriller and the other a satirical sports parable turned smash musical, found happiness here on the Eastern Shore.

Lucille Fletcher was born into a middle-class family in New York City on March 28, 1912. She grew up writing stories and plays, and as a Depression-era scholarship student attended Vassar, where she majored in English and music. Graduating in 1933, she was hired as a receptionist and typist at CBS Radio at the dawn of the industry's golden age. For five years she worked her way through various departments. While typing up the scripts for the network's radio plays, she decided she could write something at least as good, if not better, than what she was seeing.

Given a chance, Fletcher was soon submitting her own scripts and hauling in twice what she'd been earning. Her first winner, *My Client Curley,* about a talent agent and a dancing caterpillar, would be turned into a 1944 film with Cary Grant called *Once Upon a Time.* She wrote high-profile magazine articles as well and built a reputation as a reliable and polished professional. She counted among her acquaintances Orson Welles, Vincent Price, and John Houseman.

Douglass Wallop's background was more local.

John Douglass Wallop III, a native of Washington, D.C., was born on March 8, 1920 as part of a deep-rooted Eastern Shore family that owned Virginia's Wallops Island, a small barrier island south of Chincoteague from the mid-1600s through the late nineteenth century. For many years, there was a lifesaving station and then a coast guard station located there. In 1889, a dozen or so families from Philadelphia pooled their money and purchased the island to establish the Wallops Island Club. The group built a clubhouse and several cottages that they used for summer getaways and winter hunting trips. Most of Wallops was leased to the US Navy for ordinance testing in World War II. Then the forerunner of NASA took over the lower 1,000 acres for a rocket-launching facility. The basic designs of the capsule and escape systems for the Mercury flights, the first steps in our country's human exploration of space, were tested here, and now in the twenty-first century, both government and commercial rockets are launched at the facility. In 1975, NASA transferred 373 acres of Wallops Island to the Fish and Wildlife Service to create a wildlife refuge.

Wallop was raised in Washington, D.C., but his roots were in the Chesapeake. Wallop's maternal grandfather was a waterman on the western shore of Virginia, while his father's father owned the Washington Hotel in Princess Anne. The county seat of Somerset, Maryland's southernmost county, Princess Anne is located at the head of the Manokin River, halfway between the docks of Crisfield, once the "Seafood Capital of the World," and the distributors and market buyers in Salisbury. The town center has maintained its historic architectural integrity and was entered into the National Register of Historic Places in 1980.

The Washington Hotel, now the Washington Inn and Tavern, was built in the mid-eighteenth century and has been at the heart of this community ever since. It's sometimes said George Washington slept here, hence the moniker. It's also said that the novelist and Civil War correspondent George Alfred Townsend researched and wrote *The Entailed Hat, or Patty Cannon's Times*, his fictionalized account of a real-life Delmarva slave catcher and serial killer, while lodging at the Washington. More typically, the hotel was a boarding house for the traveling salesmen, the drummers, working the area.

Talking with the Salisbury *Daily Times* after publication of his first novel *Night Light* in 1953, Wallop said his most indelible childhood memories of Princess Anne were fishing "day in, day out, from the Town Bridge . . . catching a catfish about every other day" and "an old guy named McKlemmy who delivered milk to the hotel; he came in a buggy and the milk tasted like garlic."

After graduating from the University of Maryland in 1942, Wallop worked in D.C. as a United Press rewrite man and then in New York, drafting news scripts for radio announcers. It was in these days he met and became lifelong friends with David Brinkley. Brinkley went on to become a reporter and one of America's most famous and influential network news anchors. Early in 1948, when

Wallop was twenty-eight years old, he took a job with Doubleday publishers. In the scope of things, it was a short-term gig, from January to May, but what an opportunity it turned out to be. Few people get such an up-close view of history.

Five-star General Dwight D. Eisenhower, the Supreme Commander of the Allied Expeditionary Force in Europe, was stepping down as President Truman's Army Chief of Staff and felt it was time to tell his part of the World War II story. For five months, under the supervision of high-ranking editors, Wallop, who'd learned shorthand at the encouragement of his businessman father, took dictation from "The General" during the day and transcribed what he'd written at night. The next day, Eisenhower would correct the notes. According to Wallop, The General possessed a phenomenal memory, speaking off the top of his head without having to consult documents or maps, and displayed a "tremendous power of concentration." The resulting document, *Crusade in Europe*, was released in November 1948 to critical fanfare and phenomenal sales, and remains an important firsthand account from one of the era's most significant figures. In five years, "Ike" would be president of the United States.

Wallop returned home to Arlington, Virginia, to sell insurance with his dad and work on the short stories and "fragments" he toyed with in his spare time. A baseball fan, he rooted for the Washington Senators and, as always, was hoping for the best. They'd started the season winning two out of three against the hated Yankees but had struggled since. His aunt and uncle owned a seasonal business, so as in summers past, Wallop planned on spending time at their place, helping them out while dreading, yet fully anticipating, the eventual competitive collapse of his favorite team.

Lucille Fletcher and Bernard Herrmann's five-year courtship began when they worked at CBS. "Benny" was a musician and composer and when he was made the conductor of the CBS Orchestra, he'd hold the position for fifteen years. Herrmann and Fletcher married in 1939, moved to Hollywood in 1940, and had two daughters they named Dorothy and Wendy. Fletcher was always a creative night owl. In the couple's early years together, when they lived in a cramped Manhattan apartment, she wrote her scripts outside in the hallway so her typing wouldn't wake the kids. One of the most famous radio scripts she wrote was *The Hitch-Hiker*, which Orson Welles presented on his show in 1941. Based on an incident where she and her husband saw the same strange-looking man twice on their first cross-country drive, the popular episode was produced with an original Herrmann score. The play's concept was later adapted by Rod Serling into a memorable first season *Twilight Zone* episode that many fans consider among the best of the acclaimed series. Herrmann also composed that show's famous theme music.

Their marriage ended in 1948. The settlement was amicable, and after the turbulence of the breakup subsided, they remained friends until he died in 1977. During his career, Herrmann composed music for many memorable pictures. His first credit was on *Citizen Kane* for Welles, and on the night he died in December 1975, he'd just finished his work on Martin Scorsese's *Taxi Driver*. He was Oscar-nominated for five films, *Citizen Kane*, *Taxi Driver* (posthumously), *Anna and the King of Siam* (1946), Brian De Palma's *Obsession* (1976, also posthumously), and the one for which he won in 1941, *All That Money Can Buy* or *The Devil and Daniel Webster*. Herrmann also collaborated on most of

Alfred Hitchcock's classic films and is credited with scoring the iconic screaming strings that make up "The Murder" music that plays during the shower scene in *Psycho* (1962).

On the advice of a friend, after Fletcher and Herrmann fell out, she packed up their girls and traveled by ferry, train, and taxi to vacation in Ocean City, Maryland. She'd never even heard of the place before. In 1990, she told John Devine with the *Star Democrat* that it "seemed like a journey to the moon."

They stayed at the Hamilton Hotel on Third Street and Boardwalk, "a beautiful, old-fashioned sleepy beach resort" that dated back to the turn of the century. With three-and-a-half stories, 100 guest rooms, and twelve first-floor apartments, the hotel offered its clientele both elegant and simple charms. An orchestra played in the dining room while Sunday supper featured waffles and broiled chicken. The Hamilton burned down in December 1969, damaging its boarding-house neighbor the Seaview in the process. Both were demolished and replaced by the Polynesian, the first condominium project on the south end of the boardwalk.

At the time Fletcher was visiting with her daughters, though, the Hamilton was in its prime as a first-class seaside getaway. Among the hotel's amenities was a handsome younger gentleman who was working there for the summer, doing odd jobs, manning the front desk, and lending the owners, his aunt and uncle, a hand.

His name was Douglass Wallop.

It was love at first sight for them both.

Fletcher was having a heck of a 1948. The end of her marriage, a return from life on the West Coast to New York, now the beginning of another romantic relationship and, oh yeah, one of her radio plays was coming out as a major motion picture.

"The most famous radio drama of all time now electrifies the screen!" was the tagline.

Sorry, Wrong Number, Fletcher's suspenseful tale of a wealthy bedridden woman who overhears two men talking on the phone about a plan to commit murder, debuted on the radio on May 25, 1943. The presentation was so popular it was reenacted seven times over the next five years, each time with Agnes Moorehead (*Citizen Kane*, *Show Boat*, *Bewitched*) playing the desperate and infirm Leona Stevenson. In what is virtually an extended monologue, the play is a tutorial in the use of theater-of-the-mind music, sound effects, and acting. A 1959 version won an Edgar Award for Best Radio Drama, and the original was added to the Library of Congress's National Recording Registry in 2014. Welles called it "the greatest single radio script ever written."

As Fletcher's creative output increased, it became more evident that this attractive young woman's sunny disposition harbored a dark streak. *Sorry, Wrong Number* was scary in part because it was subversive. It broke the unspoken rule about bad guys being the only characters who faced violent endings. Fletcher usually said she created Leona Stevenson after a supermarket run-in with an obnoxious Manhattanite, but there's at least one account where the character is based on the mother of an old boyfriend. Either way, a little literary revenge can pack a punch.

In 1947, she'd started working on the screenplay for *Sorry* and it proved challenging to adapt the tense immediacy of a short radio play into a full-length picture. Plus, there were so many other important decisions to be made. When it came to casting, Fletcher wanted to go with the tried-and-true and put Moorehead in the lead, but the producer Hal Wallis (1899–1986) wanted to use

Barbara Stanwyck. Wallis was one of Hollywood's biggest bigwigs. He'd been making movies since 1930's *Moby Dick* and worked behind the scenes on such Warner Brothers' hits and classics as *Little Caesar, The Adventures of Robin Hood, Santa Fe Trail, Sergeant York, The Maltese Falcon*, and *Casablanca*. As an independent producer, he'd go on to make *Sorry, Wrong Number* along with scores of other films ranging from *Barefoot in the Park* to *True Grit*. Wallis produced most of the Dean Martin and Jerry Lewis comedies of the 1950s and later oversaw a string of low-budget Elvis Presley flicks that made money by the Memphis truckload. During his career, Wallis amassed 377 producing credits.

He won the casting debate.

Ukraine-born Anatole Litvak was chosen to direct the production. During World War II, Litvak, a refuge from Nazi Germany, along with Frank Capra (*It's a Wonderful Life, Mr. Smith Goes to Washington, It Happened One Night*), made a series of *Why We Fight* documentaries for the government, cinematically justifying America's entrance into the international conflict. Litvak shot films in the U.S. and Europe and was nominated for Best Director twice. *Sorry* is often noted for his closeups of the actors, use of the settings in the plot, and the imaginative and atmospheric noirish camerawork provided by Sol Polito (*The Adventures of Robin Hood, Sergeant York, Arsenic and Old Lace*).

Burt Lancaster was hired to play Stanwyck's husband. A tough New York street kid before he was a ladies' man actor, Lancaster performed as a circus acrobat and was introduced to real showbiz through the wartime USO. He was on his way up in 1948 but would go on to become one of the movies' brightest stars with a long and varied career.

Stanwyck filmed her part for *Sorry* in chronological order during a two-week period, and other than flashbacks, the film plays out in real time. For her effort, Stanwyck earned a Best Actress Oscar nomination for her fourth and last time. Though she never won, she was awarded an honorary Oscar in 1982. The completed film utilizes many conventions of noir, with its sense of dread, flashback storytelling, and the interplay of light and shadow. The picture was a critical and financial success. Adding cinematic plot points, ratcheting up the tension, Fletcher succeeded in adapting her short work into a satisfying feature film. For her efforts, she was nominated for an Edgar Allan Poe Award and for Best Drama from the Writers Guild of America.

Sorry, Wrong Number was released on September 24, 1948. On January 6, 1949, less than six months after meeting in Ocean City, Wallop and Fletcher married. She and her daughters moved to a "beautiful" historic home in Arlington, Virginia where her new husband continued to sell insurance while they both wrote.

In 1951, Fletcher worked again with Allan Ullman, her coauthor on the novelization of *Sorry, Wrong Number*, to adapt her radio play *The Night Man* into a book-length thriller. Wallop published his first novel in 1953, a mystery called *Night Light*. The book sold well for a debut and got decent reviews. Hollywood optioned the story, though ultimately no film was made. All the while, Wallop kept on selling insurance. In a 1996 *Star Democrat* story, Fletcher told novelist and biographer Roy Hoopes (*Cain: The Biography of James M. Cain*) that "those were the halcyon days. One day we drove down to Ocean City and brought back two white rockers from his uncle's hotel. We sat them side by side on our wide veranda and sat drinking coffee and discussing manuscripts."

During the tranquil months, Wallop was working on another "serious" book that he told the *Daily Times* featured a hotel very much like his grandfather's Princess Anne landmark. He was 350 pages in and thought he had about a year to go on it. All was good.

All except those Senators, that is. The year 1953 was a break-even season, but things were not looking to get better any time soon. His team was well on their way to earning its reputation as sad-sack national punchline. It'd been twenty years since they won a pennant, and he was four years old the last time they took it all. Meanwhile, those hated Yankees ended the season 99-52 and won their fifth consecutive world series. Wallop just couldn't let it go.

He stopped his work in progress and commenced writing a story about a frustrated Senators fan who sold his soul to the devil for a chance at defeating the Yankees as a big-hitting, big-league outfielder. Fletcher tried to talk him out of it. "His humorous side was rather a shock to me," she confessed to Hoopes. "I had thought of Doug as a serious writer, one in the somber tradition of Faulkner and Hemingway." He finished the book in three months.

The Year the Yankees Lost the Pennant came out in September 1954, became a pick of the Book of the Month Club and a selection for the Reader's Digest Condensed Book Club, and sold 2.5 million copies. Broadway and Hollywood came running.

Wallop quit selling insurance.

"His main interest," Fletcher said, "seemed to be waiting for the mailman to bring his royalty checks, [but] once he got involved in show biz, the coffee hours were over. The phone kept ringing, and he was always on the shuttle back and forth to New York."

Directed by the stage and film veteran George Abbott, with a book by Abbott and Wallop and music, and lyrics by Richard Adler and Jerry Ross (*The Pajama Game*), the show, now called *Damn Yankees*, featured the following stars: Ray Walston (*My Favorite Martian, Fast Times at Ridgemont High*) as the devilish Mr. Applegate; Robert Shafer as the fed-up and willing-to-make-a-deal Senators fan Joe Boyd; Stephen Douglass as the transformed slugger Joe Hardy; and Shannon Bolin as Joe's wife, Meg. The flame-haired beauty Gwen Verdon, with eyes that, according to a *New York Times* profile, changed "from the color of honey-flecked avocado to cornflower blue," was chosen to play the temptress Lola after being approved by high-strung choreographer Bob Fosse (*Sweet Charity, Cabaret, All That Jazz*). The two were married in 1960, a union that lasted until Fosse died in 1987. Their complicated personal and professional relationships were spotlighted in the 2019 miniseries *Fosse/Verdon* starring Sam Rockwell and Michelle Williams.

Damn Yankees opened on May 5, 1955. Fletcher told Hoopes that she remembered her husband standing in the back of the theater "pale as a ghost in his tuxedo, listening hopefully for the laughter and applause. After the show he and I went to a big party at George Abbott's where the cast and investors waited until morning for the reviews to come out. There were raves. It was very thrilling—and disrupting!"

The show, a crowd- and critic-pleasing triumph, ran for 1,019 performances and won seven Tony Awards, including Best Musical, Best Leading Musical Actor and Actress for Vernon and Walston, and Best Choreography. Revivals through the years included one in 1981 featuring former NFL quarterback Joe Namath as Joe Hardy. Another production featured Jarrod Emick, 1994's Tony winner for Best Featured Actor in a Musical, as Joe Hardy; Bebe Neuwirth as Lola; and Victor Garber, who was succeeded in his portrayal of Applegate by Jerry Lewis in his Broadway debut.

Warner Brothers released the film version, directed by Abbott and Stanley Donen (*Seven Brides for Seven Brothers, Singin' in the Rain, Funny Face*), in September 1958 to a responsive box office. Despite omitting five songs from the score, the movie is so faithful to the Broadway show that most critics who find fault deem it too devoted to its source. In their view, it was staged like a play and didn't take advantage of film's wider scope of possibilities.

Still and all, most takes were along the lines of the *Baltimore Sun's* Hope Pantell, who declared the film version to be "as flashy, funny, tuneful, and gaily irreverent as ever," and gave much credit to the primary cast being the same from the home-run Broadway show. The singular major replacement was Stephen Douglass losing his role of the strong, dumb, and likeable Joe Hardy to Tab Hunter, a talent agent-and-studio-groomed teen idol. Hunter kept working long after his golden boy days were over, but *Damn Yankees* was the height of his career. Stephen Douglass also continued to act. Before he retired in 1972, he would play Gaylord Ravenal in the Lincoln Center's 1966 revival of Edna Ferber's *Show Boat*.

In 1960, the Senators put Douglass Wallop out of his misery by relocating to Minnesota and changing their name to the Twins.

As the fervor of the *Damn Yankees* phenomenon died down, the Wallops anticipated getting back to a normal pace, writing and spending more time at the summer home they bought with proceeds from their hot-damn hit musical. The house they'd bought on Town Creek in Oxford.

Why Oxford?

Oxford has history. It's one of the oldest and most unique towns in Maryland. Located near the mouth of the Tred Avon River, Oxford is surrounded on three sides by water, and Town Creek on the northeast offers boaters a protective natural harbor. Settled in the mid-to-late 1600s, Oxford was Maryland's largest international port for a century. With an economy based on slavery and tobacco and all the ills and profits those trades brought, it was a boomtown with sustained prosperity.

During the American Revolutionary War, much of the Eastern Shore, conservative in nature, wanted to stay loyal to the crown, but Oxford was a hotbed of prominent insurgents including the "financier of the Revolution," Robert Morris Jr., and Tench

Tilghman, General Washington's aide-de-camp, who delivered the message of the British surrender in Yorktown, Virginia to the Continental Congress in Philadelphia.

Oxford suffered in the first years of independence. The economy slumped with the absence of British ships and the transition from tobacco to other crops. The locals began focusing on their maritime enterprises, becoming well-regarded shipbuilders and watermen who contributed much to the history and culture of the region, but day-to-day life was in shambles.

In the decades following the Civil War, the markets for Chesapeake Bay seafood opened up. With new techniques in harvesting, packaging, and delivery expanding the geographical reach of their products, the people of Oxford, like many communities connected to the mighty Chesapeake, took advantage of nature's bounty and profited from their willingness to work hard and innovate. Maryland oysters were king. Advances in canning other food allowed local farmers also to get in on the good times.

The railroad came to Oxford in 1871. From up and down the Bay, steamboats puffed in and out at two different wharves. New homes, businesses, and churches were constructed. There were up to 20 seafood-packing plants at work. Oxford boatbuilders and watermen cultivated their reputation as being among the best.

And then, once again, the bottom fell out.

By the mid-twentieth century, the Chesapeake oyster business was done for. Overfishing, environmental depredation, changing market dynamics—there's plenty of blame to go around, but the bottom line is that the days of plenty were over. There are still watermen who make a living in the seafood industry, but far fewer than the historic numbers, and very few harvest wild oysters.

Despite its relapse into slumber, Oxford hung in there and curated a charm and sense of community. As yachting and sail boating grew more popular with the middle class, tourists and travelers started discovering the charismatic waterfront village. Local families who continued to fish the waterways and build the boats were joined by folks with money to spend and a taste for the quiet pleasures of life. Movers and shakers from every walk of life became part of the scenery. The town developed an artsy reputation, and famous figures besides Fletcher and Wallop who have called Oxford home include the pioneering TV chef Graham Kerr, known as the Galloping Gourmet.

Today, Oxford continues to pay respect to its waterman and boatbuilding heritage but is now best known as a peaceful and cordial getaway for folks anxious to leave the priorities of modern life behind for a while. The place is picturesque, with elegant historic homes along the waterfront, a sandy beach, and an inviting town park. There are inns and B&Bs and excellent places to eat. The Oxford Community Center, home of the well-respected acting troupe the Tred Avon Players, is a cultural treasure. The Mystery Loves Company Booksellers is a full-service bookstore cherished by the area's community of readers and writers. The Oxford Bellevue Ferry, first launched in 1683 and operating continuously since 1836, is thought to be the oldest privately owned ferryboat in the country. A ride on this iconic little boat is short but stunningly scenic and memorable for riders of any age.

Why Oxford?

"We just fell in love with it," Fletcher told the *Daily Times* in 1976. Then she added the traditional Eastern Shore refrain: "When I'm away, I just can't wait to get over the [Chesapeake Bay] bridge and get home."

The Wallops moved to Oxford full-time in the mid-1960s. They loved to sail and explore the nooks and crannies along the tributaries of the Bay, and at home they each enjoyed their hobbies and pursuits. He was into tennis, chess, woodworking, and jazz records, while she, a lifelong music lover, sang and played piano.

But they wrote together.

Apart.

She worked at a desk in an upstairs room on the same 1925 portable Underwood typewriter she'd used since college. He composed rough drafts in shorthand and liked to move around the house, so he'd write at a card table sitting in whichever room he felt lucky. "I'm superstitious," he'd say.

They'd get together for breakfast, lunch, and dinner, and when they went back to writing, they passed the work back and forth to each other for critique. In 1985, Fletcher told the *Star Democrat*'s Martha McCormick that though they trusted each other's intentions without question, it was hard to dish out criticism and even harder to take it with grace. "If his opinion is unfavorable, it's bound to send me into a blue funk for about a week." She confided that he often found fault with the dialogue she wrote for men, saying "men don't talk that way." She'd criticize the prudish way he dressed his female characters.

Fletcher particularly could get lost in the creative process. After her death, daughter Dorothy, an author herself, told the *Baltimore Sun* that her mom's trancelike work state was a family joke. "We'd go into her office and say, "Can we have $10,000?" and she'd say, "Um-hmm. It's in my purse."

One time, husband and wife held a contest to see who could finish writing a book first. Three months later they finished on the exact same day.

Their output was impressive. After *Yankees*, Wallop wrote a dozen more novels, some serious, some not, half of them at least partially set on the Eastern Shore. 1963's *Ocean Front* and *Stone*, from 1971, take place in Ocean City. *The Regatta*, from 1981, concerns an annual sailboat race from Annapolis to Oxford and was his "oblique attempt to talk about Talbot County." His last book, *The Other Side of the River*, published in 1984, concerns a murder committed on the waterfront estate of a retired professor.

His wife liked his humor novels best. "He writes them faster," and he's "more relaxed" when he's working on them, she explained. In 1969, Wallop published *The Good Life* about a married couple who decide to get a taste of high society by hiring on as a butler and maid to a wealthy family. For a while it looked like Cary Grant might star in an MGM film adaptation, but the deal fell through. NBC did produce a sitcom based on the book with Larry Hagman, in one of his many jobs between *I Dream of Jeannie* and *Dallas*, along with Donna Mills, best known from the *Dallas* spinoff *Knot's Landing*, but it didn't last long.

In 1969, to celebrate 100 years of professional baseball, Wallop published *Baseball, An Informal History*, a loose narrative account of a sport that had given him much but was losing ground as America's National Pastime.

Fletcher wrote all kinds of things. Whatever struck her. Plays, short stories, and children's books. She worked on an autobiography. After *Night Man* with Ullman, she published seven novels on her own, almost all well reviewed. The first of those, *The Daughters of Jasper Clay* (1958), was a family drama. The Cold War espionage tale *Blindfold* was made into a mediocre movie starring Rock Hudson and Claudia Cardinale. *The Strange Blue Yawl* is about a murder witnessed on the Chesapeake Bay as imagined from her very own home's waterfront window.

In January 1972, she published *Night Watch*. The Broadway adaptation opened a month later. The story centers on a neurotic and wealthy insomniac living in Manhattan who is convinced she's witnessed a murder. Joan Hackett (*Support Your Local Sheriff*, *Will*

Penny) played the role to positive reviews and the show ran for 121 performances, but when it came time to cast the movie, Elizabeth Taylor took the role. Fletcher was not pleased.

"I've never made any bones about the fact that I detested it," she proclaimed to the *Daily Times*. "It was supposed to be a nice little murder. And Elizabeth Taylor was much too beautiful to be believable in that role." She explained that though she was the screenwriter, the director, Brian G. Hutton, was a friend of Taylor and her husband Richard Burton, and that the super-famous couple meddled so much with the plot, Fletcher stepped back and was not involved with the project after the initial phases of production.

The last film to be made from one of her books was 1982's unremarkable *Hit and Run* based on *Eighty Dollars to Stamford*, published seven years prior. When what would be her final book was rejected by her publisher, she sent it out to her daughters and their husbands for feedback. They said add more sex, violence, and strong language. She followed their advice in the rewrite, and Morrow published the thriller *Mirror Image* in 1988.

Wallop died on April Fool's Day in 1985. His buddy David Brinkley came to town to eulogize him and then again to celebrate his life and works. Wallop was known to be shy and dignified, never one to use more words than needed, but witty, with a sense of the ridiculous. Brinkley said his friend liked sailing, people, and the Eastern Shore way of life.

Fletcher made Oxford her home for about 30 years. She played the organ and sang in the choir at the United Methodist Church, and neighbors remembered her as a friendly, generous, and unpretentious member of their community. To anyone who might ask, she was also a living history of radio, television, and film and did not mind sharing a bit of showbiz scuttlebutt. She met and worked with theater groups from around the region and held a specific fondness for the Tred Avon Players. In 1994 she helped judge TAP's Lucille Fletcher One-Act Play Contest, the winner of which was *The Superhero*, written by Brent Lewis, the author of this book. The prize was the honor of sharing the bill with a production of *Sorry, Wrong Number*. A few short years later, Fletcher left the Eastern Shore to be closer to her family. On August 31, 2000, she died at St. Mary's Hospital in Langhorne, Pennsylvania, at the age of 88.

"Writing is something we have deeply in common. We love to talk about it, think about it, and work at it," Fletcher told a Friends of the Talbot County Free Library crowd at a Tidewater Inn luncheon on March 23, 1985, a little more than a week before she lost her husband, who was in the hospital. "It's part of our daily routine, our way of life."

"All the while what I thought we were doing was writing so we would have enough money so we wouldn't have to work." Wallop would often quip in response to his wife's public pronouncements before turning more serious. "To me," he'd conclude, "that is one of the nicest things about writing. Never in my life have I felt that it was work. It is work, of course, but in all honesty, it's work I would have done without making a cent."

Forever cementing the roles of Fletcher and Wallop among the great writers who have called the Eastern Shore home, *Sorry, Wrong Number* and *Damn Yankees* look like they will continue to live on in one form or another for a long time.

And as for the authors' feelings about their adopted home?

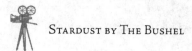

"Like Doug," Fletcher told the *Star Democrat* after her husband's death, "I feel that [the Eastern Shore] is a goldmine for writers, full of strange stories, unusual characters and rare beauty."

For creative types looking for inspiration, you can't ask for more than that.

The rest, as always, is up to you.

ON LOCATION

Ocean City is Maryland's biggest summertime draw, luring visitors by the millions to a slender coastal island renowned for its amusements, boardwalk, and seemingly endless beach. The resort has reeled in many a filmmaker and celebrity, too. (*Jeramey Lende/Shutterstock*)

DELMARVA
AND OCEAN CITY

It can be confusing, these concepts of what exactly is Delmarva and what's the Eastern Shore.

Easy part first: The Delmarva Peninsula includes almost all of Delaware and the Eastern Shores of Maryland and Virginia. Maryland makes up most of Delmarva, and most of that area is rural, with less than 10 percent of the state's population. Nine of Maryland's twenty-three counties are east of the Chesapeake Bay. Seven have Chesapeake coastlines. There are two Virginia counties on the peninsula: Accomack and Northampton. They're even more sparsely developed than those in the Maryland jurisdictions and make up a sliver of Virginia's population.

The Eastern Shore, well, that's a bit more ambiguous.

For Baysiders, there's a sense that once you're out of the Chesapeake watershed, or if, as in the case of Delaware, you don't border the Bay at all, it's difficult, if not impossible, to consider that neck of the woods the Eastern Shore. Historically, Shorefolk are hospitable but not always inclusive. We've been known to fight among ourselves. Generations of virtual isolation will do that to a people, even if they share a history, culture, and economy. There's no doubt many of the good citizens of Delaware and our coastal

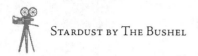
communities consider themselves part of the Eastern Shore, so as we proceed, let's include all our neighbors in our discussion.

Bordered by the Chesapeake, the Atlantic Ocean, Delaware Bay, and the Delaware River, the Delmarva Peninsula is a little more than 180 miles long and up to seventy at its widest. Down at its southern point below Cape Charles, Virginia, there's no more than a couple miles of wetlands separating the bay from the ocean. It's here you'll find the Chesapeake Bay Bridge-Tunnel, the 17.6 mile feat of engineering superstructure that connects Delmarva to the western shore of Virginia and makes a cameo appearance in 2006's *Mission: Impossible III*. In the beginning of the movie's second act, Tom Cruise's superspy Ethan Hunt and his team are transporting a captured villain across the bridge-tunnel when their convoy is attacked in a drone strike. When the black-ops mayhem kicks off, there are explosions, flipping cars, helicopters, high-tech weaponry, danger from above and below, and close calls galore. There is also, of course, extended footage of Tom Cruise running, then leaping, then running some more.

It's a short but important sequence, filmed in October 2005, but the stars were never actually on location. They did their work on a studio set in California. Old-fashioned Hollywood trickery and sophisticated computer-generated images conspire to trick the senses into believing the excitement is happening on the bridge-tunnel, but all that was shot here were establishing shots of the convoy crossing westbound. It took a second-unit crew a mere day's work to get what they needed, but for a cinematic debut, it's hard to beat being featured in a Tom Cruise blockbuster.

To show they appreciated the cooperation they received, Paramount Pictures donated $30,000 to the Eastern Shore United Way Campaign, and when *MI3* opened, the studio invited 900 bridge-and-tunnel employees and their families to a premiere screening at the Idle Hour Theatre in Belle Haven, Virginia.

Chincoteague, Virginia, located about forty miles northeast of Bell Haven, is the hometown of Bill and Skip Hinnant. Growing up along with their older sister Jean, these children of the town's long-time pharmacist loved movies and built a stage in their parents' home where they performed in productions they also wrote. Bill, born John F. Hinnant, Jr, short-of-stature but not of talent, was the older of the two boys, while Joseph, Skip, the more outgoing. Both attended the Yale School of Drama, and as a sophomore Bill won a part on Broadway in *No Time for Sergeants* with a young Andy Griffith. The school recommended he submit a leave of absence and accept the role. Other cast members included Don Knotts and Roddy McDowell. The show ran for two years from 1955-1957. When the production closed, Bill returned to Yale and graduated in 1959, Skip's freshman year.

Over the next decade, Bill appeared on various television shows, and from 1963 to 1965, Skip played a boyfriend to one of the twin cousins Patty Duke portrayed on *The Patty Duke Show*. In 1967 the brothers originated roles in the inaugural off-Broadway run of the hit musical *You're a Good Man, Charlie Brown* based on the characters in Charles M. Schulz's *Peanuts* comic strip. Gary Burghoff, who would later become famous as Radar O'Reilly in the TV version of *M*A*S*H*, played the "round-headed" title character while Skip was cast as the Beethoven-obsessed piano prodigy Schroeder and Bill was the first to interpret for the stage the world's most whimsical beagle, Snoopy.

Skip went on to become best known as a member of the cast of *The Electric Company*, a PBS show designed to help kids become more interested in reading. He also became a well-respected voice actor, and though credited for playing such wholesome characters as The Easter Bunny and Pogo Possum, his most famous voice characterization was the lead in Ralph Bakshi's 1972 X-rated animated feature *Fritz the Cat* and its 1974 sequel. Skip Hinnant's last on-screen roles were in episodes of *As the World Turns* and the sitcom *Kate & Allie*. Bill Hinnant drowned in 1978 at the age of 42 while vacationing in the Dominican Republic. His final major role was a reprisal of his turn as Snoopy in the 1973 animated version of *You're a Good Man, Charlie Brown*.

Across the state line, actor-producer Dale Midkiff spent part of his youth in Chance, Maryland (2021 population: 470). Chance is twenty minutes from the Somerset County seat of Princess Anne. Members of Midkiff's family here built boats and worked the water. The actor visited often as a child, on occasion as an adult. After graduating from Salisbury University, Midkiff spent the summer in Ocean City "waiting tables at night and painting condos by day" before heading to New York to start his career. He spent five years there, working, going to classes, and acting in off-Broadway productions. His first onscreen appearance was playing a violence-prone pimp in independent producing trailblazer Roger Corman's 1985 low budget potboiler *Streetwalkin'*, starring the eventual Oscar winner Melissa Leo. He followed that up with the second lead again in a ratings-grabbing TV movie about the early years of the characters on *Dallas*. His next break was playing Elvis Presley in 1988's *Elvis and Me* based on a memoir by the King of Rock and Roll's ex-wife Priscilla (*The Naked Gun* movies), who was also a producer on the picture. Midkiff was cast two weeks before filming began. He's perhaps most well known as the star of the original 1989 adaptation of Stephen King's *Pet Sematary*.

Bernice Frankel was born in New York City in 1922 and came to Cambridge, Maryland, with her family during the Great Depression. Frankel would make her mark on Broadway and then hit it big on TV, starring in two classic sitcoms. Known for her comedic chops, outspoken characters, and a voice that commanded attention, Frankel grew up to become one of the most famous stars ever to have lived on the Eastern Shore.

Most people knew her as Bea Arthur.

Frankel was the middle daughter of three. She, along with her parents Philip and Rebecca, and her younger sister Marian, moved to Cambridge in the early 1930s. Older sister Gertrude might have lived with them at their home on Mill Street for a time as well. Her father, a tall, distinguished man with a cordial demeanor and a noted sense of humor, opened a clothing store called P. Frankel's and then in 1948 opened a second shop in the remodeled Grand Opera House on Race Street.

Friends and classmates of Frankel remember her as a statuesque and good-looking girl, a brunette with dark brown eyes and a funny, self-assured nature. She resembled her dad in personality and appearance. With her family in the clothing business, she was always well put together. She hated phys ed and was known to push back against authority. She did a remarkable impression of Mae West and was voted the wittiest girl in class. One old acquaintance said she had a reputation as a "hot potato."

Shirley Spedden, a close companion from those days, told Brice Stump of the *Salisbury Daily Times* how Frankel would get friends to push her dad's silver Packard out of the driveway so her parents wouldn't hear when she started the motor. One time she got pulled over by a state trooper on Route 50. As the officer approached, Frankel instructed one of her accomplices in the backseat to lay down. She told the trooper she was sorry, but she was speeding because the girl in the backseat was giving birth and she was trying to get to Easton hospital as quickly as possible. He told her to follow him. As he escorted them to the hospital, the friend wondered aloud what they were going to do upon arrival. Frankel said they'd figure that out when they got there. As they pulled into the parking lot, the cop waved at them and drove away. Her friends couldn't believe she'd pulled it off.

She performed with a group of friends, singing the hits of the day at dances and in the nightclubs of Ocean City. Those who knew Frankel in her teen years thought of her more as a singer than an actress, but they weren't surprised someone of such apparent talent and strong will would succeed in the entertainment field. She once hosted a sellout talent show in a long sapphire blue dress. Spedden called her "absolutely ravishing."

Ravishing doesn't seem like a word Bea Arthur would ever use to describe herself unless she were making a self-deprecating joke. Seems she never felt any of those things her Cambridge High classmates remembered. Arthur later described her younger self as being a painfully shy misfit. She spent most of her time reading movie magazines and dreaming of being a "little, short, blonde movie star." Perhaps what others saw as an attractive confidence, wit, and moxie were just ways a teenage girl might camouflage her insecurities.

Before her senior year, Frankel left Cambridge to graduate from a girls school in Liberty, Pennsylvania. Then she went to a junior college in Virginia. When the United States entered World War II, she was among first to enlist in the Marine Corps Women's Reserves. She worked at Marine Headquarters in D.C. and came back to visit Cambridge on occasion. She was granted a transfer to the Motor Transport School, and after graduating she served as a stateside truck driver and dispatcher. She received her Honorable Discharge in 1945.

Frankel attended the Franklin Institute of Science and Arts in Philadelphia, where she became a licensed medical technician. She returned to Cambridge to work in that field for a few months and then told her parents she wanted to pursue a career in show business. She left for New York to "become someone else."

She changed her name to Beatrice Arthur after marrying fellow marine Robert Alan Aurthur in 1947. Their union lasted three years. He worked in films, primarily as a writer, including on several projects with Sidney Poitier, and died of lung cancer at age fifty-six. Aurthur received two posthumous Academy Award nominations for writing and producing his last film, *All That Jazz*.

Besides moving to the big city and getting hitched, 1947 was an important year for Arthur in another way. She'd also been accepted into the New School's prestigious Dramatic Workshop. Brando studied there. Her student contemporaries included Harry Belafonte, Tony Curtis, Walter Matthau, and Rod Steiger.

Within months of divorcing Aurthur, Arthur married fellow workshop actor Gene Saks, and they stayed together for twenty-eight years. Saks was a prolific theater professional, first onstage and then as a three-time Tony Award–winning director. He was nominated four other times. He was a friend and collaborator of Neil Simon for more than two decades and three of the eight films he directed—*Barefoot in the Park*, *The Odd Couple*, and *Brighton Beach Memories*—were written by Simon.

In 1954, Arthur reaped enthusiastic notices as an outrageous scene stealer named Lucy Brown in a smash off-Broadway production of Bertolt Brecht's *The Threepenny Opera*. In 1956, she found herself in the strange situation of being the understudy of Tallulah Bankhead in a Boston-based rip-off production of the *Ziegfeld Follies*. In 1964, she created the role of Yente the Matchmaker in *Fiddler on the Roof.*

Arthur and Saks adopted two sons, and with her workload increasing, Arthur's rare return trips to the Eastern Shore ended.

She was up for the lead role in the Broadway musical *Mame*, but even though her husband was directing, the part went to Angela Lansbury. Arthur took on the sarcastic and faithful sidekick character instead. It worked out. Both actresses won Tony awards that year and became lifelong friends. Saks was tapped to direct the movie version as well, and despite her reservations, Arthur let him pressure her into reprising Vera for the screen. Lansbury was replaced by a miscast Lucille Ball. The movie turned out to be a box office and critical disaster and ended any possibility of the film career Ball was looking to revive.

Though she made an occasional TV appearance to help pay the bills, Arthur thought of herself as a New York stage actor. Now, nearing fifty, she was approached by a producer and admirer who had a guest part on one of his shows that he felt she'd be perfect in.

The producer was Norman Lear. His show, *All in the Family*.

Norman Lear began in TV as a writer and moved into development. His biggest shows would include *Sanford and Son*, *The Jeffersons*, and *One Day at a Time*. Driven by controversy over content, *All in the Family* premiered to high ratings in January 1971, but after the initial publicity and curiosity died down, enough viewers lost interest that the show hardly seemed worth the trouble to renew. Then it caught on in summer reruns. When it returned for its second season, it was the number-one show on TV and stayed that way for six years.

In December, Arthur was brought in to play the perfect foil to Carroll O'Connor's bigoted grump Archie Bunker: Archie's wife

Edith's outspoken liberal cousin, Maude Findlay. Arthur knew O'Connor from their theater days, and Jean Stapleton, who played the ditzy and loveable Edith, had been a recognized comic entity at least since playing Sister Miller in the 1958 film version of Douglass Wallop's *Damn Yankees*, a role she had originated on Broadway three years prior. With Arthur's stinging line readings, deadpan delivery, and husky voice, Maude was an immediate sensation. The network bosses ordered a spin-off posthaste.

Though Norman Lear's shows always made comedy a priority and were rarely saddled with that "Very Special Episode" vibe, they did address serious topics and discussed American life in a way TV never had before. Religion and politics, civil and equal rights, the Vietnam War, and substance abuse were storytelling fodder. Sometimes they made headlines, as when *Maude* introduced an abortion plotline two months before the *Roe v. Wade* Supreme Court decision in January 1973. In 1977, Arthur won the Emmy for lead comedy actress. *Good Times* was a spinoff about the family of Maude's maid, and *Maude* was still popular when the show's star pulled the plug after six seasons.

Arthur moved to Los Angeles in 1972. She and Saks split up and divorced in 1978. Saks died in 2015 at the age of ninety-three.

The Golden Girls premiered in September 1985, lasted until 1992, and was a winner right off the bat. Created by Susan Harris, a writer and show runner who had penned *Maude*'s abortion episode, the sitcom took place in Miami and was about four older women sharing a home. Arthur played the divorced schoolteacher, Dorothy Zbornack, the show's anchor. Rue McClanahan was the southern belle Blanche, and Betty White the naïve and off-center Rose. Despite being a year younger than Arthur, Estelle Getty played Dorothy's mother Sophia, who moves in after her nursing home burned down in the first episode.

A top-ten show for six of its seven seasons, *The Golden Girls* collected 58 Emmy nominations, with eleven wins, including twice for Outstanding Comedy Series. Each primary actor won Emmys, the only comedy show cast besides *All in the Family*, *Will & Grace*, and *Schitt's Creek* ever to do so. After seven seasons and 180 episodes, as she'd done with *Maude*, Arthur left the show when she knew it had peaked. The other three characters opened a hotel called *The Golden Palace*, with Don Cheadle and Cheech Marin, but it closed after one season.

After *The Golden Girls*, Arthur made guest appearances on TV and toured in a couple of one-woman shows where she sang and told stories. Her last role was playing Larry David's mother in a 2005 episode of *Curb Your Enthusiasm*.

"I've been in the business so long, I've done everything but rodeo and porno," she'd wisecrack. Though she excelled at playing strong, brassy women who pulled no punches and left no doubt where they stood, her loved ones and closest friends knew her as tender, introverted, and unpretentious. She was an animal rights activist and an advocate for the elderly and Jewish communities. She cared about LGBTQ youth homelessness and bequeathed part of her estate toward that cause. When she died in 2009, Broadway dimmed its lights in her honor. She holds the record for the third-most Emmy nominations for lead comedy actress, with only Julia Louis Dreyfus and Mary Tyler Moore having more. She was inducted into the Television Hall of Fame in 2008.

Though she lost touch with the Shore as her star ascended, her ex-running buddies never lost their feelings for her or the stock they put in their relationships. Back in 2003, Arbutus Anderson Fehsenfeld told the *Salisbury Daily Times* that no matter what, "she will always be Bernice to me."

For a small state, Delaware has produced its share of creative talent, and Wilmington, the state's largest and most populated city, seems to be a fertile cradle for the artistically inclined. Valerie Bertinelli (*One Day at a Time, Touched by an Angel, Hot in Cleveland*) was born in Wilmington, as was Elizabeth Shue (*Adventures in Babysitting, Leaving Las Vegas, CSI: Crime Scene Investigation*) and her younger brother, Andrew (*Melrose Place*). Judge Reinhold is also a native, though like the others, he did not grow up there. He got his first major exposure playing the "single, successful guy" Brad Hamilton in *Fast Times at Ridgemont High*. With more than 100 credits to his name, Reinhold is perhaps most recognizable as Detective Billy Rosewood in Eddie Murphy's *Beverly Hills Cop* films and as the stepdad Neil in three *Santa Clause* movies with Tim Allen.

Wilmington's Kathleen Widdoes started in a short-lived 1959 daytime serial called *Young Dr. Malone*, which took place in a fictional Maryland town, and worked continually in the business for another fifty years, capping her career with 1,480 appearances as either Emma Snyder or Emily Stewart in *As the World Turns*.

Five-time World Champion Grand Master martial artist and actress Cynthia Rothrock was also born in Wilmington. After excelling in her sport, she enjoyed a successful B-movie career. In 2014, she was the first martial artist to be inducted into the prestigious International Sports Hall of Fame.

Sean Patrick Thomas was raised in Wilmington, where his parents, immigrants from Guyana, worked for DuPont. Thomas landed his breakout role in 2001's *Save the Last Dance* as the love interest of star Julia Stiles. He was Detective Temple Page in all eighty-nine episodes of *The District* and will play Monteith in producer Joel Coen's 2021 production of *Macbeth* starring Denzel Washington and Frances McDormand.

Yvette Freeman played Nurse Haleh Adams on 184 episodes of *ER* through fifteen seasons and nine as Irma in seasons two and three of *Orange Is the New Black*. She's a native of Wilmington and an art and theater graduate of the University of Delaware.

The current most famous actor from Delaware is Aubrey Plaza. Born and raised in Wilmington, Plaza worked as an NBC page while attending New York University's Tisch School of the Arts and she performed with the improv sketch group Upright Citizen's Brigade. Her first paid gig, for which she earned membership in the Screen Actors Guild, was being typecast as an NBC page in an episode of *30 Rock*. She wore her own her day-job uniform. In 2008, she met a casting director named Allison Jones. Jones's resume goes back to when she worked for shows such as *The Golden Girls*, *Family Ties*, and *The Fresh Prince of Bel Air*. Her instinct for spotting talent is uncanny and she's built her reputation on her ability to help put together knockout ensemble casts.

When she met Plaza, Jones was casting Judd Apatow's *Funny People* starring his roommate from their early days in showbiz, Adam Sandler. She and Apatow (*40-Year Old Virgin*, *Knocked Up*, *Bridesmaids*) had collaborated since she'd put together a company of youthful unknowns, most all of whom went on to noteworthy careers, for his now cultishly beloved show *Freaks and Geeks*.

Around the same time as *Funny People*, Jones was also casting a new series for Greg Daniels and Michael Schur, creators of *The Office*, another series Jones casted to phenomenal success. Jones told Schur that she'd met "the weirdest girl" and arranged a face-to-face between him and Plaza. Schur came out of their meeting saying the actress spent their time together making him feel "really uncomfortable for like an hour." He then wrote a character designed just for her.

Parks and Recreation, starring Amy Poehler, premiered in April 2009, ran for seven seasons, and among a slew of standout performances, Jones had again worked her magic. Plaza was a fan favorite as the dark and droll but nougat-centered April Ludgate, aka Janet Snakehole, aka Judy Hitler, aka Satan's Niece. The role and the show made Aubrey Plaza a star.

She got the job on *Funny People* too.

In 2010, Plaza was part of *Scott Pilgrim vs. the World* (Jones scores again!) and in 2012 starred in the off-kilter but sweet time-travel romance *Safety Not Guaranteed*. She was the lead in 2013's *The To Do List*. In 2017, she produced and starred in *The Little Hours* and *Ingrid Goes West*. As of 2020, she has no less than five projects in production. Two of those projects, *The Ark and the Aardvark* and *Little Demon* are animated, and Plaza is a featured voice, a style of performance that appeals to her.

Her first notable voicework was as internet superstar Grumpy Cat (2012–2019) in Lifetime's 2014 cable movie *Grumpy Cat's Worst Christmas Ever*. She's also the voice of Nocturna on *Spongebob Squarepants* and the home operating system called Lucy on the cop romance *Castle*. When she was voted Delaware's Most Famous Person by readers of her hometown paper in 2018, Plaza promised to do her best to represent the state in "the strangest way possible."

Wilmington is also a locale, though not a filming location, in the plots of *Fight Club* and *The Wrestler*, but did stand in onscreen as the fictional town of Arcadia in establishing shots for the 2003–2005 series *Joan of Arcadia*.

New Castle's Ryan Phillippe's (*Crash*, *Flags of Our Fathers*) first substantial role was playing daytime TV's first gay teen on *One Life to Live*. His earliest feature film appearance was in 1995's

Crimson Tide. He scored with *I Know What You Did Last Summer* and *Cruel Intentions.* He was the fictional sniper Bob Lee Swagger in the 2016–2018 series *Shooter*, based on the action novels by former *Baltimore Sun* and *Washington Post* film critic Stephen Hunter. In 2020, he appeared in two films, *The 2nd* and *The Sound of Philadelphia*, as well as the crime show *Big Sky.* From 1999 to 2008 Phillippe was married to Academy Award–winning actress Reese Witherspoon.

Other notable actors from Delaware include Doug Hutchins (*The Green Mile, Lost, 24*) and Teri Polo (*Meet the Fockers, The West Wing, The Fosters*), both born in the state capital of Dover.

William Alland (1916–1997) was born in Delmar, Delaware, and moved with his family to Baltimore when he was a kid. With ambitions to make it on Broadway, Alland headed to New York at his first opportunity. He took acting classes, met a developing auteur named Orson Welles, and worked his way into the Mercury Theater Group that Welles founded with John Houseman. As an assistant director and voice actor, Alland was in the studio that Halloween in 1938 when the group staged a radio adaptation of H. G. Wells's *War of the Worlds* realistic enough to frighten listeners into believing an actual alien invasion was under way. When Welles went to Hollywood, Alland went with him. He plays a critical role in Welles's masterpiece *Citizen Kane.* As Jerry Thompson, the journalist delving into the life mysteries of newspaper magnate Charles Foster Kane, Thompson is never seen in close-up but is shot from behind or in the shadows.

Alland enlisted in the Army Air Corps in World War II and served as a pilot with more than fifty missions in the South Pacific theater. After the war, he moved to a producing position with Universal-International, where he became known for cranking out low-budget "nine-day wonders" that were, for the most part, either cowboy or sci-fi pics. In 1953, he released *It Came from Outer Space*, based on a story by Ray Bradbury. His *Creature from the Black Lagoon* came out in 1954. Its sequel, *Revenge of the Creature* in 1955, gave Clint Eastwood his first screen credit. Alland's output for the next two years include *This Island Earth*, *Tarantula*, and *The Mole People*. He got caught up in the Red Scare of the early 1950s and named names behind closed doors, but when he died, he was best remembered as an affable guy who loved show business to his core.

And out of all the dogs who have appeared onscreen, few have made as indelible an impression from one performance as the American Pitbull from Delaware named Sayuri, who played Brandy in Quentin Tarantino's 2019 magnum opus *Once Upon a Time in Hollywood*. Sayuri belongs to Delaware Red Pit Bulls owners Matt and Monique Klosowski. For fifteen years, the Klosowskis had been breeding and training dogs on a small scale, mostly for friends and family, when out of the blue Hollywood came calling. Dedicated to the breed, the Klosowskis were known for raising loving, smart, athletic, and hard-working canines.

The Klosowskis and the filmmakers came to an agreement and the Hollywood trainers drove "cuddle-happy" Sayuri, a 55-pound three-year-old, and a stunt double named Cerberus, to California for filming. They were joined on set by a third dog, Siren, who also portrayed Brandy in some shots.

Filming wrapped in February 2019, and Sayuri and Cerberus returned home. *Once Upon a Time in Hollywood* opened in late July to strong reviews and Tarantino's biggest box office ever. Sayuri was a scene-stealer. The loving and semi-neglected pet of Brad Pitt's Cliff Booth, Brandy spends her day watching TV in a filthy trailer while her owner, an unemployable stuntman, cruises L.A. running errands for his boss Rick Dalton, played by Leonardo DiCaprio,

and encountering the Charles Manson cult along the way. When he finally returns home to have dinner with Brandy, Cliff makes her wait as he dumps a can of Wolf's Tooth Dog Food—it comes in various flavors including rat, raccoon, and lizard—but she lets him know she's displeased. In the picture's hyperviolent and alternate history final act, Brandy comes through like a champ. When the 2020 Oscar nominations were announced, *Hollywood* received ten, including Best Motion Picture, Director, Lead Actor, Original Screenplay, and Cinematography. Though the film only took home two awards, for Production Design and Supporting Actor for Pitt, Sayuri had already won her accolades. When the picture premiered at the Cannes Film Festival back in the spring, she was named recipient of the Palm Dog Award for Best Performance by a Canine. Tarantino accepted on her behalf. He remarked that though they'd struggled a bit to get Sayuri "to do this or that" during filming, in the end, "when I was editing the movie, I realized she's a great actress. I actually started seeing things in her face when I was cutting it together that I didn't see on the day, so whatever little difficulties we had on the set just really melted away when I saw what a great performance she gave."

1915's *Emmy of Stork's Nest* starred Mary Miles Minter (1902–1984). This lost silent picture was filmed in Delaware and along the Delaware River in Pennsylvania and New Jersey. Based on a popular romantic novel about a naïve child-of-the-woods blossoming into womanhood, a bear cub called Billy Bruin was a featured player. Minter, promoted to be the next Mary Pickford, was a child star with a domineering stage mom whose career was ruined by her connection to the scandalous unsolved 1922 murder of director William Desmond Taylor.

The first feature film shot entirely in Delaware starred Robin Williams and was directed by Peter Weir (*Witness, Green Card, Master and Commander: The Far Side of the World*). Set in the 1950s, 1989's *Dead Poets Society* tells the story of a dedicated English teacher at an elite high school who ignites the imagination of his students. The movie was shot on location for more than ten weeks, with most filming taking place at St. Andrews, a private boarding school in Middletown.

St. Andrews was established in 1929 by philanthropist A. Felix DuPont. Alumni include the musician-actor Loudon Wainwright III; John Seabrook, author of the *New Yorker* article *The Flash of Genius* that inspired the 2008 film about inventor and Eastern Shore resident Robert Kearns; as well as the Shore natives news anchor Erin Burnett and singer-songwriter Maggie Rogers. The school was also used in a 2001 episode of *The West Wing* titled "Two Cathedrals."

Another location in Middletown that was used for *Dead Poets Society* is the Everett Theatre (c. 1922), where a student production of *A Midsummer's Night's Dream* is performed. The Everett is on the National Register of Historic Places and still operates as a theater and community cultural center under the auspices of a nonprofit organization. Scenes were also shot around Wilmington and New Castle, and more than 1,000 locals were used as extras, including many students from area schools.

The first movie produced from a script by Tom Schulman (*Honey I Shrunk the Kids, What about Bob?*), *Dead Poets Society* was nominated for Best Actor, Best Director, and Best Picture Oscars, and won Schulman a best screenplay award. It was the tenth-biggest moneymaker of the year in the United States and the fifth in the world and still holds high scores on review-aggregating websites. "O Captain! My Captain!" and "Carpe diem. Seize the day, boys. Make your lives extraordinary" are, respectively, the title of a Walt Whitman poem and a riff on an adage coined by the Roman poet Horace, but *Dead Poets Society* made both among the most memorable movie lines of all time.

Though not listed as a shooting location, the Dover International Speedway in Delaware's state capital, nicknamed the Monster Mile for its challenging treatment of cars and drivers, shows up onscreen during a fast, funny, and action-packed racing montage in 1990's *Days of Thunder* starring Tom Cruise and directed by Tony Scott (*Top Gun, True Romance, Crimson Tide*).

Beloved was an acclaimed and bestselling 1987 novel by the esteemed author Toni Morrison (1931–2019). The book is emotional, intense, and profound, and won the 1998 Pulitzer Prize for fiction. In 1993, Morrison became the first black woman to be awarded the Nobel Prize in Literature. Like many readers, Oprah Winfrey fell in love with *Beloved*. She dreamed of adapting the book to screen, envisioning herself and Danny Glover in the leading roles, and worked for ten years to get the movie made the way she wanted it. Directed by Jonathan Demme (*Stop Making Sense, Philadelphia, Adaptation*), who'd won almost every award possible for 1992's *Silence of the Lambs*, *Beloved* did not fare well with critics or audiences. Filmed in Pennsylvania, as well as in the historic section of New Castle on the Delaware River, some outdoor scenes were captured at the Fair Hill Natural Resource Area in Cecil County, Maryland. Parts of Disney's *Tuck Everlasting* from 2002 were also filmed at Fair Hill.

Director M. Night Shyamalan (*The Sixth Sense, Unbreakable, Signs*), was born in India, raised in Philly, and likes to tell stories with a twist that take place around his hometown. In 2004, he released *The Village*, partially shot in Centerville, Delaware, an eighteenth-century village in the Brandywine Valley, and starring such major talent as Bryce Dallas Howard, Joaquin Phoenix, Adrian Brody, William Hurt, Sigourney Weaver, and Broadway star Cherry Jones. The year after *The Village*, Jones would play an important role in Eastern Shoreman Doug Sadler's indie film, *Swimmers*, shot in Talbot County, Maryland.

The one time Hollywood flirted with Delmarva and got the cold shoulder was in 1998 when scouts were looking for places to film the adaptation of Nicholas Sparks's *Message in a Bottle* with Kevin Costner, Robin Wright, and Paul Newman (1925–2008), who was hot off a 1995 Oscar win for *Nobody's Fool*. *Message in a Bottle* tells the story of a divorced mom who finds the titular bottle on a beach with a heartbreaking love letter inside from a widowed fisherman and shipbuilder to his deceased wife. One filming location under consideration was Tangier Island in Accomack County, Virginia.

Tangier Island is in the mid- to lower Chesapeake, fifteen miles or so from the mainland, and is as isolated as one gets in this already remote area. No more than four feet above sea level, Tangier can be walked in half an hour. Approximately 700 people lived there in the late 1990s, and most residents then and now belong to long-established island families who have worked the surrounding water for generations. Religion is important to the islanders, and many identify as conservative Christians.

When Hollywood approached, leadership was intrigued at first, but after reading the screenplay the town council voted unanimously against the proposal to film on the island. They objected to the drinking of beer and wine (alcohol sales are prohibited on Tangier), some cussing (taking the Lord's name in vain was especially offensive), and a mild love scene between

301

unmarried characters. After the vote, the council held out hope that the studio might change the script to alleviate their concerns. They thought they were giving Hollywood an opportunity to show that the industry was listening to an audience looking for a movie "that's been cleaned up for the moral-minded family."

Hollywood went elsewhere.

Most of the film was shot in Maine and North Carolina.

Tangier Island's stance made news from Alberta, Canada to Honolulu, Hawaii and beyond. Not every islander supported the council's decision. Many were disappointed in losing the financial boon that would have come with the film's production and any promotional value for the island that might have followed.

Before the council vote, Newman (*The Hustler, Cool Hand Luke, The Sting*), assuming he'd be working there soon, made plans to come down and check the island out. When he heard that the town fathers rejected the filmmakers' advances, he came anyway. Incognito and armed with a sense of humor, he took in the reaction of the islanders and asked officials if he could make a pitch to persuade reconsideration but was told not to bother.

In the end, *Message in a Bottle* is a tame PG-13 romance in the style of most movies made from the works of Sparks (*A Walk to Remember, The Notebook, Dear John*) and is, by most standards, innocuous. It is also Sparks's largest-grossing film ever.

Ocean City, or O.C. to its friends, is a resort town located on an Atlantic Ocean barrier island with a history as a rest-and-recreation destination going back more than 150 years. Consisting of less than five square miles, with less than 10,000 full-time residents, the population can swell up to 350,000 on summer weekends. Eight million vacationers visit in a typical year. From June to August, Ocean City is the second-most-populated municipality in the state of Maryland, behind only Baltimore. Families return year after year, generation after generation. With its own flavor, icons, and rites of passage, it holds a special place in the hearts and memories of an unknowable number of individual stories.

The Atlantic Ocean is the majestic main attraction, and its appeal is powerful. Once a quiet getaway for "people of refinement," a visitor to today's up-and-running Ocean City might have to give their senses a chance to acclimate to the town's perpetual undercurrent of stimulation, the splashes of noise and color, the boundless tastes and smells. It's an indisputable fact that one of things people love most about the place is the wafting smell of freshly applied salt and malt vinegar to hot boardwalk French fries. The pleasures here are simple but enduring.

With a sharply focused, decades-long resolve to promote their town as a family-friendly vacation haven, the civic leaders of Ocean City have worked hard to carve out a reputation as the place to go for good clean fun in the sun. Ocean City sentimentalists tend to think of the era of their youth as the time to which all other generations pale in comparison. When it comes to Ocean City, there's always going to be at least a hint of romantic nostalgia floating in the air along with that salt and vinegar.

Where Ocean City sits used to be part of one long barrier island that stretched from Indian River Bay, Delaware down to Tom's Cove, Virginia at the southern tip of Assateague. Folks have been eyeballing ways to monetize this coastline since Day One. "Ocean City is a history of investments," said John Dale Showell

III, a descendent of some of the resort's earliest proselytizers, in Mary Corddry's *City on the Sand: Ocean City, Maryland and the People Who Built It*. It wasn't until after the Civil War, in the time of the railroads, however, that things started coming together for this isolated and uninhabited outpost on the Atlantic Ocean.

Property was cheap in the late 1860s, when a New York businessman named Stephen Taber obtained deeds to most of the island that was within Maryland. One of the parcels was a 280-acre oceanfront site that he picked up for less than dollar an acre. A shrewd investor, he was not, however, adept at naming things, as evidenced by his designating this tract "Ladies Resort to the Ocean." Nevertheless, the piece of property was across from the narrowest stretch of Sinepuxent Bay, which looked like a fine place to maybe build a bridge someday.

In 1869, a local named Isaac Coffin opened a beachfront guest cottage and barroom in what would soon become known as Ocean City. More hunting lodge than hotel, the Rhode Island Inn was the first accommodations here to house paying customers.

Colonel Lemuel Showell (1822–1902) owned a little place on the beach too. Showell, from an old Eastern Shore family, became obsessed with the idea that the island could be built into something special. In July 1872, Showell and his colleagues organized a meeting with potential investors. Stephen Taber was there too, and he listened to the organization's pitch to kickstart a resort town. Taber told them that if the company could raise enough funds to build a hotel, they could have a ten-acre parcel of their choice. If they were successful on the hotel project, Taber would then deed over another fifty acres to build a town around their venture.

The name "Ocean City" came from a stockholder meeting where other names were considered and rejected, including Beach City, Sinepuxent City, even Ladies Resort to the Ocean.

The Atlantic Hotel opened to stupendous fanfare on Independence Day 1875. Four stories tall and stretching a whole block from Baltimore Avenue to the beach, the Atlantic was among the finest of grand East Coast hotels. In 1923, the hotel was sold to a Dr. Charles Purnell and has been owned by members of his family since. The Atlantic burned down in a 1925 fire that destroyed three blocks of the fledgling resort, but the proprietors rebuilt and it stands today as an esteemed boardwalk landmark.

When construction of the original Atlantic was completed, Taber stuck by his word and turned over fifty acres to the hotel company, which subdivided the parcel into 205 building lots.

In the early 1880s a wooden railroad bridge was constructed across Sinepuxent Bay. Railroad companies teamed with Chesapeake steamboat outfits and offered excursions to this new city by the sea. For the populations of rural Eastern Shore towns such as St. Michaels and Preston, watching the Ocean City Flyer chug past was a weekend highlight.

Ocean City catered to "the financially elite." Hoteliers installed an elevated, removable boardwalk. Swimming wasn't really a thing yet. Visitors rented modest Victorian-style bathing suits and there were ropes leading from the shore into the water that brave early adapters held onto as they stood in the surf. In 1907, the next coterie of founding fathers built Ocean City's first fishing pier where anglers could rent gear and tackle. There was a roller-skating rink. At the foot, where a giant four-ton mechanical shark now bursts through the walls of the Ripley's Believe It or Not attraction, there were refreshments available, a silent movie theater, and a bowling alley. Big-name orchestras and topnotch singers performed in the Pier Ballroom. Local girls were on hand to sell clams, crab cakes, and saltwater taffy to the tourists who dressed for dinner and then went dancing or strolling the boardwalk as the evening lengthened.

The first car bridge into Ocean City opened in 1916. As auto ownership increased and Americans enjoyed more free time, new highways shortened distances and expanded the average family's horizons. Ocean City was waiting for them with open arms.

After years of its citizens petitioning the government to build a harbor on the bay side of Ocean City, a 1933 hurricane of epic proportions cut an inlet fifty feet wide and eight feet deep, which opened up a whole new source of pride and income to the citizens of Ocean City.

The first recorded white marlin caught off the city's coast was in 1934. Commercial fishermen had long been a part of the community, but sport fishing like this was new. The inlet provided harbor for the boats that anglers needed to access the fishing grounds some eighty to 100 miles offshore. These days Ocean City is one of the sport's most popular fishing ports and is called the White Marlin Capital of the World. With millions of dollars in prize money, the Ocean City White Marlin Open, held every August, brings in anglers from around the world and is the number-one blue-water fishing competition anywhere. The Chesapeake Bay Bridge, connecting Annapolis with the Eastern Shore, opened in 1952, replacing an outdated ferry system and creating a connecting roadway for vacationers and day-trippers from the Baltimore-Washington metro area. The Chesapeake Bay Bridge-Tunnel between the Virginia Eastern Shore and Hampton Roads was completed in 1964, opening a southern-based market for promoting Ocean City. In the 1960s and 1970s, the resort continued to grow. Unlike its more-protective Delaware neighbors to the north, Rehoboth and Bethany Beaches, which were founded for church getaways and summer camps, Ocean City embraced the great consumer surge in the form of condominium projects, shopping centers, golf courses, restaurants, amusement parks, and real estate offices. People came from everywhere to take in the many pleasures the old Ladies Resort to the Ocean had to offer. More and more memories were made.

"There's a summer you'll always remember, and a hope that if you go back, it will happen again. *Violets Are Blue*. Nothing ever felt better."

That's a tagline most every romantic can relate to.

Starring Sissy Spacek and Kevin Kline, *Violets Are Blue* was the second of five films directed by Jack Fisk. Most accomplished as a production designer, Fisk has been nominated for design Oscars twice, first for *There Will Be Blood* in 2008, then again in 2016 for *The Revenant*. His directorial debut was 1981's *Raggedy Man*, which also starred Spacek, whom he happens to have been married to since 1974. For *Violets Are Blue*, the couple and their two children were in town a few weeks prior to filming, he hard at work on preproduction duties, she soaking in the atmosphere, talking to people to help give her character authenticity, and learning to sail. Fisk told reporters they found the locals welcoming and gracious and that he thought of his crew's presence in town as being like any other group of people working a summer job. It's just that their summer job in Ocean City would be making a movie.

Filming began on August 6, 1984 and was scheduled to run through September. As production geared up, Ocean City Mayor Harry Kelley, one of the movie's greatest backers, organized a press conference and meet-and-greet and gave the primary players keys to the city. Bonnie Bedelia, who portrayed Kline's character's wife raved, "This is the best location I've ever been on. I don't even feel like I'm working." Around the resort, the locals referred to the cast and crew as "the movie people." Though they were curious and often awestruck when there was a celebrity sighting, a visiting correspondent from Easton's *Star Democrat* reported that except for the excitement in the mayor's voice and a parking lot full of brand new rental cars on 1st Street, "You'd hardly know there's a Hollywood film company in town."

Sequences were filmed at various locations, including on the beach at Assateague, the boardwalk, Trimper's Amusement Park, Fager's Island restaurant and nightclub, the West Ocean City fishing pier, and the Cropper house (c. 1912), on the south side of Division Street, which was the home of Sissy Spacek's character's parents. For scenes of the home where Kline's and Bedelia's characters live, a 3,000-square-foot, two-story house with an artificially weathered exterior was built across the bay in West Ocean City on what locals refer to as Stinky Beach. The house was damaged by arsonists the following winter, and the fire department burned down the rest later in a training exercise.

Longtime local broadcasting personality and venerable Master of Ceremonies Wayne Cannon, the "Voice" of Ocean City who died in April 2021, was always one of his town's most enthusiastic cheerleaders. When the cast and crew started rolling film on *Violets Are Blue* here, Cannon was on air at radio station WETT and was a member of the both the Tourism Commission and the Ocean City Chamber of Commerce.

"They used hundreds of locals as extras," Cannon said in a 2019 interview. "I was in two scenes: the sailboat race scene at Fager's Island and the opening scene on the boardwalk. For the Fager's Island shoot, our thing was after the race. They were coming back, and we all ran out to greet the sailboats and the sailors and shake hands and all that stuff. I got a hundred dollars from Columbia

Pictures. I should have kept the check. Now it'd be better to have than the $100.

"With the other scene, I just happened to be riding in Ocean City one day and somebody said, you know they're filming on the boardwalk. So, just on a whim, I went down and got myself in the shot. It's in the beginning of the movie, in the opening credits, and Sissy Spacek is walking the boards. She's coming one way and I'm walking the other and I'm wearing my WETT shirt. Watching the movie, I always tell my kids, that's your father there."

Ocean City was determined to hold a premiere for the film and on Sunday, April 6, 1986, five days before its official release, the film was shown twice for local audiences. A "black-tie optional" event was held at the Sun & Surf Cinema with a reception afterward at the Carousel Hotel, where open bars, buffets, and the nostalgic sounds of the band Junior Cline and the Recliners awaited. Tickets benefitting five local charities sold out in two weeks and 1,200 people attended the glitzy red carpet and champagne festivities. Hollywood-style searchlights lit the sky.

The second showing that evening was attended by the invited celebrities. Guests included Sissy Spacek, Jack Fisk, and Bonnie Bedelia. Kevin Kline was unable to attend due to a work conflict. Spacek was quoted as saying the premiere was like coming home; Bedelia joked that she was disappointed in the town for torching the Stinky Beach house in her absence and thought they should have waited for her so that she could have participated in the "big bonfire." When the credits rolled, locals were pleased to see a prominent thank you dedicated to the late Mayor Kelley, who died before *Violets* was released.

Doing press for the picture, Kevin Kline expressed his belief that in its efforts to "explore and illuminate the myth of first love," there was something "intrinsically honorable" about the movie.

Spacek hoped viewers would be drawn to the universal nature of the story and the characters' emotions.

And the fans?

Violets Are Blue is a favorite of many. One IMDB reviewer giving the movie a ten out of ten posted that she and her husband first met in Ocean City and were together for thirty-three years before he died. "I find myself traveling to the ocean to recapture that peace and tranquility we both had there," she wrote. "The movie lets me see and remember those things young people experience in a small resort town. We lived there during the late 60's and early 70's . . . what a pleasure it was to watch the actors walk through places that my husband and I had shared many years ago."

Romance runs deep on the Eastern Shore.

So does nostalgia.

Ping Pong Summer is a 2014 independent family comedy written and directed by Marylander Michael Tully. Tully graduated from the University of Maryland with a degree in visual arts and film production. His first directing effort, featuring amateur actors, was 2006's *Cocaine Angel*, a detailed look into the life of a junkie. His second feature, *Septian* (2011), which he also wrote and acted in, is his take on the themes and motifs of the Southern Gothic. Tully's third project, *Ping Pong Summer*, was based on a screenplay he'd been working on since he was a teenager.

Inspired by 1980s teen flicks along with trips Tully's family took to Ocean City when he was growing up, *Ping Pong Summer* looks back on a time when whatever was on MTV ruled pop culture. The story centers around Rad Miracle, who, despite his gnarly, funky-fresh name, is an awkward thirteen-year-old experiencing that transformative summer between middle and high school. Part coming-of-age film, part underdog sports movie, Rad encounters several teenage milestones during a week in O.C., including forming new friendships, interactions with bullies, and his first crush on a girl very much out of his league.

After working on the screenplay for years and never having enough resources to produce the movie the way he wanted, everything came together after Tully reached out to his friend Jay Duplass, a writer, actor (*Transparent*), director (*Cyrus*), and producer (*Safety Not Guaranteed*), who connected Tully with Susan Sarandon. Sarandon (*The Rocky Horror Picture Show, Thelma & Louise, Dead Man Walking*) liked the story's sweetness and as co-founder of Spin, an international chain of table tennis social clubs, the ping pong angle spoke to her. Once Sarandon, who agreed to work below her usual fee, was onboard as Rad's mentor Randi Jammer, the elements of production fell into place.

Other known actors joined the cast in both important roles and cameos. Lea Thompson and John Hannah play Rad's parents. Thompson is memorable from 1980s classics such as *Red Dawn, Back to the Future,* and *Some Kind of Wonderful,* as well as the television series *Caroline in the City* and *Switched at Birth.* Scottish actor John Hannah got his break playing Matthew in *Four Weddings and a Funeral* and he was Jonathan Carnahan in Universal's three mummy movies from 1999 to 2008.

The actor, stand-up comedian, Maryland native, and ping pong aficionado Judah Friedlander from *30 Rock* has a cameo as Anthony from Anthony's Liquors deli, the landmark business located at 33rd Street and Coastal Highway that's been in operation since the end of World War II. Amy Sedaris and Robert Longstreet play Aunt Peggy and Uncle Jim, oddball relatives living the laidback beach lifestyle. Sedaris is a comedic icon with 111 acting credits, ranging from her early cult favorite *Strangers with Candy* to the surreal hospitality show *At Home with Amy Sedaris.* Longstreet had worked with Tally in *Septian.* His first credit was on a 1993 episode of Andy Griffith's *Matlock*. Since *Ping Pong Summer*, he's most notably been in *Aquaman* and *Sorry to Bother You*, both from 2018. In fall 2021 he appears in the horror sequel *Halloween Kills*.

For the teenage members of his *Ping Pong* cast, Tully sought unknown amateurs. He wanted the energy, genuineness, and look of newcomers, and as much as possible, he wanted them to be from the Delmarva area. He auditioned many young actors before choosing newcomers Marcello Conte for the lead, Myles Massey as Rad's new best-bud Teddy, and Helena Seabrook as his eye-rolling vegetarian-slash-goth sister. Most impressively, perhaps, is the performance given by then-fourteen year old Ocean City native Emmi Shockley who plays Rad's resort town dream girl Stacy Summers.

Shockley first heard about *Ping Pong Summer* while working as an extra on an ultra-low budget film in Baltimore. "I was on the set and I mentioned I was from Ocean City and someone said, "They're shooting something there!" I'd missed the auditions, but then I just emailed Michael Tully." Shy when she was little, "I guess I'd grown brave by 14."

Tully's reaction was immediate. He knew there were steps to be taken but felt instinctively that he'd found his Stacy Summers.

As with many O.C. kids, Shockley was raised in a service oriented family business, and she credits the resort town at least in part for her artistic streak. "Maybe because everyone goes to work at an early age," she says, "we might also have more responsibility and a sense of freedom and independence than teenagers in other communities. Whatever it is, kids there tend to be very creative." Shockley found her own self-confidence and identity filming short comedy sketches through the lens of a flip video camera with her brother and friends.

On set and off, the young actors bonded with their peers and interacted with the seasoned pros with whom they shared the screen. One of Shockley's most memorable moments with one of her more famous costars came when she was seated next to Susan Sarandon during a cast dinner. "We talked about how nervous I was anticipating my first onscreen kiss," Shockley says. "I mean I was just figuring out how to kiss people in real life! What she told me was not to worry, to think of kissing on screen as choreography, but with the mouth, the body. It was really good, simple advice."

A graduate of the Tisch School of the Arts at New York University with a degree in film and television production, and with interests both in front of and behind the camera, Shockley is now pursuing a career in the entertainment industry.

Beginning on September 19, 2012 with Rad and Teddy eating ice cream from Dumser's Dairyland, *Ping Pong Summer* was, by all accounts, fun to shoot. In an article for locationshub.com, an online marketplace for filmmakers and potential shooting locations, Lea Thompson said she was impressed by how much character the town of Ocean City possesses. She said she loved being at the beach, she'd seen dolphins offshore just that morning, and enjoyed being in a fun place that despite being a tourist destination had a small town's sense of community.

Suiting the filmmakers' budget, many of the most recognizable landmarks in the movie haven't changed in decades. Ocean City adapts but also works hard to hold onto its timeless aura. Not much needed to be done to travel back cinematically from 2012 to 1985.

Ocean City has always been known for its food, so it's appropriate *Ping Pong Summer* audiences get a taste. Paul Revere's Smorgasbord in the Plim Plaza Hotel on the boardwalk, home of the Early Bird Special, hits a specific nostalgic beat for viewers familiar with the resort, as does a crab feast scene at Hooper's Crab

House. Phillips Seafood Restaurant is the perfect location for a fancy teenage dinner date. Mere glimpses of culinary mainstays such as the Greene Turtle and Dough Roller Pizza and Pancakes make the viewer want to ask for a menu.

There's a funny sequence shot at Old Pro Golf, a family-owned and -operated mini-golf course that's been in business since 1965. The Miracle family shops at the Gold Coast Mall. Teddy and his dad stay at the King's Arms Motel. Rad catches Stacy making out with his rival up against the boardwalk's one-of-a-kind art shop, the Ocean Gallery World Center.

The movie gets much of the era's styles right, the clothes, the hair, and the music, along with teen nightclubs, video games, and skateboards, but also nails the location-specific details such as pool hopping, Mike "DJ Batman" Beatty, and the tan and brown cars once used by the Maryland State Police. Tully's father was a trooper, and John Hannah wore the director's dad's retired uniform in the film. Hip hop music is an important part of *Ping Pong Summer's* ambiance. The soundtrack features musical acts such as The Fat Boys, Mary Jane Girls, and New Edition, along with mainstream pop-rock bands like Mr. Mister and Kiss.

Ping Pong Summer finished filming on schedule and within budget on October 26, 2012. The last scene was shot on the fishing pier, which was practically wiped out a few days later when Hurricane Sandy blew into town.

Tully's ode to Ocean City premiered at the Sundance Film Festival in 2014 and was picked up for distribution by Gravitas Ventures. Intentionally rough around the edges, Tully's stated goal was always to shoot the movie as though it were made in the 1980s from the perspective of a real thirteen-year-old and not from an adult looking back and making "hindsight humor."

Most viewers familiar with O.C. in the time of breakdancing, pleather clothing, and first-generation arcade video games, back when the pier featured a giant straight-down waterslide of terrifying height and an infamous walk-through haunted house, should be able to plug into the sentimentality that *Ping Pong Summer* serves up.

You can almost smell those french fries from here.

FEATURE PRESENTATIONS

Before Fay Wray met King Kong, she was given the silent treatment
by Gary Cooper in *The First Kiss,* shot on location in St. Michaels,
Maryland. (*The Hollywood Archive / Alamy Stock Photo*)

THE FIRST
KISS
(1928)

The First Kiss is a lost silent picture about how a Chesapeake Bay waterman's romantic interests in an Eastern Shore belle are complicated by his family loyalties and his dream to build a world-class schooner.

Also, he's a pirate.

The film's plot is based on a short story called "Four Brothers" by occasional Marylander Tristram Tupper (1884–1955), a Mexican border and World War I veteran who would serve as an Army brigadier general in World War II. Tupper is said to have written his melodramatic bay yarn while vacationing at Maple Hall in Claiborne, Maryland. In the late nineteenth and early twentieth century, resort hotels and boarding houses, accessed via steamboats and railroads, dotted the Chesapeake shoreline. Maple Hall was among the finest.

Two months after publication of Tupper's story, however, when it came time to find accommodations to house the cast and crew coming to Talbot County to film *The First Kiss*, the proprietors of Maple Hall, holding themselves to very proper moral standards, exercised their right to refuse service. They were not going to put up with any showbiz shenanigans. Gary Cooper and Fay Wray and the rest of their Hollywood cohorts were invited to find lodging elsewhere.

For the three weeks or so they were on the Eastern Shore, most of the several dozen crew members working on *The First Kiss* stayed at the Pasadena Inn in Royal Oak. According to Dickson J. Preston's *Talbot County, A History*, Royal Oak is an "ancient" community that flourished when the steamboats and railroads started bringing vacationers to the area. "Half a dozen old homes opened their doors to paying guests," wrote Dickson, and "best known was the Pasadena Inn." Once part of a larger land grant dating back to circa 1680, this forty-two-acre parcel was subdivided off and sold to farmer John Harper in 1884. His son Frederick took over the property from his father a few years later, and when his brother Albert moved his family to California, Fredrick decided he'd stay and build his own 'Pasadena' here. In 1902, Frederick and his wife, Florence, took in their first paying guests at five bucks a week. Today, the property is the site of the Oaks Waterfront Inn, an upscale getaway, conference, and wedding destination.

In 1973, the *Baltimore Sun* Sunday magazine published a nostalgic *I Remember* . . . column written by Pauline Harper Vaillant, one of the six Harper children. Looking back to that spring when Royal Oak was home to the stars, Pauline, in her mid-twenties at the time and a hostess in the Pasadena Inn's dining room, wrote that her family was impressed by how hard everyone worked and that the stars of the film "weren't a bit like Hollywood actors were supposed to be. No wild parties, no drinking, no carrying on."

In the film, Cooper plays Mulligan Talbot, a waterman from one of Maryland's oldest families, now several generations past their prime. Mulligan's doing his best to look after his drunken widower of an old man and three good-for-nothing brothers. He's also got a thing for Wray's Anna Lee, the daughter of the richest man in town, but she spurns his advances. When "Pap" Talbot dies, Mulligan decides it's up to him to better his family name. He insists his brothers go to college and to finance their education Mulligan takes up pirating under the alias of the Black Duck. Don't get him wrong, though, he's secretly building a fancy schooner he plans to sell to pay back what he steals. Except he gets caught. His brothers—now a minister, a doctor, and a lawyer—come home to show support. A secret buyer purchases Mulligan's schooner, giving him an opportunity to make restitution. During his trial, Anna Lee, pillar of society, testifies on his behalf, and Mulligan is paroled in her care. The twist? She was the boat's anonymous buyer. The end? They're married by his brother the preacher and they sail off into the Chesapeake Bay sunset.

The plot of *The First Kiss* centered on Cooper's Mulligan Talbot character, but Fay Wray scored top billing. "She was then a much better-known star than Gary Cooper," wrote Pauline Vaillant. "In fact, he was so obscure that the local paper called him "Gary Copper" when it was first announced the movie would be made." Wray was also paid more than her leading man. On-location scuttlebutt had it that she didn't let him forget she was the star of the show. *The First Kiss* was the second of four movies the two would act in together.

Though she'll always be second-banana to the screen's greatest great ape, Fay Wray (1907–2004) amassed 123 acting credits in the course of a fifty-seven-year career. Her appearances in *Doctor X* and *The Most Dangerous Game* in 1932, and *The Vampire Bat* and *The Mystery of the Wax Museum* in 1933, the same year *King Kong* was released, contribute to her status as one of the horror genre's earliest "Scream Queens." *King Kong* is number forty-one on the

American Film Institute's Top 100 Movies of All-Time, number twelve on their list of top thrillers, and the number twenty-four love story. As impressive as he is, the big hairy suitor at the top of the Empire State Building has to share some of the movie's success with his onscreen crush.

In her *Sun* article, Pauline Vaillant noted that Wray's mother Vina was with her daughter the whole time the production team was on the Shore. She says Vina Wray "kept a pretty sharp eye on Fay ... but she needn't have worried" because Fay was in love with someone back in California. John Monk Saunders (1897–1940) wrote the war picture *Wings,* which starred It-Girl Clara Bow and Charles "Buddy" Rogers, with Gary Cooper in a bit part. *Wings* had just been named Best Picture at the very first Academy Awards. He'd also scripted the first film to costar Wray and Cooper, *Legion of the Condemned* (1928), and it was on that picture the couple-to-be met. According to Vaillant, while she was working here on the Shore, Wray talked to Saunders on the phone every evening.

The twenty-year-old Wray, as described by an unnamed reporter for Salisbury's *Daily Times,* was small and slender, wholesomely beautiful, with soft, wavy hair, large gray-blue eyes, and a firm, delicate smile. Her voice was soft and low-pitched, "which is a part of her charm that film audiences are denied." In the interview, she told the journalist that she thought the Eastern Shore was "perfectly wonderful" and pointed out that what impressed her most was the "tranquility of the water and the quietude of the towns." Cooper verified he liked it here too but wanted to know "why don't you have more sunshine?"

For his first four years in the movie business, Gary Cooper showed up mostly in Westerns. His first major break came in that two-minute appearance in *Wings,* directed by William "Wild Bill" Wellman. Wellman, a hell-raising, "shoot up the town kind of fellow," later directed *Buffalo Bill,* starring Joel McCrea as the legendary leader of the world-famous Wild West Show, and *The Story of G.I. Joe*, which would make a star out of Robert Mitchum.

Cooper's first talkie was *The Virginian (1929)*, a romanticized western that helped solidify the image of the cinematic cowboy for decades to come. His star rose through the years of the Great Depression. In the 1940s, as war once again engulfed the world, Cooper portrayed heroic American figures in 1941's *Sgt. York*, one of the most decorated soldiers of the previous War to End All Wars, and baseball's inspirational "Iron Horse" Lou Gehrig in *Pride of the Yankees* in 1942. In 1952, he would play Marshall Will Kane in *High Noon*, number two on the American Film Institute's list of outstanding westerns, after John Wayne's *The Searchers* (1956). Cooper would win Best Actor Oscars for *Sgt. York* and *High Noon* and is still considered to be among the greatest movie stars of any generation.

Vaillant described Cooper, who was a few years older than Wray, as quiet, tall, and awkward. The first time the Harper family saw him, he was coming through their front door "wearing white duck pants six inches too short, a blue shirt open all the way down the front, and tennis shoes—and promptly hit his head on our best chandelier." The embryonic matinee idol spent much of his downtime "curled up in a chair reading a book, with his long legs dangling over the arms." He also took an early morning swim in Oak Creek every day. After his climb to the top, groups of girls would come to Pasadena Inn and ask to be assigned the room where Gary Cooper slept while making *The First Kiss*. "We gave them whatever room was vacant," Pauline Harper Vaillant, whose parents owned the Pasadena, later admitted. "I guess over the years every room in the inn was known as Gary Cooper's room."

Filming began in St. Michaels on May 28, 1928. It was the most exciting thing to happen there since the War of 1812. When word got out that *The First Kiss* filmmakers were working on the Eastern Shore, thousands of curious spectators came from miles around to get a peek. On the weekends there might have been as many as 2,500 onlookers. According to Pauline Vaillant, "They swarmed over here. You could scarcely get around for the sightseers' cars." Being a silent picture, if bystanders stayed out of camera range, they could be as noisy as they wanted.

Back in Royal Oak, "a temporary Beverly Hills," the owners and staff at the Pasadena Inn grew fond of their Tinseltown guests. Quiet and hardworking, "the movie crowd" enjoyed little time to partake in such activities as the tennis, boating, fishing, or shooting that were offered by their hosts. The man in charge, the director Rowland V. Lee, ran a tight ship. Everybody was expected to be out of bed by 6:30 a.m. One of the tasks assigned to Pauline's twin brother Paul was to march up and down the halls ringing a bell like a human alarm clock. Breakfast was at 7:00. Everyone had to be on set by 8:00. One of the inn's cottages was converted into a screening room, and everybody "without exception" was required to report there at 8:00 p.m. to look at the rushes—the raw, unedited footage filmed that day.

"And everybody in Talbot County wanted to have a party for the stars." Pauline Vaillant added. "They could have been out every night if Mr. Lee let them."

Toward the end of the shoot, Saunders came to visit Wray, and they got married by Reverend Edgar T. Read at Calvary Methodist Church (a precursor to St. Mark's United Methodist Church) in Easton on Friday, June 15, 1928. The bride wore her costume, "a sort of afternoon dress." Still in movie makeup and the oysterman overalls of his character, Gary Cooper acted as best man. The *Baltimore Sun* noted he resembled a "poor but honest bivalve snatcher." The director Lee "appeared in knickers and other appurtenances of harried genius, omitting only the folding chair and megaphone." Following the ceremony, the wedding party drove to St. Michaels, where the newlyweds took pictures on the footbridge that connects Cherry Street to Navy Point. Now called Honeymoon Bridge in the couple's honor, it is still a popular location for wedding photos. Then they celebrated aboard a skipjack anchored in the harbor. Afterward, Mr. and Mrs. Saunders spent a weekend honeymooning at the Pasadena Inn.

Long-term, the marriage was not a happy one. Three years after they divorced in 1939, Wray married another writer, Robert Riskin. Riskin was most noted for working on Frank Capra classics such as *It Happened One Night* and *Mr. Deeds Goes to Town*, the film that put Gary Cooper on top of the Hollywood heap. As chronicled in a 2019 memoir by their daughter Victoria, theirs was a loving and supportive relationship until Riskin died in 1955.

From 1953 to 1980, Wray acted in tons of TV shows, everything from *Alfred Hitchcock Presents* to *Wagon Train* to *Perry Mason*, and appeared in motherly roles in several youth-oriented features such as *Tammy and The Bachelor*. After her passing in 2004 at the age of 96, the lights of the Empire State Building were dimmed in her honor. Cooper died from cancer in 1961.

When filming of *The First Kiss* finished, Vaillant was one of the few people to see the unedited footage. "On the last night the company was at the Pasadena," she wrote in the *Baltimore Sun* in1973, "they showed the entire picture just as it had been made, and it was a wonderful film." Cast and crew rolled out of town on June 17, 1928, and the movie premiered at Easton's New Theatre (later renamed the Avalon) on August 20. "This week," reported the *Star Democrat*, "Talbot countians have received the movie treat of their lives." The theater booked nine showings of the film, three a day for three days, though there are reports that at least on the first day of screening, the theater sold out five shows.

Though the plot had been tinkered with, and many sailing scenes were cut, the local audience wasn't disappointed in the sequences shot in St. Michaels. What is sure to have taken some of the air out of the party was the fact that the scenes filmed at the courthouse, with all those local extras, were unusable. Dickson says the reason was bad film stock. Dawson says all that expensive lighting they'd brought in hadn't worked. Either way, the courtroom scenes needed to be reshot on a Hollywood set. A few weeks after the premiere, Lee forwarded the scrapped footage back to the Shore, and the New Theater ran it for four nights to appreciative moviegoers.

Moviegoers here might have liked *The First Kiss*, but most critics were unimpressed. The New York *Morning Telegraph* declared that the movie's single redeeming factor was the exquisite Chesapeake Bay photography. The reviewer also gave the lead actors back-handed compliments like "Gary Cooper does an awful lot of chest-heaving, but gives an all-around good characterization," and "Fay Wray photographs beautifully and acquits herself creditably, her tendency to over-emote notwithstanding." Closer to home, Louis Azrael, a columnist for the *Baltimore Daily Post*, started his review by writing that "the pleasant, patriotic thing would be to state that the film which was made in Maryland is a masterpiece; that the Maryland product leads the world. It would not, however, be the true thing."

Veteran Baltimore newspaperman Richard D. Steuart, who wrote under the pen name Carroll Dulaney, recommended the picture while also noting the Eastern Shore background scenery as being a highlight of the production. In discussing the plot, Dulaney put a regional spin on the drunkenness of a character by saying ol' Pap Talbot was "too fond of Talbot County corn—the bottled kind" and that when Pap drinks too much and dies, he is "gathered to that country where all Eastern Shoremen, wet or dry, go finally."

A surviving print of *The First Kiss* would be the Holy Grail to Eastern Shore film buffs. Even Robert Mitchum had an interest in finding a copy. A 1988 *Star Democrat* article about Bill Newnam, owner-operator of Maryland Airlines and twenty-year manager of Easton Airport/ Newnam Field, focuses on how he'd been shuttling the rich and famous to the Shore since the 1940s. Newnam met everybody from JFK and Richard Nixon to Elizabeth Taylor and Paul Newman. He was also friends with Mitchum when the movie star and his family lived in Trappe, and taught their oldest son to fly. He affirmed Mitchum called him once to report that while in Hollywood, he'd been putting out feelers to find a copy of *The First Kiss* but was told that the building where it had been stored burned down.

The Library of Congress estimates that due to the extremely flammable nature of the film stock or simple neglect, more than 8,000 silent films, about 75 percent of the total made, are among the lost.

The First Kiss is the one the Eastern Shore would, in our cinematic heart of hearts, most love to find.

Kevin Kline and Sissy Spacek, playing former high school
sweethearts, renew their acquaintance after fifteen years in *Violets
Are Blue*. The poignant romantic drama was shot on location
in Ocean City, Maryland. *(Columbia Pictures/Photofest)*

VIOLETS ARE BLUE
(1986)

Released by Columbia Pictures, *Violets Are Blue* explores themes of freedom, fidelity, and the universal consequences of choice. It's about the different kinds of love a person can feel. The triangle created by the characters played by its two stars, Sissy Spacek and Kevin Kline, and the wife of Kline's character is compelling and human.

Spacek plays Augusta "Gussie" Sawyer, an international photojournalist who grew up in the Maryland resort town of Ocean City, but who's seen too much since and yearns for the comfort of the familiar. Spacek first caught everyone's attention in Stephen King's *Carrie* and won an Academy Award for her portrayal of country music star Loretta Lynn in 1980's *Coal Miner's Daughter*. *Violets* was the third movie of hers released in 1986 after *'night Mother*, a drama costarring Anne Bancroft, and *Crimes of the Heart*, in which she costarred with Diane Keaton and Jessica Lange and won another Oscar nomination.

Kline was smack-dab in the midst of a star-making career run. He'd held his own with Meryl Streep in *Sophie's Choice* in 1982 and had been front and center in the terrific ensemble cast of the giant hit *The Big Chill* in 1983. After *Violets*, he would make the western *Silverado*, *Cry Freedom* with Denzel Washington, and *A Fish Called Wanda*, for which he won the Best Supporting Actor Oscar, a rarity for a comedy role. In *Violets*, Kline plays Henry Squire, editor of local newspaper the *Maryland Coast Dispatch*, and Gussie Sawyer's long-lost love.

Bonnie Bedelia, playing Ruth Squires, Henry's uber-patient wife and third wheel in this deal, was hot off her Golden Globe–nominated role as drag racer Shirley Muldowney in 1983's *Heart Like a Wheel*. Bedelia, aunt of McCauley Culkin and his six siblings, made her professional stage debut at nine and for five years was a teenage soap opera actress. She impressed in *They Shoot Horses Don't They?* in 1969 and in 1970 appeared in the comedy *Lovers and Other Strangers* with Bea Arthur. After *Violets Are Blue*, Bedelia was action-hero John McClane's estranged wife Holly in 1988's classic Bruce Willis Christmas film *Die Hard* and its 1990 sequel. She played a more pivotal role as Harrison Ford's wife in *Presumed Innocent*. She portrayed matriarch Camille Braverman in TV's acclaimed family dramedy, *Parenthood*, from 2010 to 2015.

Fourteen-year-old Jim Standiford of Baltimore landed his role as Henry and Ruth's son by responding to an open casting call. *Violets* is his only professional credit. John Kellogg played Gussie's dad Ralph, who works at Trimper's Rides on the Boardwalk and doles out fatherly guidance with quiet strength. Kellogg had been acting in movies since 1940, appeared unbilled as a fraternity boy in *The Pride of the Yankees* (1942) and as a pilot in *Thirty Seconds Over Tokyo*, the film where Robert Mitchum first turned heads. Kellogg has 142 credits to his career, four after filming *Violets Are Blue*.

The person most responsible for bringing the movie to both life and the Eastern Shore was Hollywood producer Marykay Powell.

Powell, born and raised in Baltimore, visited Ocean City growing up and had a nugget of an idea for a story she'd thought she might like to tell. Despite a limited budget of ten million dollars, "as low as you could go" at the time, Powell was the person who made sure the movie happened and happened here. She always felt it was important that the resort was "actually a character in the movie, not just a background," and fought to have the movie made on location.

After studying radio and television production at Baltimore Junior College, Powell landed a gig at WBAL Radio producing commercial spots and overseeing sports broadcasts for the Baltimore Orioles, Colts, Clippers, and Bullets. When the boss added music director to her job description, she got ink in *Billboard* magazine as the youngest music director of a 50,000-watt radio station in the USA "and the ONLY Girl!" From there she went to work in New York and transitioned from the radio to the record industry, where she impressed Metro-Goldwyn-Mayer CEO James Aubrey, who'd been brought in to save a rudderless and sinking corporate ship.

James Aubrey, nicknamed the Smiling Cobra, was such a Hollywood archetype he's been fictionalized in novels and films, including Jacqueline Susann's *The Love Machine*. Tall, thin, and good-looking, Aubrey was Ivy League–polished and sharp. He found his first niche in television programming, where his blue-collar–based "broads, bosoms, and fun" formula raked in ratings and profits and brought him significant influence and power. As the "world's No.1 purveyor of entertainment," his talent was targeting the lowbrow, and he brought such memorable shows to the small screen as *Gilligan's Island*, *The Beverly Hillbillies*, *The Andy Griffith Show*, *Mister Ed*, and *The Dick Van Dyke Show*.

In 1969, he was hired to save MGM from bankruptcy. Among his first decisions, Aubrey moved the corporate offices from New York to the studio's facilities in Culver City, California. He took Marykay Powell with him, and he commandeered Louis B. Mayer's old office. Once there, he closed whole departments, oversaw the sale of the studio's backlot to developers, and, most egregiously to fans, sold off the studio's historic collection of props and costumes.

He brought all current production to a standstill. He canceled twelve pictures in preproduction and clashed with filmmakers who resented his bloodbath tactics. For the next few years, Aubrey's MGM focused on turning out low-budget sci-fi, westerns, and exploitation flicks. His brutal managerial style, along with the profits from the MGM Grand Hotel in Las Vegas, put the studio back in the black. He resigned in 1973, saying his job was done.

Marykay Powell still had lots to do, though. Under Aubrey, she'd been promoted to unit publicist, where her job was to support individual movies with marketing and publicity. Much travel was involved, and it was in this assignment where she began "to get the hang" of on-set production, "its rigors as well as its delights."

With an expanding love of art films, Powell left the studio system to work for and promote the Los Angeles Film Festival, which was the largest of its kind. "In the movie capital of the world," she writes in a 2020 email, "it was devoured whole." One big wheel paying attention to the hype and hoopla of FILMEX was Ray Stark of Rastar Productions.

Stark was another notoriously successful Hollywood dealmaker. Calculating, witty, and massively influential, he started in showbiz as a literary agent, became a talent agent, and then an independent producer whose intellect, eye for talent, and legendary under-the-radar prowess in the game of industry politics gave his opinions undeniable sway and made him a force to be reckoned with. One day Powell got a call from Stark. He said, "I hear you're the girl

getting all this great publicity for all these TERRIBLE movies....
I'd like to talk with you."

Of his vast output during a six-decade career—he'd had a
hand in bringing more than 250 films to screen—Stark was most
noted for 1968's *Funny Girl*, the property that launched Barbra
Streisand's star. Based on the biography of the comedienne, singer,
and popular Ziegfeld Follies star Fanny Brice, who also happened
to be his mother-in-law, Stark decided to produce *Funny Girl* first
as a Broadway musical. It was his first play. He cast Streisand. It was
her first play too. And it was colossal, lasting 1,348 performances
and locking the film into the sure-thing category.

Powell was asked to join Rastar in 1976 as the vice president
overseeing publicity and marketing. The job was a huge opportunity
in many ways. Most important to Powell at the time, it provided
a regular paycheck. But Stark's reputation proceeded him. "One
friend who had experience with Ray told me, 'You won't last a
week . . . he's a monster!' I remember saying, 'Well, it will probably
take him a couple of weeks to fire me and he'll still have to pay
me, right?'" Except for a break to make some movies outside her
relationship with Rastar, Powell stayed almost twenty-eight years.

In her tenure with the company, a company she'd preside over
for a term, Rastar released many notable motion pictures, including
The Goodbye Girl, *The Electric Horseman*, and *Richard Pryor: Live
on the Sunset Strip*. Powell became a producer with *Violets Are Blue*.
Later, with Rastar and independently, she produced films such
as *Biloxi Blues*, *White Fang*, *Harriet the Spy*, and Harrison Ford's
Random Hearts, which was filmed around Washington, D.C. and
Baltimore. In 1993, Powell and Stark, along with two co-producers,
Thomas M. Hammel and Glenn Jordan, won an Emmy Award for
HBO's *Barbarians at the Gate*. Her final credit before retirement
was 2008's *The Curious Case of Benjamin Button*.

Powell's memories of vacationing in Ocean City as a teen stuck with her. She spoke with several potential screenwriters until she found Naomi Foner, a former member of the Children's Television Workshop who had been involved in the development of *Sesame Street* and *Electric Company*. Foner had written some television; an episode of *Secrets of Midland Heights* featuring a youthful Eastern Shore actress named Linda Hamilton was on her resume. *Violets Are Blue* would be her first script to make it to the big screen. Powell read some of her work and found she liked the writer's sensibilities. "She was a very sensitive woman," Powell said. "She understood what I was talking about." To Powell, the story was about people making choices. Foner understood that, and she got the job. She herself would later go on to produce films.

When Foner wrote *Violets,* she had two young kids. Their dad was film and TV director Stephen Gyllenhaal. The kids were named Maggie and Jake. Readers of this book may have heard of them.

Marykay Powell's "little movie" was not a box-office smash and was never expected to be. Reviews were mixed, but influential critics Gene Siskel and Roger Ebert gave *Violets Are Blue* two thumbs up. Ebert was enthusiastic in his appreciation of the grown-up take on the film's emotional themes. "*Violets Are Blue* establishes its events within a vivid sense of time and place. We get a real feel for the close-knit seaside community," Ebert wrote. "You meet the person you loved when you were seventeen, and now you are thirty-three, and a lot of your life's history has been written. And yet, as your eyes meet, your last kiss is as clear as yesterday."

Shot in and around St. Michaels, Maryland, family drama
Clara's Heart starred one of the world's most recognizable actresses,
Whoopi Goldberg, and served as the film debut for a then-unknown
major star on the rise, Neil Patrick Harris. *(Warner Bros./Photofest)*

CLARA'S HEART
(1988)

A screenwriter writes. An actor acts. A camera operator operates the camera. There's makeup, hair, and costume departments. A set designer. A prop manager. A stunt coordinator.

Many job titles in the movie business are self-explanatory and easy to wrap one's head around, but not all of them. The gaffer is the head electrician. The key grip supervises the other grips who do any physical work required on set, except for what falls under the domain of the gaffer. The best boy can be the right-hand man to either the gaffer or the key grip.

The director oversees a movie's artistic vision and the technical crews required to pull that vision off and is a key decision maker in the production of a film. The director directs.

And then there's the producer. A producer, of course, produces.

Among many credits and accomplishments, Marianne Moloney was the executive producer of *Clara's Heart*, a movie filmed in Talbot County in 1987. *Clara's Heart* starred Whoopi Goldberg and introduced audiences to Neil Patrick Harris.

In a 2020 e-mail interview, here's how Marianne Moloney describes her role: "A Producer conceives or identifies a story one wants to tell on screen . . . secures a Writer with whom the Producer develops the screenplay (narrative and characters) . . . secures the Director, whose vision will put the story on the screen, to commit to the screenplay . . . secures the financing to mount the production, hires the cast and crew, supervises the actual production (artistically and financially), as well as the post production (editing, scoring, sound mixing), and then sees the project through all distribution channels through which it is marketed and released."

We're not kidding when we say a producer produces.

Born in Brooklyn, New York, Moloney grew up on Long Island. After graduating from college and earning a master's degree at Columbia, her first job was at Charles Scribner's Sons publishers, where her responsibilities included the sale of subsidiary rights, the licensing of books to paperback publishers and book clubs, as well as to film, television, and stage producers.

With a stop at Crown Publishers after leaving Scribner's, Moloney moved on to Viking Press as subsidiary rights director. A few successful campaigns under her belt, she helped her editorial colleague Patricia Irving market an "over the transom" book titled *Ordinary People*, written by an agent-less newcomer named Judith Guest.

It was the first time in twenty-seven years they'd published an unsolicited manuscript. Despite a plot some critics would consider too much of a downer, mass market publishers loved what they read, and a spirited auction resulted in a "handsome price" for the rights to paperback publication. Movie rights were a tougher sell; that raw and tragic plot scared off a few potential buyers. Nevertheless, the book made it into the right hands, and next thing Moloney knew, she was in her boss's Madison Avenue office meeting with representatives from Robert Redford's production company.

Guest's fictional family drama served as Redford's directorial debut and was adapted for the screen by Alvin Sargent, the screenwriter of 1973's *Paper Moon* and 1977's *Julia* (for which he'd won his first Oscar). *Ordinary People* won four Academy Awards— Best Picture, Best Director, Best Adapted Screenplay, and Best Supporting Actor for Timothy Hutton. Nominated cast members Mary Tyler Moore and Judd Hirsch enjoyed whole new careers after the film struck a chord with critics and the public alike.

"Soon after," Moloney says, she moved from New York to L.A. Within a year, she left her position as a literary agent to become vice president for production at Universal Studios under the wing of studio head Ned Tanen. The first film Moloney worked on in her role as a studio executive was *Raggedy Man*, which starred Sissy Spacek and was directed by her husband Jack Fisk. Fisk would go on to direct his wife in *Violets Are Blue*. *Raggedy Man* costarred Eric Roberts and Sam Shepard, and it featured the film debut of Henry Thomas, who in the next year would become famous as the best friend of everyone's favorite lovable stranded alien, *E.T. the Extra-Terrestrial*.

It was during Moloney's next gig, as president of motion pictures at Mary Tyler Moore's MTM Enterprises, that her friend and colleague producer Martin Elfand (*Dog Day Afternoon, An Officer and a Gentleman*) asked her to read a script he was developing with playwright Mark Medoff from a novel by Joseph Olshan called *Clara's Heart*. It was the story of a family dealing with the trauma of losing a child. "Marty felt I might respond to the material," says Moloney, "and perhaps encourage MTM to partner with Warner Bros. in financing the film project. I remember sharing the script with MTM's Chairman Arthur Price, who proclaimed 'Moloney, this is no small movie! GO!'"

With most of the story taking place on the Eastern Shore, and with a solid community of film professionals based in the region, a location shoot was deemed necessary and affordable. "I was aware of the Eastern Shore," says Moloney, "because my dad collected duck decoys and sporting prints and maps, and the bay area was prominently featured in his collection. Also, I was a zealous teen equestrian and member of the U.S. Pony Club, so the Chincoteague ponies were in my ken too."

"We were fortunate to get Robert Mulligan as our director. His ability to realize a performance, particularly from our first-timer Neil, was extraordinary. But if you know his work with young actors — *To Kill a Mockingbird, Summer of '42,* and later, *The Man in the Moon,* where he gave Reese Witherspoon her start—this is no surprise!"

Moloney visited the Eastern Shore set for a few weeks during production and says she felt like part of a welcome invasion. "The place is gorgeous," she says, "so playing against the darkness of the family's narrative it's haunting." Mulligan and Elfand were there "24/7," along with cinematographer Freddie Francis. A two-time Academy Award winner, Francis had a career behind the camera going back to 1937. One of his most noted works is Martin Scorsese's 1991 *Cape Fear* remake, which featured cameos by the original picture's stars, Gregory Peck and Robert Mitchum.

With regard to her lead actor, Moloney says "Whoopi did it beautifully. Look at that moment in the film when she tells the young boy she too is leaving. He feels abandoned, by his parents and the one person he is close to, Clara. Betrayed . . . he calls her that 'N' word, a powerful moment from writer Medoff, and Whoopi embraces him, understanding where his anger comes from ... and forgives him. She captured it all in a simple gesture."

After *Clara's Heart*, Whoopi Goldberg won a Supporting Actress Oscar for *Ghost* in 1991, rocked a habit in 1992's *Sister Act*, and added more than 150 onscreen credits to her resume. She's hosted the daytime talk show *The View* since 2007 and is one of the most recognizable people on the planet.

The costars playing Bill and Leona Hart, grieving parents who have lost a child to Sudden Infant Death Syndrome, were Michael Ontkean and Kathleen Quinlan, and Moloney remembers them fondly. Ontkean had broken out as Officer Willie Gillis in the hit cop show *The Rookies*. He followed up *The Rookies* with the hockey movie *Slap Shot*, starring Paul Newman, which almost always lands at the top of Best Sports Movie lists. Quinlan made her professional debut in *American Graffiti*, was nominated for a Golden Globe for her work in *I Never Promised You a Rose Garden*, and would earn an Academy Award nomination for her role as Marilyn, the wife of Tom Hanks's astronaut Jim Lovell in *Apollo 13*. Since 1994, she has been the wife of actor Bruce Abbot, who from 1982 to 1989 was married to the Eastern Shore's own Linda Hamilton.

The revelation of *Clara's Heart* was Neil Patrick Harris. "I believe Neil was attending a theatre camp in New Mexico," says Moloney. "A tape of his work was sent to Marty and to me from Mark Medoff. I remember how smart and quick Neil was. He had an ability to be natural, as though he did not know a camera was watching. He traversed the comic and tragic moments with wisdom beyond his years and Bob Mulligan guided all of it.

"I can also tell you that my MTM colleague Steven Bochco asked me about Neil in connection with a series he was developing [called] *Doogie Howser*. We showed Steven some of our footage during our post-production at MTM ... and you know the rest."

Neil Patrick Harris found fame playing a teenage physician in *Doogie Howser, M.D.* (1989–1993), and though he worked consistently after the show's cancellation, it wasn't until he played a sex-and-drugs-driven version of himself in the 2004 stoner comedy *Harold & Kumar Go to White Castle* that he made another mark on pop culture. He then played womanizer Barney Stinson on *How I Met Your Mother* for seven seasons.

In the end, *Clara's Heart* wasn't a big hit, but no one involved ever thought it would be. The creators of the film were trying to tell a small story with deep affection about real people facing life-changing circumstances. The movie is sad, but not humorless, and touches real human emotions. Most of the film's success rests on the chemistry and capable acting shoulders of Goldberg and Neil Patrick Harris. After several iffy comedies underperformed prior to this film's release, Goldberg gives what more than a few critics called a stunning display of dramatic talent. Harris was noted for his impressive debut performance and in fact was nominated for a Best Supporting Actor Golden Globe.

Moloney produced several more films after *Clara's Heart* including the romance *Mr. Wonderful*, *A Soldier's Sweetheart*, based on the story "Sweetheart of Song Tra Bong" by National Book Award Winner Tim O' Brien in his semiautobiographical Viet Nam collection *The Things They Carried*, and *Out of the Ashes*, a biographical drama that starred Christine Lahti as Holocaust concentration camp survivor Gisella Perl.

When asked what she learned working on *Clara's Heart*, Moloney says it's the "power of words on both the page and the screen . . . a story's capacity to move people."

A screenwriter writes.

Richard Dreyfuss plays a psychiatrist who is trying to unlock the traumatic memories of Ben Faulkner, a young boy who has seen too much, in this murder mystery set in Easton, Maryland. *(Warner Bros. Pictures/Photofest)*

SILENT FALL
(1994)

In 1993, *Silent Fall*, a whodunit murder mystery with the tagline "A Savage Crime—A Silent Witness" came to Easton for a three-week location shoot.

Silent Fall was directed by Australian Bruce Beresford, a two-time Oscar nominee best known for *Tender Mercies* (1983) and *Driving Miss Daisy* (1989), and written by Akiva Goldsman, now a highly credited script-doctor, producer, and director who would write the Oscar-winning screenplay for 2001's *A Beautiful Mind*.

Starring Richard Dreyfuss, John Lithgow, and the Eastern Shore's own Linda Hamilton, *Silent Fall* also introduced to the screen, in his first and only film role, nine-year-old Ben Faulkner, and Liv Tyler, daughter of Aerosmith lead singer Steven Tyler and model Bebe Buell.

In *Silent Fall*, the relationship between Tim and Sylvie— found at the murder scene covered with blood and cowering in a closet— is at the core of the story. Reading for the role at age sixteen, Tyler had dabbled in modeling and was attending a private New York high school. She's quoted as saying to embody her first role, she found the emotions she needed from her belly and her involvement with the character.

Dreyfuss explained in interviews that he chose to do the film because he wanted to work with director Bruce Beresford, a two-time Oscar nominee, and because he liked the main character, a "serious fellow with a problem in his past." He said Beresford was a director who knew what he wanted but was open to suggestions. In the finished film, Beresford is most effective when using his creative focus to delve into the mysteries of autism and addressing the sensitivity of a fragile child's psyche. Beresford created a movie that captures the moody juxtaposition of Easton's tranquil leaf-strewn lawns and richly appointed country houses with dark family secrets.

Dreyfuss's character, retired after the death of a child in his care, is called in by the local lawman (the always watchable J. T. Walsh) to interact with Tim and help the boy unlock and share with the authorities what he saw at the crime scene. Dreyfuss's character reluctantly agrees. While he works on getting the traumatized child to open up to him, various suspects emerge. Unfortunately, by the time his character pieces the puzzle together, there isn't much left to surprise audiences. For most viewers, the solution to the murder mystery has been made all but obvious from the opening scenes.

Silent Fall was not received well by critics or film fans. Michael Wilmington of the *Chicago Tribune* suggested nature lovers try forgetting the actors onscreen and focusing on the trees behind them. Hal Hinson of the *Washington Post* confessed that despite being so predictable you'd almost swear you'd seen it before, *Silent Fall* manages to suck you in with "quiet seductiveness of atmosphere." Hinson also opined that though Dreyfuss was playing his character by rote, the reviewer was struck by Liv Tyler's presence, saying that she and her character's "haunted eyes" exhibited "a provocative sensuality." Even Dave Williams, the *Star-Democrat's* entertainment editor, couldn't find much to recommend. Rottentomatoes.com rates the movie at 22 percent with critics and at 39 percent in audience reviews.

The movie didn't make much of an impression at the box office either. In a year when *The Lion King*, *Forrest Gump*, and *True Lies* held the top box office positions, *Silent Fall* came in number 168 out of 259 movies released. With a budget of $30 million, *Silent Fall* grossed $3,180,674, half in its opening weekend.

No one's career seemed particularly damaged by the critical and financial failure of *Silent Fall*. Liv Tyler went on to perform in many high-profile roles including in *Armageddon*, *The Lord of the Rings* trilogy, and *The Incredible Hulk*. Lithgow would soon begin his five-season television run as an alien in 3rd *Rock from the Sun*, and his ensuing career has been vast, diverse, and heavy on awards. Since *Silent Fall*, her cinematic return to the Eastern Shore, Linda Hamilton worked in movies and on TV, mostly on her own terms, for another quarter century. In 1995, the very next year, Dreyfuss scored an Oscar for his performance in *Mr. Holland's Opus*.

Though the official premiere was held in Los Angeles, Morgan Creek Productions arranged a special screening of *Silent Fall* for the town of Easton at the Avalon Theatre on Thursday, October 22, 1994. Invited guests included Maryland Governor and Eastern Shoreman Harry Hughes and his wife Patricia, the movie's Ben Faulkner, now ten and in fifth grade, along with his parents and brother, and James Robinson, the CEO and president of Morgan Creek Productions. Robinson spent part of his childhood in Easton, and in his remarks that night lauded Talbot Countians for their hospitality and support. He called the Eastern Shore the "center of the universe" and with searchlights scanning the skies over the town and the Easton High School Band playing *Hooray for Hollywood*, for at least one evening, it felt like he may have been right.

Skittish bride Julia Roberts and smitten groom Richard Gere
pose with director Gary Marshall in one of the runaway hits of
1999, set in Berlin, Maryland—which was given a makeover and
dubbed *Hale* for its star turn. (*Paramount Pictures/Photofest*)

RUNAWAY BRIDE
(1999)

Julia Roberts wasn't the first *Runaway Bride*, and the 1999 follow-up to *Pretty Woman*, her smash rom-com hit with Richard Gere, wasn't the first motion picture to use that title.

1930's *Runaway Bride* was produced by RKO Radio Pictures and starred Mary Astor as a flapper socialite named, coincidently one assumes, Mary. Mary runs off to marry her caddish rich boyfriend Dick and then runs off again when she sees this Dick for what he really is. She meets the man of her dreams, takes on a fake identity, and gets caught up with gangsters and fake hospitals and all kinds of nonsense. The story is ludicrous in every way, but RKO was only in its second year of making movies. The studio wasn't yet the creative powerhouse behind such glory as *King Kong* and *Citizen Kane*, and hadn't yet made stars out of Tarzan, Astaire and Rogers, or Robert Mitchum.

In her career, Mary Astor (1906–1987) was in more than 100 films from 1921 through 1964. Unlike many of her silent-film peers, she was able to mature out of ingénue roles and transitioned to talkies with relative ease. Her talent and beauty afforded her a career that survived even the scandal of a nasty divorce and child-custody trial where her diary was leaked to the press. In 1941 she'd not only win a Best Supporting Actress Oscar for her role in *The Great Lie*, but she'd also star opposite Humphrey Bogart in *The Maltese Falcon*.

The plot of the *Runaway Bride* starring Gere and Roberts, one of the biggest stars in the world at the time, is nothing like the earlier version. In this one, Gere's character, New York newspaper columnist Ike Graham writes a story about Roberts' Maggie Carpenter, a small-town girl who has repeatedly left her grooms-to-be standing at the altar. When his readers take interest, Ike travels to quirky little Hale, Maryland—played by the Eastern Shore town of Berlin—to cover Maggie's impending fourth attempt at walking all the way down the aisle. Giving nothing away, it's fair to say true love wins out.

The movie had been in development for a decade or so. A wide range of screen personalities were reportedly attached to the project at various times including Sandra Bullock, Demi Moore, and Ellen DeGeneres as the "normal, but with a twist" country girl Maggie. Ben Affleck, Michael Douglas, and Harrison Ford were considered for the role of the smooth and jaded Ike. A version of the script that Gere liked landed on his desk and he said he'd do it if the producers could get Roberts. She'd read an earlier draft and passed, but at Gere's request took another look and agreed *Runaway Bride* could work for the two of them.

Together they contacted the trusted third leg of their trinity, *Pretty Woman*'s director Garry Marshall (1934–2016). The creator of *Happy Days*, *Laverne & Shirley* (which starred his sister Penny), and *Mork & Mindy*—Marshall had directed films that included *Young Doctors in Love* (1982), *The Flamingo Kid* (1984), and *Overboard* (1987), before putting Roberts and Gere together for

Pretty Woman. Even as Marshall was itching to work with the crowd-pleasing pair again, he also had been planning to take his wife Barbara on a long-promised vacation. Roberts and Gere convinced Barbara to let her husband "come play" with them instead, and the deal was sealed. "People have been trying to get them back together for nine years," producer Tom Rosenberg told the *LA Times*, "and suddenly it happened—it was all settled in a week."

Along with Roberts and Gere, *Runaway Bride* featured Joan Cusack as Maggie's best friend, Paul Dooley as her widowed dad, and Christopher Meloni as her matrimonially doomed current fiancé. Laurie Metcalfe has an uncredited role as baker Betty Trout and, as always, she's a scene-stealer. Sticking with what works, Marshall cast *Pretty Woman* actors, including Hector Elizondo and Larry Miller, in *Runaway Bride*, and as was his custom, put himself and family members into roles too. Marshall himself is the third baseman in the baseball game sequence. His daughter Kathleen is Cousin Cindy, his son's the clerk at the Atlantic Hotel, and his granddaughter, along with other children belonging to members of the cast and crew, attends the Hale Sunday School.

Toward the end of July 1999, as the film's release neared, promotion for *Runaway Bride* was pervasive. Garry Marshall appeared on everything from the morning news shows to the late-night talk shows. Julia Roberts showed up on Rosie O'Donnell's afternoon talk show and chatted about buying that year's Christmas presents in the shops of Berlin. *Entertainment Weekly, TV Guide,* and *People* were some of the magazines that ran cover stories. A gala Los Angeles premiere was held on Sunday, July 25. Roberts attended with her boyfriend Benjamin Bratt (*Law & Order, Miss Congeniality, Traffic*), and Gere with Cary Lowell (*Law & Order, License to Kill, Sleepless in Seattle*), whom he would marry and then battle in a headline-making divorce. In the audience were various studio chiefs, Garry Marshall and his wife Barbara; his sister, the actress and film director Penny Marshall (1943–2018), Roberts's brother Eric (*The Pope of Greenwich Village*, *Raggedy Man*, *Star 80*), and Henry Winkler (Fonzie from Marshall's *Happy Days*). Eric Clapton was there too. He had a song on the soundtrack, which included such on-the-nose tunes as *Ready to Run* by the Dixie Chicks, U2's *I Still Haven't Found What I'm Looking For*, and a Billy Joel cover of Lloyd Price's *Where Were You (on Our Wedding Day)?* Attendees were served soft crabs, crab cakes, and meatloaf under signs that read "Welcome to Hale, MD, Home of the Sweet Peach." The following day Gere participated in the time-honored Hollywood tradition of having his hand and footprints embedded in the concrete at Grauman's Chinese Theatre. In November, he would be named *People* magazine's Sexiest Man Alive.

The Eastern Shore staged its own premiere on July 29, the night before *Runaway Bride* opened nationwide. The Chamber of Commerce rented out a West Ocean City theater, and hosted three sold-out showings. Susan Taylor, the curator at Berlin's Taylor House Museum, says that when the first scene showing Berlin came up, "you could feel the whole theater gasp." Cheers went up whenever a recognizable face or place showed up onscreen After the first screening, everyone went back to town and had a luau celebration to match one of the wedding themes from the film. Perhaps because the movie didn't land with the box office or cultural impact of *Pretty Woman*, it's easy to forget how successful a film *Runaway Bride* turned out to be. It made more than $35 million in its first weekend. It was Roberts's biggest opening up to that time and still is Gere's biggest opening ever by far. *Runaway Bride* ended up grossing more than $300 million worldwide and continues to show up on lists as one of the romantic comedy genre's fan favorites.

Lovable scoundrels Owen Wilson and Vince Vaughn plot their next moves in *Wedding Crashers*, the talk of the town when it was filmed on location in St. Michaels, Maryland. *(New Line Cinema/Photofest)*

WEDDING CRASHERS

(2005)

Wedding Crasher Rule #4: No one goes home alone.

Raunchy and hilarious. Those seem to be the two words moviegoers use most when describing *Wedding Crashers*, the R-rated comedy starring Owen Wilson and Vince Vaughn as John Beckwith and Jeremy Grey, the uninvited merrymakers in the title.

The two leads first turned heads in a pair of 1996 indie films, *Bottle Rocket* for Wilson and *Swingers* for Vaughn, but since then had followed different career paths. Wilson showed up in a string of high-profile projects like *Armageddon*, *Shanghai Noon* with Jackie Chan, and *Meet the Fockers*, and was Oscar-nominated for co-writing 2001's *The Royal Tenenbaums*, while Vaughn struggled to find his footing after a number of missteps. He'd recently scored with *Old School*, *Dodgeball: A True Underdog Story*, and *Mr. & Mrs. Smith*, which opened the month before *Wedding Crashers*, but at the time of casting, Vaughn was by no means a sure bet. Decision makers weren't even certain the two actors' contrasting senses of humor and odd-couple chemistry would work either. The director, however, David Dobkin, wasn't one of those people. Dobkin, whose first credits were on videos for Tupac Shakur songs, had directed exactly two movies before being selected to helm *Wedding Crashers* —1998's *Clay Pigeons* with Vince Vaughn and Wilson's 2003 sequel to *Shanghai Noon, Shanghai Knights.*

Once their director was chosen and their stars were cast, producers had to fill the other important onscreen roles in the film. Rachel McAdams won the role of Claire Cleary, Wilson's romantic Achilles heel. In a breakout performance, Isla Fisher plays her dangerously sexy sister. The eternally-fun-to-watch Christopher Walken is their dad and the Secretary of the United States Treasury. Jane Seymour, most famous for her six-season run as *Dr. Quinn, Medicine Woman,* plays his hot-to-trot trophy wife. Keir O'Donnell, whose most prominent appearances up to then had been on an episode each of *Lost* and *8 Simple Rules,* was cast as the peculiar artist brother Todd Cleary, and billed ninth, Bradley Cooper is in full-on yuppie jackass mode as Claire's fiancé Sack.

Wedding Crashers came out on July 15, the same day as *Charlie and the Chocolate Factory* with Johnny Depp. *Charlie* was number one for two weeks, and then an unheard-of phenomenon happened. In its third week of release, *Wedding Crashers* found itself going from number two in ticket sales to the top spot.

That's what good word-of-mouth can do for a movie.

About the time it looked like this rowdy-little-flick-that-could was catching on, *Entertainment Weekly* magazine, which used to come out weekly, predicted that this "buzz-free, moderately budgeted farce has emerged as the vehicle that could just drive its stars to the upper reaches of the Hollywood A-List." Wilson, the bigger name at the time, was paid $10 million for his role as John Beckwith in *Wedding Crashers,* while Vaughn earned three million playing Jeremey Grey. The movie grossed $288,467,645.

Much of that haul was a payoff on the bet that the contrasting personalities and humor of the two leads—Wilson's laidback cool versus Vaughn's full-steam-ahead bluster—would win the day, but the rest of the cast contribute their share of funny to the proceedings. The turning point in the main characters' lives is when they crash the wedding of a daughter of the secretary of the treasury, William Cleary, and cross paths with the bride's sisters and bridesmaids, Claire and Gloria. John is taken in by the charms of Claire. He convinces Jeremy to bend the Wedding Crasher rules (Rule #22: You have the wedding and the reception to seal the deal. There's no overtime) and accept an invitation to join the eccentric Clearys on a weekend retreat to their estate on the Eastern Shore.

Character actor extraordinaire Christopher Walken plays Treasury Secretary Cleary and Jane Seymour (*Live and Let Die*, *Somewhere in Time*, *Dr. Quinn, Medicine Woman*) is his randy second wife Kathleen. Rachel McAdams snagged the coveted part as Claire Cleary before audiences saw her in 2004 *Mean Girls* and *The Notebook* breakout roles and, luckily for the filmmakers, before her price went up. McAdams took to the Chesapeake Bay lifestyle and trained for a sailing certification because her character was supposed to be an expert sailor. In the sailing scenes aboard the charter schooner *Woodwind II* out of Annapolis, McAdams took the helm for real. On the other hand, when Walken was at the wheel, an employee of the charter company knelt out of frame and steered the boat for *The Deer Hunter* Oscar winner.

Isla Fisher steals scene after scene as the younger sister and lovable maniac Gloria. Critic Pete Travers of *Rolling Stone* wrote that she conveyed "just the right notes of erotic dazzle and fatal-attraction menace." Before *Wedding Crashers*, Fisher had appeared in bit parts on American TV and film, but in her native Australia she was known as a teenage soap opera star and the author of two bestselling young adult romance novels. Around the same time *Wedding Crashers* was coming together, she became engaged to the British comedian Sacha Baron Cohen of Ali G and Borat fame. For her role as Gloria, Fisher won the 2006 MTV Movie Award for Best Breakthrough Performance and collected two Teen Choice Awards: one for Choice Breakout and one for Choice Hissy Fit.

In between games of off-camera backgammon and ping pong, Wilson and Vaughn worked on their characters and got to know each other better by taking the script and improvising new dialogue to try out once the cameras rolled. On top of the bawdy onscreen shenanigans, the banter between the two leads provides much of the comedy fans responded to, both in the movie's first run and in the years since. Most of the memorable lines belong to Vaughn's character. For quotability, it's hard to beat such Jeremy Grey go-tos as "A friend in need is a pest," "I'm a little too traumatized to have a scone," and "I got to get out of here, pronto. I got a stage five clinger. Stage five, virgin, clinger."

Vaughn doesn't get all the classic dialogue, though. It's Will Ferrell, who, after turning down the role Wilson accepted, shows up as Chazz Reinhold. Chazz, an aging "crasher," still living at his mom's and crashing funerals now instead of weddings who yells the immortal line, "Hey, Ma! Can we get some meatloaf?"

And Flip, Sack's overexuberant toady, yells out at one point: "Yeah! Crab cakes and football! That's what Maryland does!"

Debbi Dodson, director of tourism for Talbot County at the time, remembers that once the *Wedding Crashers* gears were set in motion, it was all-systems-go. She was surprised by how quickly the decision-making process went from identifying and submitting potential locations for the filmmakers' consideration to cameras rolling. Dodson was a primary coordinator when it came to communications between the *Crashers* filmmakers and local government, businesses, and community partners.

"The first callback," Dodson says, "was from the Director of the Maryland Film Commission Jack Gerbes letting me know St. Michaels was of great interest to the filmmakers. The next call was from New Line Cinema's location chief in California, followed by a call from the Location Manager Carol Flaisher. The following day, Flaisher's team arrived, and I met them at the Tidewater Inn where most of the film crew eventually stayed. Everything fell into place. We began locking down the lodging for everyone. Most of the A-List stayed at the Inn at Perry Cabin, but Vince and Owen preferred to stay in private homes. Carol Flaisher and the finance staff set up offices at the Tidewater. Shortly thereafter, the crews arrived and the following week the actors arrived."

Flaisher has been on many sets through the years, and she knows when something's clicking. "When the films are actually shooting, I'm usually on set all day every day," she says. "With *Wedding Crashers*, the script was pretty good, but these kids, they were on point every single time. They were great. We were laughing the whole time. That little girl, Isla Fisher, she killed me. Every time she came out her timing was right on. I fell in love with her in about one second. The scene on the deck at the house with the guys, we fell over each other laughing. The cute little dark-haired girl, Rachel McAdams, nobody knew who she was at the time and I've done two movies with her since. She was the cutest, the brightest, she worked hard, and she had that big smile and you just have to eat her up. Christopher Walken knocked us over. I mean the whole thing was great. And you just knew it. When you work on a show that you know is going to be a hit, it's really fun. I made a lot of everlasting friends on that show."

"This film was such a great experience for everyone," Dodson remembered in a 2020 email. "The residents and businesses were warm and welcoming, while the crew members, producers, directors, and actors made Talbot County their home for approximately six weeks. Owen and Vince enjoyed dining out at local restaurants. The outdoor dining space at the Tidewater Inn was always bustling in the evening with the crew and sometimes actors. They shopped, ate, and lived here as if they were home.

"Several members of the crew were musicians who loved going to Carpenter Street (Saloon, in St. Michaels) to play on open mic nights, and they always remembered to invite us. Most nights after work, we would spend an hour or two with everyone on the terrace of the Tidewater Inn. Vince and Owen often dined at Mason's. Owen could be seen around town walking his dog. Jayne Seymour, an artist herself, frequented the local art galleries and purchased several paintings. She enjoyed talking with artists about their work. Vince hosted a pool party at the Tidewater Inn that was a big hit with everyone."

Inarguably crowd-pleasing, the critical reception of *Wedding Crashers* was mixed. Roger Ebert called it all runway and no takeoff. Pete Travers of *Rolling Stone* said it was hot, rowdy fun. Anthony Lane from the *New Yorker* split the difference with a riff on a line from the movie: "Sometimes 10 percent of your brain is just enough."

Those that flat-out didn't like the movie were also divided: it was either too vulgar for them or they believed the filmmakers hedged their bets on salaciousness and wrapped things up with an overly sentimental, predictable Hollywood ending. Moviegoers didn't seem to pay much attention to criticism. *Wedding Crashers* finished 2005 in fifth place, one spot ahead of its debut-weekend competitor, *Charlie and the Chocolate Factory*.

In the eyes of some, *Wedding Crashers* hasn't aged well, but there's no doubt the movie retains many loyal fans and in 2020, sixteen years after the release of the original, word got out that a sequel was in development.

Because as decreed in Crashers Rule #115: Never walk away from a crasher in a funny jacket.

A bit adrift in their fictional lives, Matthew McConaughey and Sarah Jessica Parker sparkled together in the waterfront setting of Oxford, Maryland, in *Failure to Launch*. *(Paramount/Photofest)*

FAILURE TO LAUNCH

(2006)

Oxford, Maryland is a jewel of the Eastern Shore, a sailing and yachting haven with a history going back to our nation's beginnings. For the past fifty years or so, Oxford's population has remained between 600-700. That's about the same as the number of boat slips there. On any given day, there are probably more boats than cars, possibly more boats than people, in Oxford.

Like *The First Kiss* and *Runaway Bride*, *Failure to Launch* is a Paramount Pictures romance. It's the story of a thirty-five-year-old man who still lives with his parents and falls for the 'interventionist' they hire to trick him into standing on his own two feet. The movie's tagline is: "To Leave the Nest, Some Men Just Need a Little Push." Sarah Jessica Parker's character Paula provides that push to Matthew McConaughey's unwitting Peter Pan, Tripp. Things go sideways of course when true love, as it tends to do, intervenes in the proceedings.

Directed by Tom Dey, *Failure to Launch*'s supporting players include the esteemed Kathy Bates and football legend and TV announcer Terry Bradshaw as Tripp's mom and dad, Justin Bartha

363

and Bradley Cooper (in his first movie after *Wedding Crashers*) as Tripp's buddies, and Zooey Deschanel as Paula's quirky roommate. McConaughey's Tripp is a boat builder. Boats are important to the story, and the freedom of being on the water is a thematic undercurrent of the movie. So, when it comes to boats, as locations manager Carol Flaisher asked Christine Neff of the *Star Democrat* in 2005: "Where better to go than here?"

"When you're making a movie," Flaisher said in our 2020 interview, "most people on set don't have to speak to another human being outside the movie, but I deal with the outside world. When I do locations, my entire job is outside the movie. When I find a place they want to shoot, I'm the one who knocks on the door. A lot of people can't do that. I can talk to a tree, man. Then, when the films are shooting, you're on set eighteen hours sometimes. I always have a good team. we just organize the time."

Regarding how she approaches the Eastern Shore in her professional role, Flaisher is straightforward. "It's beautiful, it's lovely, it's wonderful, but I'm not *selling* the Eastern Shore to anybody. It would have to be a script that needs the Eastern Shore. For example, with *Failure to Launch*, they shot that mostly in Louisiana and Alabama. But they didn't want it to be a New Orleans film. They wanted it to be closer to D.C.; they wanted it to be the Chesapeake Bay and so you had to go to the Bay to get the Bay. You're not going to get the Bay in New Orleans. You're not. It's a different terrain. It's just a different place.

"The water's a big draw. These days, I do a lot of scouting in the air. We fly over and my eyeballs fall out! Who are these people who live, have lived, in these houses? The history! I think it's fascinating. And Oxford," she adds, "is gorgeous, just a really interesting little town. I have mixed feelings about the whole world knowing about it."

The Chesapeake Bay, the Eastern Shore, or Oxford are never mentioned in *Failure to Launch*, but there is a quick shot with a sign that reads Oxford Boatyard in the background. Though the story has a small-town feel, some scenes suggest the characters live in a much larger municipality than exists on this part of the Shore.

Filming took place during the first couple weeks of August 2005. Some early setups were captured at Bachelor Point and then the production moved over to the Mainstay restaurant, now Doc's Sunset Grille, where a scene of the two stars eating steamed crabs—she's banging the heck out of those shells with that mallet—was filmed. Then they went on to shoot scenes at the boatyard and at Cutts & Case Shipyard. "Oh my god," Carol Flaisher said, "the boat makers. It was terrific. There are some famous boatbuilders in Oxford, and we got to visit with them, talk to them, and see the boats. It was a knockout. Everybody was blown away. The boats were a big draw on that show."

During the shoot, the *Star Democrat*'s Neff reported that the crew—who came from all over the country—were enjoying themselves while in town and were going out nightly to local bars and restaurants and taking boat trips on the area's waterways. Despite some challenges of working in a rural area—like access, accommodations, and the lack of parking lots for storing equipment—the *Failure to Launch* cast and crew found the local people and area businesses fun to work with and very welcoming. "They're thrilled," Flaisher told Neff. "They're eating crabmeat every day."

The scenes captured here did not require many extras, so few locals were cast, but word got out that movie stars were in orbit. The locals weren't the only ones interested in the presence of celebrity. One day the Oxford Police Department were required to shoo away some out-of-town paparazzi. David Parkerson, skipper of the St. Michaels Water Taxi at the time, said that though McConaughey was considered a down-to-earth guy who fit in well with the locals, Parkerson's wife Leslie made sure he knew that if the sex symbol actor were to board his boat and Parkerson not call her, he needn't bother coming home.

Nonetheless, the stars were friendly with the people they interacted with. "He [McConaughey] was lovely," Flaisher remembered. "And she was very friendly. It was the first thing she did after *Sex in the City* hit, so the girls went nuts for Sarah Jessica Parker, not so much the men, but any group of girls who would come by would be happy. And you know, when she was walking back to her trailer or whatever, she took pictures with everybody and she would smile and be friendly. He stayed more to himself. But he was, I thought, very charming."

Tourism director Debbi Dodson was directly involved with the *Failure to Launch* filmmakers. Looking back, Dodson recalled a special day on set. "There's a shot in the movie of Matthew McConaughey lying in a boat and it's raining. The water was actually coming from Fire Department hoses. There were a zillion boats in the harbor and to minimize the number in the shot, some were covered with black cloth so they wouldn't show up. It was dusk but there were so many lights it looked like broad daylight.

"As the crewmembers were leaving for the day, Matthew McConaughey walked by a lady with a camera and two beautiful little nine- or ten-year-old girls in gorgeous little sundresses. The lady was obviously nervous and unsure whether she should approach the actor, when he stopped and asked if she'd like to take a picture of him with the girls. Afterwards he hung around and talked for a few minutes. I thought that was really nice and says a lot about how comfortable we can make visitors feel."

Carole Flaisher knows that feeling. "I tell you what it's all about," she says. "It's all about relationships. My best pal from all of this was Debbi Dodson. Let me tell you about Debbi. There would be no Eastern Shore film business without Debbi. She opened every door for me. I couldn't do anything without her. There are so many hidden-away things that you don't know, down these little roads that you don't even know leads to something or other. She knew everybody. She made things happen that we could not. She got prices down. She got people to cooperate. She got people who said no, no, no to say yes. Debbi was not only instrumental; she accomplished the most important parts and she always stayed in the shadows. She had a wonderful attitude. I never saw her unhappy. Frankly, I couldn't wait to get up the next day to deal with her. That's how much fun she was. She and I laughed and laughed. Not only do I love her, I couldn't have done it without her. And you can tell her I said so."

Flaisher continued. "Jack Gerbes, the director of the Maryland Film Office, was wonderful too. He really worked really hard for us. He wanted these movies made in Maryland, and he bent over backwards for us a lot. Dependability is the most important thing. And if Jack said he would do something; I didn't have to call him fifty times asking did you deal with it? I knew that he would. And Debbi, I didn't even have to finish the sentence.

"We all became good friends. We trusted and depended on each other, and we had each other's back for damn sure."

Regarding the film crews she's worked with over the years and the relationships she's built with her coworkers, Flaisher says, "you never know when one of them is going to come back as your producer. You don't know who they're gonna be, and then they turn out to be these wonderful, hard-working, successful, fabulous people. And so, the friends you made on the movie a million years ago that you haven't seen since, it doesn't matter. It's like a family. You're all cousins. We're all a bunch of cousins."

When it came out, *Failure to Launch* was not well reviewed, but audiences liked it and fans of the genre defend the film. Perhaps most notable for the star power of the leads (and Terry Bradshaw's character's "nude room"), *Failure to Launch* was nominated for Best Comedy at the 2007 People's Choice Awards and AARP Movies for Grownups Awards, and as Choice Chick Flick at the Teens Choice Awards. With a budget of $50 million, the film made almost half that back in its first weekend and grossed $130 million.

Gerbes extolled the area's hospitality toward filmmakers: "I can't speak highly enough about the beauty and the people of the Shore. They welcome these creative people into the community with open arms. They go out of their way to show the charms of the Eastern Shore. There's excitement about being immortalized on screen."

Dodson adds, "It's fun to see something you worked hard on succeed. Filmmaking encourages pride in the scenery of the area that we often take for granted. A lot of the actors and technical people talk about how lucky we are to live here."

And most of us fortunate enough to do so couldn't agree more.

ACKNOWLEDGMENTS

All plans for researching this book, like everything everywhere, changed in March 2020. Nevertheless, the show must always go on, so with the circumstances and challenges, as well as the opportunities, that the first year and a half of the COVID-19 pandemic presented, I'm particularly grateful to all those who took the time to speak with me for this project, including:

William Bankhead, for his gracious hospitality while spending a cold winter day on his Eastern Shore family farm warmly telling me firsthand stories of his mother and his aunt Tallulah. **Wayne Cannon** (1949-2021), the decades-long voice of Ocean City and its most enthusiastic cheerleader, for being so friendly, informative, and excited about the idea of this book. May he rest in peace and on the air. **Debbi Dodson**, the champion of Eastern Shore filmmaking, for being supportive from even before the beginning. I first interviewed Debbi over a decade ago for a magazine article I was writing. She was the best then and still is. This would have been a much shorter book without Debbi's efforts and successes as the longtime Director of Tourism for Talbot County. Her encouragement in the writing of this book has been indispensable. **Carol Flaisher,** for giving me colorful insight as to how the behind-the-scenes business of moviemaking functions, for taking time out of her busy schedule to talk with me a few times, and for being a living reminder that all this stuff is supposed to be fun. **Jack Gerbes**, the director of the Maryland Film Office, for his dedication to Maryland filmmaking and his red carpet enthusiasm for my vision as to what this book could be.

Linda Harrison for all the time she spent with me on the phone over the last couple years and for just being her awesome self. When I was a kid, *Planet of the Apes* was one of my favorite things ever. Still is. If I'd known then that I'd one day call "Nova" a friend, that would have been the only thing I would have ever talked about. **Patrick Henry**, artist extraordinaire and one of the nicest people you could ever meet, for providing a *Runaway Bride* story that hadn't been written about dozens of times before. **Tim Kearns** for talking candidly and with love about his dad Robert and the experiences of his family before, during, and after the filming of *Flash of Genius*. **William "Bill Mac" McAllister** (1928-2020) and his son **William "Sandy" McAllister** for sharing their memories of their family's friendship with Robert and Dorothy Mitchum and their children. The three of us talked in person in late 2019 and I remember leaving Bill McAllister's house thinking I might be on to something good with the concept of this book. R.I.P, Bill Mac, I know you will be missed by many.

Petrine Mitchum for helping me make sure I had her family's story straight and for some extremely encouraging feedback after reading the chapter I wrote about her mom and dad, feedback that helped me confirm I was on the right track. **Marianne Moloney** for sharing her incredible life and career stories with me and being my firsthand source for everything *Clara's Heart*. **David Parkerson** for being my man in St. Michaels and one of the most knowledgeable and friendliest guys around, as well as the **Parkerson family** in general for always having my back. **Marykay Powell**, another filmmaking insider with an exciting and consequential career who provided me with so much backstage insight regarding Hollywood and the making of *Violets are Blue*. **Emmi Shockley**

for enthusiastically talking to me about her hometown of Ocean City, her experiences playing the quintessential resort town crush in *Ping Pong Summer*, and her goals both in front of and behind the camera. I can't wait to see what's in store for you and look forward to your future successes.

Unable to visit all the museums and locations I'd planned to prior to COVID, I especially appreciate the help provided by **Becky Riti**, the librarian of the Maryland Room at the Talbot County Free Library in Easton and **Susan Taylor** of the Calvin B. Taylor House Museum in Berlin. These dedicated ladies and the historical resources they oversee are Eastern Shore treasures.

I'm grateful to my wonderful editor **Susan Carini**, a movie fan as well as an advisor and organizer beyond compare, who helped me work the kinks out and made sure this book wasn't a hodgepodge of trivia, mixed-up grammar, and puzzling Eastern Shore syntax. Susan's efforts made this a better book than it ever could have been without her.

I'd especially like to thank Secant Publishing's **Ron Sauder** for not only nurturing *Starlight by the Bushel* from seed to harvest to market, but for giving me the opportunity to spend my time during a global pandemic being both entertained and productive. This is our book, Ron, and I cannot thank you enough for believing in me and the viability of this, our book.

And finally, thanks to everyone who has encouraged and supported my writing efforts over the years. Ya'll are the greatest of friends and always will be.

BIBLIOGRAPHY

THE WHIP

Books

Brady, William A. *Showman*. Philadelphia: Curtis Publishing Company, 1936.

Rhodes, Harry C. *Queenstown: The Social History of a Small American Town*. London, UK: Queen Anne Press, 1981.

Newspaper Articles

"Camera Battery Films Realistic Railroad Wreck Near Queenstown." *Centreville Observer*. January 6, 1917.

Tinee, Mae. "It's No Mystery—But You'll Like June Elvidge." *Chicago Tribune*. April 19, 1917.

Internet Sources

Arthur Lloyd. The Music Hall and Theatre History Site Dedicated to Arthur Lloyd, 1839–1904. http://www.arthurlloyd.co.uk/DruryLane/TheWhip.htm.

Grost, Mike. "The Films of Maurice Tourneur." http://mikegrost.com/mtour.htm.

International Boxing Hall of Fame. "William A. Brady."

ibhof.com/pages/about/inductees/nonparticipant/brady.html.

Snow, Richard F. "American Characters: William A. Brady." *American Heritage*. American Heritage.com. April/May 1980. https://www.americanheritage.com/william-brady.

ON LOCATION: BERLIN

Books

Taylor, Susan. *Images of America: Berlin*. Mount Pleasant: Arcadia Publishing, 2007.

Internet Sources

Bayside Gazette. "Berlin: The First 150 Years." https://baysideoc.com/berlin-the-first-150-years/.

Calvin B. Taylor House Museum. taylorhousemuseum.org.

Maryland Film Office. http://marylandfilm.org/Town of Berlin, Maryland. berlinmd.gov.

Welcome to Berlin. berlinmainstreet.com.

ROBERT MITCHUM

Books
Charles River Editors. *American Legends: The Life of Robert Mitchum.* CreateSpace Independent Publishing Platform, 2001.

Love, Damien. *Robert Mitchum: Solid, Dad, Crazy.* London, UK: B. T. Batsford, 2002.

Roberts, Jerry, Editor. *Mitchum: In His Own Words.* Montclair, NJ: Proscenium Publishers, 2000.

Server, Lee. *Robert Mitchum: Baby, I Don't Care.* New York: St. Martin's Press, 2001.

Newspaper Articles
Champlin, Charles. "Mitchum: Hollywood's Enduring Bad Boy." *Los Angeles Times.* July 2, 1997.

Rasmussen, Fred. "Maryland Was Home to Tough-Guy Actor." *Baltimore Sun.* July 20, 1997.

Thomas, Bob. "Life in Maryland Is to Mitchum's Liking." *Evening Sun* (Baltimore, MD). December 6, 1960.

Magazines, Promotional Material
Albright, David. "The Man Who Dared to Sue." *Photoplay.* January 1956.

Chappell, Helen. "Robert Mitchum Slept Here." *Tidewater Times.* January 2013.

Crust, Kevin. "On His 100th Birthday, Here's to Legendary Hollywood Tough Guy Robert Mitchum." *Los Angeles Times.* August 4, 2017.

Davidson, Bill. "The Many Moods of Robert Mitchum." *Saturday Evening Post.* January 1, 1962.

Lewis, Grover. "Robert Mitchum: The Last Celluloid Desperado." *Rolling Stone.* March 15, 1973.

Internet Sources
Ebert, Roger. Robert Mitchum: "One of the Greatest Movie Stars was Rin Tin Tin. It Can't Be Too Much of a Trick." Rogerebert.com. October 10, 1993. https://www.rogerebert.com/interviews/robert-mitchum-one-of-the-greatest-movie-stars-was-rin-tin-tin-it-cant-be-too-much-of-a-trick.

McNulty, Anne. "The Two Sides of Former Trappe Resident Robert Mitchum." Whatsupmag.com. February 21, 2007. https://whatsupmag.com/culture/the-two-sides-of-former-trappe-resident-robert-mitchum/.

Seymore, James W., Jr. "Rough, Tough and Rowdy Robert Mitchum." People.com. February 14, 1983. https://people.com/archive/cover-story-rough-tough-and-rowdy-robert-mitchum-vol-19-no-6/.

Ward, Robert. "Robert Mitchum Was Mr. Bad Taste and Trouble Himself." Thedailybeast.com. July 19, 2014; updated March 10, 2020. https://www.thedailybeast.com/the-stacks-mr-bad-taste-and-trouble-himself-robert-mitchum.

LINDA HARRISON

Books

Dunne, John Gregory. *The Studio*. New York: Vintage Books, 1998.

Heston, Charlton. *In the Arena*. New York: Simon & Schuster, 1995.

Heston, Charlton and Jean-Pierre Isbouts. *Charlton Heston's Hollywood: 50 Years in American Film*. New York: GT Publishing Corporation, 1998.

Pendreigh, Brian. *The Legend of the Planet of the Apes or How Hollywood Turned Darwin Upside Down*. Clerkenwell, London, UK: Pan Macmillan, 2001.

Rinzler, J. W. *The Making of the Planet of the Apes*. New York: HarperCollins, 2018.

Russo, Joe, Larry Landsman, and Edward Gross. *Planet of the Apes Revisited: The Behind-the-Scenes Story of the Classic Science Fiction Saga*. New York: St. Martin's Press, 2001.

Newspaper Articles

Crockett, Sandra. "A Cinderella Homecoming." *Baltimore Sun*. February 23, 1992.

Wilkes, Paul. "Linda Harrison: Maryland Beauty." *Baltimore Sun/Sun Magazine*. August 25, 1968.

Magazines

Cinefantastique 2, no. 2 (1972): 17-37

Winogura, Dale. "Dialogues on Apes, Apes, and More Apes."

Internet Sources

The Forbidden Zone: Planet of the Apes. theforbidden-zone.com

Hunter's Planet of the Apes Archives. pota.goatley.com

Video

Behind the Planet of the Apes. Directed by Kevin Burns and David Comtois. Los Angeles: Twentieth Century Fox Film Corporation, 1998.

LINDA HAMILTON

Books

Shay, Don and Duncan, Jody. *The Making of Terminator 2*. New York: Spectra, 1991.

Newspaper Articles

"Area Girl Appears in Movie." *Daily Times* (Salisbury, MD). October 24, 1984.

Fleming, Dick. "Shore Native Is TV Series Star." *Daily Times* (Salisbury, MD). September 20, 1987.

Harris, Harry. "Linda Hamilton." *Kingsport Times-News*. January 16, 1981.

"Salisburian Linda Hamilton Is Emmy Nominee." *Daily Times* (Salisbury, MD). August 4, 1989.

Magazines

Bradshaw, Paul. "Back to the Future." *Total Film* 209, October, 2019.

Internet Sources

Buchanan, Kyle. "Linda Hamilton Fled Hollywood, but 'Terminator' Still Found Her." *New York Times*. nytimes.com. September 3, 2019. https://www.nytimes.com/2019/09/03/movies/linda-hamilton-terminator.html

CNN Larry King Live Interview with Linda Hamilton. https://transcripts.cnn.com/show/lkl/date/2005-10-14/segment/01

"*Depression Takes Its Toll.*" *Linda Hamilton on the Oprah Winfrey Show*. https://www.oprah.com/spirit/depression-takes-its-toll/all

Floorwalker, Mike. "Why Linda Hamilton Didn't Want To Watch Terminator: Dark Fate." Looper.com. February 19, 2020.

Kit, Borys. "Linda Hamilton Set to Return to 'Terminator' Franchise." *Hollywood Reporter*. hollywoodreporter.com. September 19, 2017. https://www.hollywoodreporter.com/heat-vision/linda-hamilton-set-return-terminator-franchise-1040948.

Linda Hamilton Monologue – Saturday Night Live. https://www.youtube.com/watch?v=NHNRiRun_cI

McLeavy, Alex. "Sarah Connor Doesn't Thrash." film.avclub.com. February 13, 2020. https://www.hollywoodreporter.com/heat-vision/linda-hamilton-set-return-terminator-franchise-1040948.

"What the Hell Happened to Linda Hamilton?" lebeauleblog.com. June 15, 2014. https://lebeauleblog.com/2014/06/15/what-the-hell-happened-to-linda-hamilton/.

White, Adam. "Linda Hamilton: 'Everyone's terrified of James Cameron. I'm not.'" indepndent.co.uk. October 21, 2019. https://www.independent.co.uk/arts-entertainment/films/features/linda-hamilton-interview-terminator-dark-fate-james-cameron-sarah-connor-release-date-a9165636.html

TALLULAH BANKHEAD

Books

Bankhead, Tallulah. *Tallulah: My Autobiography*. Rev ed. Jackson: University Press of Mississippi, 2004.

Bradshaw, Jon. *Dreams That Money Can Buy: The Tragic Life of Libby Holman*. New York: William Morrow and Company, 1985.

Bret, David. *Tallulah Bankhead: A Scandalous Life*. London: Robson Books, 1998.

Flamini, Roland. *Scarlett, Rhett, and a Cast of Thousands: The Filming of Gone with the Wind*. New York: Macmillan Publishing Company, 1975.

Gottlieb, Robert. *Lives and Letters*. New York: Farrar, Straus, and Giroux, 2011.

Herrmann, Dorothy. *With Malice Toward All*. New York: G. P. Putnam's Sons, 1982.

Israel, Lee. *Miss Tallulah Bankhead*. New York: Dell Publishing Company, 1972.

Lang, Rocky, Barbara Hall, and Peter Bogdanovich. *Letters from Hollywood: Inside the Private World of Classic American Moviemaking*. New York: Abrams Books, 2019.

Lobenthal, Joel. *Tallulah! The Life and Times of a Leading Lady*. Rev. ed. New York: HarperCollins Publishers, 2008.

Madsen, Axel. *The Sewing Circle: Hollywood's Greatest Secret: Female Stars Who Loved Other Women*. New York: Birch Lane Press, 1995.

Rawls, Eugenia. *Tallulah: A Memory*. Birmingham: UAB Press, 1979.

Newspaper Articles

Shaffer, Rosalind. "New Tallulah Bankhead Seen in Second Hollywood Visit." *Arizona Republic*. October 31, 1943.

Thompson, William. "In Life, a Love of 'Excess' in Death, a Lasting Allure." *Baltimore Sun*. December 12, 1993.

"262-Acre Estate Given to Easter Seal Society. *News Journal* (Wilmington, DE). February 22, 1954.

Magazines

"The Little Foxes: Tallulah Bankhead Has Her First U.S. Hit." *Life*. March 6, 1939.

"One Woman Show." *Time*. November 22, 1948.

Internet Sources

Biscuit: For Women Who Won't Pick a Side. "Bi 40s screen queens—Part 1: Tallulah Bankhead ('I'm ambisextrous, dahling!')." www.thisisbiscuit.co.uk. October 24, 2014. http://www.thisisbiscuit.co.uk/bisexual-40s-screen-queens-part-1-tallulah-bankhead-im-ambisextrous-dahling/.

Encyclopedia of Alabama. encyclopediaofalabama.org.

Gill, Brendan. "Making a Noise in the World—I." *New Yorker.* newyorker.com. September 29, 1972. https://www.newyorker.com/magazine/1972/10/07/making-a-noise-in-the-world-i.

Gottlieb, Robert. "Dah-ling, The Strange Case of Tallulah Bankhead." *New Yorker.* newyorker.com. May 8, 2005. https://www.newyorker.com/magazine/2005/05/16/dah-ling.

St. Paul's, Kent. stpaulkent.org.

Tallulah Bankhead: A Passionate Life. tallulahbankhead.weebly.com.

Williams, Tennessee. "A Tribute from Tennessee Williams to 'Heroic Tallulah Bankhead.'" *New York Times.* nytimes.com. March 4, 1956. https://archive.nytimes.com/www.nytimes.com/books/00/12/31/specials/williams-bankhead.html.

ON LOCATION: EASTON

Books

Fujiwara, Chris. *Jacques Tourneur: The Cinema of Nightfall.* Jefferson, NC: McFarland & Company, 1998.

Ingraham, Prentiss. *Land of Legendary Lore: Sketches of Romance and Reality on the Eastern Shore of the Chesapeake.* Charleston: Nabu Press, 2013.

Newspaper Articles

"Cowboy Actor Joel McCrea Dies at 84." *Los Angeles Times.* October 21, 1990.

Gardner, R. H. "Easton-Area Folk Turn Out for 'Hit The Deck' Premiere." *Baltimore Sun.* February 26, 1955.

Harrington, Norman. "The Movie Almost No One Remembers." *Banner* (Easton, MD). April 4, 1975.

Howell, Peter. "Ann Miller Brought Glamour to Easton in '55." *Star Democrat* (Easton, MD). January 30, 2004.

Kathman, Harold. "Living Happily Ever After: Joe David Brown." *Star Democrat* (Easton, MD). April 21, 1950.

"Highlights of Brown's 'Stars In My Crown.'" *Star Democrat* (Easton, MD). April 21, 1950.

La Prade, Joy. "The Avalon Theatre. Easton Landmark Celebrates a Milestone." *Star Democrat* (Easton, MD). October 15, 2006.

"Mayor Thanks Ann Miller For Appearance Here." *Star-Democrat.* (Easton, MD) March 4, 1955.

"MGM's 'Hit the Deck' Has World Premiere in Easton." *Star-Democrat.* (Easton, MD) March 4, 1955.

"MGM's Production 'Hit the Deck' Has Premiere Here." *Star Democrat* (Easton, MD). February 26, 1955.

"Town Honors Author on Day of Premiere." *Star Democrat* (Easton, MD). April 28, 1950.

Williams, Dave. "Hurry and Wait." *Star Democrat* (Easton, MD). October 17, 1993.

—. "Moviegoers Will Find Little Action, no Sex in Movie at Avalon." *Star Democrat* (Easton, MD). October 27, 1994.

Magazines
Dawson, James. "Talbot County Goes to the Movies." *Tidewater Times*, June 2016.

Internet Sources
Absher, Frank. "Junkin Was in the Right Place at the Right Time." St Louis Media History Foundation. stlmediahistory.org. https://www.stlmediahistory.org/index.php/Radio/RadioArticles/junkin-was-in-the-right-place-at-the-right-time1.

Avalon Foundation. avalonfoundation.org

Chennault, Nicholas. "Stars in My Crown." thegreatwesternmovies.com. May 16, 2014. http://thegreatwesternmovies.com/2014/05/16/stars-crown/.

Easton, Maryland. eastonmd.org.

Hill, Charlie. "Biography of Prentiss Ingraham." Mississippi Writers and Musicians. mswritersandmusicians.com/mississippi-writers/colonel-prentiss-ingraham.

"Ingraham, Prentiss." The House of Beadle and Adams and Its Dime and Nickel Novels: The Story of a Vanished Literature. A Project of the Northern Illinois University Libraries.ulib.niu.edu/badndp/ingraham_prentiss.html.

Sanchez-Saavedra, E. M. "Col. Prentiss Ingraham, Adventurer, Novelist and Buffalo Bill's Publicity Man." Yesterday's Papers.. January 10, 2012. http://john-adcock.blogspot.com/2012/01/col-prentiss-ingraham-1809-1860.html.

Slater, Tom. "Corinne Griffith." *Women Film Pioneers Project*, ed. Jane Gaines, Radha Vatsal, and Monica Dall'Asta. New York: Columbia University Libraries, 2013.

https://wfpp.columbia.edu/pioneer/ccp-corinne-griffith/.

Talbot County, Maryland. talbotcountymd.gov.

Tidewater Inn. Tidewaterinn.com.

HARRIET TUBMAN
Books
Bradford, Sarah. *Harriet Tubman: The Moses of Her People.* New York: Dover Publications. 2004.

Clinton, Catherine. *Harriet Tubman: The Road to Freedom.* New York: Little, Brown and Company, 2005.

Dunbar, Erica Armstrong. *She Came to Slay: The Life and Times of Harriet Tubman.* New York: Simon & Schuster, 2019.

Humez, Jean M. *Harriet Tubman: The Life and the Life Stories.* Madison: University of Wisconsin Press, 2003.

Larson, Kate Clifford. *Bound for the Promised Land: Harriet Tubman, Portrait of an American Hero.* New York: Ballantine Books, 2004.

Newspaper Articles

Finseth, Ian. "Douglass and the Legacy of Mount Misery." *Baltimore Sun.* August 20, 2006.

Opilo, Emily. "Tubman, Douglass Statues Make Debut at State House." *Baltimore Sun.* February 11, 2020.

Internet Sources

Bhatti, Umber. "'Harriet': The Real-Life Inspirations behind the Characters." *Hollywood Reporter.* hollywoodreporter.com. December 23, 2019. https://www.hollywoodreporter.com/news/true-story-harriet-how-accurate-are-characters-1253182.

Frederick Douglass. frederickdouglassbirthplace.org.

Gasca, Noel. "Harriet Tubman and Frederick Douglass Statues Unveiled at Maryland State House." NPR. npr.org. February 12, 2020. https://www.npr.org/local/305/2020/02/12/805279006/harriet-tubman-and-frederick-douglass-statues-unveiled-at-maryland-state-house

Greenburg, Evan. "Inside the Creation of the Tubman and Douglass Statues at the Maryland State House." *Baltimore Magazine.* baltimoremagazine.com. February 26, 2020. https://www.baltimoremagazine.com/section/community/inside-the-creation-of-the-tubman-and-douglass-statues-at-the-maryland-state-house/.

Maryland State Archives. msa.maryland.gov.

National Park Service: Harriet Tubman Underground Railroad. nps.gov/hatu.

Stiehm, Jamie. "Parallel Lives from the Eastern Shore." *New York Times.* opinionator.blogs.nytimes.come. June 24, 2011. https://opinionator.blogs.nytimes.com/2011/06/24/parallel-lives-from-the-eastern-shore/.

Harriet Tubman. harriettubman.com.

Harriet Tubman Underground Railroad Byway. harriettubmanbyway.org.

ANNIE OAKLEY

Books

The Autobiography of Annie Oakley. Greenville, OH: Darke County Historical Society, 2006.

Kasper, Shirl. *Annie Oakley*. Norman: University of Oklahoma Press, 1992.

McMurtry, Larry. *The Colonel and Little Missie*. New York: Simon & Schuster, 2005.

Musser, Charles. *Thomas A. Edison and His Kinetographic Motion Pictures*. New Brunswick, NJ: Rutgers University Press, 1995.

Riley, Glenda. *The Life and Legacy of Annie Oakley*. New ed. Norman, OK: University of Oklahoma Press, 2002.

Robbins, Marilyn, editor. *Personal Pages from Annie Oakley & Frank Butler*. Greenville, OH: Darke County Historical Society, 2006.

Swartout, Annie Fern. *Missie: Life and Times of Annie Oakley*. Greenville, OH: Coachwhip Productions, 2013.

Newspaper Articles

Dean, Gail. "Oakley Memorabilia Shared at Fest." *Star Democrat* (Easton, MD). August 11, 2010.

Lieber, Leslie. "Annie, Watch Your Pigtails!" *Baltimore Sun*. June 10, 1956.

Moore, Dick. "Annie Oakley House for Sale." *Daily Times* (Salisbury, MD). January 14, 1982.

Oakley, Annie. "Every Woman Should Learn to Shoot." *Baltimore Sun*. October 28, 1923.

Poole, Gray Johnson. "A Long-Neglected Heroine." *Evening Sun* (Baltimore, MD). July 30, 1946.

Rasmussen, Frederick N. "Annie Oakley Lived on the Eastern Shore." *Baltimore Sun*. May 23, 2010.

Wharton, Carol. "Echo of Annie Oakley." *Baltimore Sun*. June 16, 1946.

Magazines, Promotional Material

The Academy Foundation Presents a 50th Anniversary Screening of *Annie Get Your Gun* featuring Miles Kreuger. Program. 2000.

Annie Oakley of Darke County: Little Miss Sure Shot. Darke County Historical Society. Greenville's Garst Museum.

Internet Sources

American Experience: "Annie Oakley Becomes a Movie Star." *PBS*. pbs.org. https://www.pbs.org/wgbh/americanexperience/features/oakley-star/.

The Annie Oakley Center Foundation. annieoakleycenterfoundation.com.

Asleson, Robyn. "Faster than a Speeding Bullet: Thomas Alva Edison Shoots Annie Oakley." The National Portrait Gallery, *Smithsonian Institution*. npg.si.edu. https://npg.si.edu/es/node/7189.

Bowden, Denny. "Annie Oakley was Almost Crushed to Death Near Daytona Beach." *Florida History Network*. floridahistorynetwork.com. Undated. http://www.floridahistorynetwork.com/blog---annie-oakley-was-nearly-crushed-to-death-near-daytona-beach.html.

Caroline County Historical Society. choptankriverheritage.org.

Eisenberg, Susan Dormady. "On the Trail of Annie Oakley in Cambridge, Maryland." *Huffington Post*. Huff.post.com. November 10, 2010. https://www.huffpost.com/entry/on-the-trail-of-annie-oak_b_781040.

Koenig, Helmut. "West Orange, N.J., the Original 'Hollywood.'" *Chicago Tribune*. chicagotribune.com. January 8, 1989. https://www.chicagotribune.com/news/ct-xpm-1989-01-08-8902230599-story.html.

Myers, Caron. "Buffalo Bill Derailed in Davidson County." *Our State*. ourstate.com. October 2011. https://www.ourstate.com/buffalo-bill-wild-west-show/.

Oklahoma Historical Society. okhistory.org.

Righthand, Jess. "How Annie Oakley, 'Princess of the West.' Preserved Her Ladylike Reputation." *Smithsonian Magazine*. smithsonianmag.com. August 11, 2010. https://www.smithsonianmag.com/history/how-annie-oakley-princess-of-the-west-preserved-her-ladylike-reputation-55701906/.

ROBERT KEARNS

Newspaper Articles

"Announce Sale of Cheston-on-Wye." *News Journal* (Wilmington, DE) March 29, 1930.

Klein, Alec Matthew. "Millions of Dollars Can't Wipe Away Pain." *Baltimore Sun*. March 26, 1995.

Maki, Greg. "Two Picks for Film Fest Have Local Ties." *Star Democrat* (Easton, MD). August 21, 2008.

—. "Hollywood Western Will Premiere at Fest." *Star Democrat* (Easton, MD). September 9, 2008.

—. "Film Festival Opens to Rave Reviews." *Star Democrat* (Easton, MD). September 21, 2008.

"Inventor Wins $11.3 Million from Chrysler in Wiper Case." *Californian* (Salinas, CA). June 12, 1992.

McCauley, Mary Carole. "Family's Heritage." *Baltimore Sun*. November 30, 2014.

"Robert Kearns, Inventor of Intermittent Wipers Who Battled Car Companies, Dies." *Star Democrat* (Easton, MD). February 27, 2005.

Standish, Frederick. "Patents, Autos and the Courts." *Fort Worth Star-Telegram*. November 18, 1990.

Tabler, Dan. "Andrus, 'Boy Wonder of Wall Street' Dies at 101." *Star Democrat* (Easton, MD). November 22, 1989.

—. "The Long Life of an Extraordinary Man." *Record Observer*. (Centreville, MD). September 2, 2010.

Internet Sources

Benedetti, Marti. "Kearns Shows Flashes of Genius, Years of Turmoil." *Auto Week*. autoweek.com. September 28, 2008. https://www.autoweek.com/news/a2046496/kearns-shows-flashes-genius-years-turmoil/.

Crockett, Zachary. "The Epic, Decades-long Battle between Ford and a Small-time Inventor." *The Hustle*. thehustle.co. September 2, 2019. https://thehustle.co/windshield-wiper-inventor-robert-kearns/

Dennis Kearns. Dennis-kearns.com.

"Greg Kinnear Has 'Flash of Genius' in New Movie." *NPR*. npr.org. September 28, 2008.

Johnson, Reed. "The Cantankerous Man behind the Wipers." *Los Angeles Times*. Latimes.com. October 3, 2008. https://www.latimes.com/archives/la-xpm-2008-oct-03-et-kearns3-story.html.

"Lauren Graham has emotional meeting with Kearns family on 'Flash of Genius.'" Gilmore Girls. Gilmoregirls.org. September 22, 2007. http://www.gilmoregirls.org/forum/index.php?PHPSESSID=h9rtvv97arhh1tvviuaen2lgh5&topic=8435.msg381312#msg381312

Seabrook, John. "The Flash of Genius." *New Yorker*. newyorker.com. January 3, 1993. https://www.newyorker.com/magazine/1993/01/11/the-flash-of-genius.

"Windshield Wipers Invented In 'Flash of Genius.'" *NPR*. npr.org. October 3, 2008. https://www.npr.org/templates/story/story.php?storyId=95344135.

MISTY OF CHINCOTEAGUE

Books

Amrhein, John, Jr. *The Hidden Galleon*. Kitty Hawk, NC: New Maritima Press, 2007.

Henry, Marguerite. *Misty of Chincoteague*. Chicago: Rand McNally & Company, 1947.

—. *A Pictorial Life Story of Misty*. Chicago: Rand McNally & Company, 1976.

Mariner, Kirk. *Once upon an Island: The History of Chincoteague*. Onancock, VA: Miona Publications, 2010.

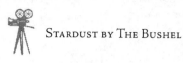
Newspaper Articles

Burroughs, Betty. "The Legend Lingers." *Morning News* (Wilmington, DE). October 28, 1972.

"Chincoteague Gets Set for Premiere of 'Misty.'" *Daily Times* (Salisbury, MD). June 13, 1961.

Henry, Marguerite. "A Closed Door Opened by a Providential Wind." *Chicago Tribune.* November 10, 1963.

Hillinger, Charles. "Horse Lovers 'Dear Abby': Life Is a Fast Track for Author." *Los Angeles Times.* November 11, 1979.

Lansberg, William R. "Author of Misty." *Star-Gazette* (Elmira, NY). April 1, 1962.

Layton, Bob. "Famous Story of Misty Put on Film." *Daily Times* (Salisbury, MD). December 1, 1960.

Loring, Kay. "Author Henry, Like Readers, Charmed by Her Animals." *Chicago Tribune.* April 11, 1962.

"'Misty' Author Gone, But Not Forgotten." *Chincoteague Beachcomber.* July 23, 1999.

"'Misty' Filming To Start Monday." *Daily Times* (Salisbury, MD). August 19, 1960.

"'Misty of Chincoteague' Is Being Made into Movie." *Baltimore Sun.* September 14, 1960.

"Misty of Chincoteague Is Living Proof of her Legend." Morning News (Wilmington, DE). August 23, 1972.

"Misty of Chincoteague, Storybook Pony, Is Dead." *Baltimore Sun.* October 17, 1972.

Mooar, Brian. "'Misty' Author Marguerite Henry Dies at Age 95." *Washington Post.* November 27, 1997.

Moore, Dick. "Background Given on 'Misty' Story." *Daily Times* (Salisbury, MD). June 19, 1983.

Perry, Helen J. "Author Waits Expectantly for Famed 'Misty's' First Foal." *News Journal* (Wilmington, DE). March 17, 1960.

Rasmussen, Fred. "'Misty of Chincoteague' Tale Gallops On." *Baltimore Sun.* December 28, 1997.

Reppert, Ralph. "Chincoteague's Ponies in a Movie." *Baltimore Sun.* November 6, 1960.

Saunders, Mark. "Misty's Mystique." *Daily Times* (Salisbury, MD). July 21, 1996.

"Special Carnival Whoops It Up for Film Company Shooting 'Misty.'" *Daily Times* (Salisbury, MD). August 29, 1960.

Stump, Brice. "Chincoteague Pony Is Subject of Book, Film." *Daily Times* (Salisbury, MD). July 6, 2004.

—. "Book and Movie about Misty Changed the Island." *Chincoteague Beachcomber*. July 22, 2006.

Williams, Douglas. "He Came to Sell Batteries and Stayed." *Northwest Herald* (Woodstock, IL). June 22, 1987.

Internet Sources

Amrhein, John. "Mystery Solved: Assateague Island's Wild Ponies Have Spanish Origins." *Horsetalk*. horsetalk.co.nz. July 27, 2015. https://www.horsetalk.co.nz/2015/07/27/mystery-solved-assateague-islands-wild-ponies-spanish-origins/.

"Chesapeake History: The Ash Wednesday Storm of 1962." *PropTalk*. proptalk.com. https://www.proptalk.com/ash-wednesday-storm-1962.

Chincoteague Chamer of Commerce and Certified Visitor Center. chincoteaguechamber.com.

Chincoteague Island, Virginia. chincoteague.com.

Chincoteague Volunteer Fire Department. https://www.cvfc3.com.

The Hidden Galleon. thehiddengalleon.com.

Hugo, Kristen. "Inside the Famous Chincoteague Pony Swim." *National Geographic*. Nationalgeographic.com. August 1, 2016. https://www.nationalgeographic.com/animals/article/chincoteague-famous-pony-swim-horses.

International Museum of the Horse. imh.org.

McGraw, Eliza. "The True Story of Misty of Chincoteague, the Pony Who Stared Down a Nor'easter." *Smithsonian Magazine*. smithsonianmag.com. October 26, 2018. https://www.smithsonianmag.com/history/real-misty-chincoteague-once-stared-down-barrel-storm-180970557/.

The Misty of Chincoteague Foundation. mistyofchincoteague.org.

Misty's Heaven. The official website for Misty's family. mistysheaven.com.

Museum of Chincoteague Island. chincoteaguemuseum.com.

National Park Service. nps.gov.

Staton, John W. "Most Quaint Island on Virginia Coast: Chincoteague One of Virginia's Most Interesting Spots." *Times* (Richmond, VA). January 11, 1903.

The Countryside Transformed: The Railroad and the Eastern Shore of Virginia, 1870–1935. http://eshore.iath.virginia.edu.

http://eshore.iath.virginia.edu/node/1858.

ON LOCATION: ST. MICHAELS

Newspaper Articles

Goad, Meredith. "Newnam Still Shuttles Rich, Famous to Shore." *Star Democrat* (Easton, MD). January 12, 1988.

Griffith, Jean. "Baltimore Clippers and Thomas Kemp of St. Michaels." *Star Democrat* (Easton, MD). May 18, 2012.

Howell, Peter. "Whoopi Back in Dramatic Groove." *Star Democrat* (Easton, MD). October 9, 1988.

—. "Whoopi's Film Opens in Easton." *Star Democrat* (Easton, MD). October 9, 1988.

Layburn, Jennifer. "Pasadena Inn and the Harpers: One Is Synonymous with the Other." *Star Democrat* (Easton, MD). March 3, 1995.

Mills, Eric. "Movie Premieres in Easton Oct. 7." *Star Democrat* (Easton, MD). August 23, 1988.

Scheuerman, Jane. "Extra, Extra, Talbot Goes Hollywood . . ." *Star Democrat* (Easton, MD). October 29, 1987.

Internet Sources

Chesapeake Bay Maritime Museum. cbmm.org

Experience St. Michaels. stmichaelsmd.com.

Flaisher, Carol. "I Wanted to Be a Movie Star." *ByGeorge: Stories of Georgetown.* georgetowndcblog.com. August 8, 2019.

Goldstein, Steve. "A Conversation with Carol Flaisher." *Location Managers Guild International.* locationmanagers.org (reprinted from *Bethesda Magazine* March/April 2017). https://locationmanagers.org/conversation-carol-flaisher/.

Inn at Perry Cabin. innatperrycabin.com.

Killham, Nina. "D.C.'s Liaison to La-La Land." *Washington Post.* washingtonpost.com. May 24, 1987. https://www.washingtonpost.com/archive/lifestyle/style/1987/05/24/dcs-liaison-to-la-la-land/9904dd0b-e567-4d74-b0a5-d786dc2eae68/.

The Oaks. the-oaks.com.

Saints Peter & Paul Parish & School. ssppeaston.org.

St. Michaels, Maryland. Business Association. stmichaelsmd.org

Taylor, Peter Lane. "Welcome to the New Hamptons (Crabs and Politics Included)." *Forbes.* forbes.com. July 12, 2017. https://www.forbes.com/sites/petertaylor/2017/07/12/welcome-to-the-new-hamptons-crabs-and-russian-politics-included/?sh=1229e8481a7d.

Worrall, Simon. "Clipper Ship Owners Made Millions. Others Paid the Price." *National Geographic*. nationalgeographic.com. August 31, 2018. https://www.nationalgeographic.com/science/article/news-clipper-ship-opium-trade-gold-rush.

https://www.historichotels.org/us/hotels-resorts/inn-at-perry-cabin/history.php

JAMES M. CAIN AND FILM NOIR
Books
Cain, James M. *Three of a Kind*. New York: Alfred A. Knopf, 1944.

Charles River Editors. *American Legends: The Life of Barbara Stanwyck*. CreateSpace Independent Publishing Platform, 2001.

Hoopes, Ray. *Cain: The Biography of James M. Cain*. New York: Holt, Rinehart and Winston, 1982.

—. *60 Years of Journalism by James M. Cain*. Popular Press, 1985.

Madden, David. *The Voice of James M. Cain*. Washington: Rowman & Littlefield Publishing Group, 2020.

Newspaper Articles
Birnbaum, Stuart. "The James M. Cain Revival." *LA Weekly*. Los Angeles, CA. October 2, 1980.

Bode, Carl. "Let's Lift a Glass to James M. Cain." *Baltimore Sun*. June 25, 1978.

Dorsey, John. "The Writer Never Gives Up." *Baltimore Sun*. March 29, 1970.

Hoopes, Roy. "Cain: The Maryland Years." *Baltimore Sun/Sun Magazine*. October 4, 1981.

—. "The Early Cain." *Baltimore Sun. Sun Magazine*. September 27, 1981.

Warren, Tim. "James M. Cain Exhibit at Pratt Recalls His Impact on American Literature and Culture." *Baltimore Sun*. August 16, 1992.

Journals
Zinsser, David. "James M. Cain: The Art of Fiction, LXIX." *Paris Review* no. 73 (1978): 117-38.

Internet Sources
Als, Hilton. "This Woman's Work: James M. Cain on the Grass Widow." *New Yorker*. newyorker.com. March 21, 2011. https://www.newyorker.com/magazine/2011/03/28/this-womans-work.

Anthony, Scott. "A Film to Remember: 'Double Indemnity' (1944)." *Medium*. medium.com. February 12, 2019. https://medium.com/@sadissinger/a-film-to-remember-double-indemnity-1944-e3a1eab9dcb5.

Churchill, Sarah. "Rereading *Mildred Pierce* by James M. Cain." *The Guardian.* theguardian.com. June 24, 2011. https://www.theguardian.com/books/2011/jun/24/mildred-pierce-sarah-churchwell-rereading.

Dissette, James. "Op-Ed: When Is Washington College Going to Show Love for James M. Cain." *Chestertown Spy.* chestertownspy.org. May 29, 2015. https://chestertownspy.org/2015/05/29/op-ed-when-is-washington-college-going-to-show-the-love-for-james-m-cain/.

Healey, David. Delmarva Accents: Delmarvese Is a Language unto Its Own." *Healey Ink.* davidhealeyauthor.com. May 2, 2017. https://davidhealeyauthor.com/2017/05/02/delmarva-accents-delmarvese-is-a-language-unto-its-own/.

Hendon, Ann. "Remembering American Mercury Writer James M. Cain." americanmercury.org. October 27, 2010.

https://theamericanmercury.org/2010/10/remembering-american-mercury-writer-james-m-cain/

Lippman, Laura. "Laura Lippman on James M. Cain's Transgressive Noir: Crime Fiction's Most Reluctant Icon." *Crime Reads.* crimereads.com. March 7, 2018. https://crimereads.com/laura-lippman-on-james-m-cains-transgressive-noir/.

—. "Raising Cain to Higher Levels of Recognition." *Baltimore Sun.* baltimoresun.com. March 3, 1994. https://www.baltimoresun.com/news/bs-xpm-1994-03-03-1994062153-story.html.

Murphy, Dwyer. "The Wit, Wisdom, and Noirs of James M. Cain." *Crime Reads.* crimereads.com. July 1, 2019.

"Prince of Darkness." *The Guardian.* theguardian.com. April 12, 2001. https://www.theguardian.com/film/2001/apr/13/features.

Washington College. washcoll.edu.

EDNA FERBER AND THE JAMES ADAMS FLOATING THEATRE

Books

Ferber, Edna. *A Peculiar Treasure.* New York: Doubleday & Company, 1938; rev. eds., 1939, 1960.

Gillespie, C. Richard. *The James Adams Floating Theatre.* Centreville, MD: Tidewater Publishers, 1991.

Meade, Marion. *Bobbed Hair and Bathtub Gin: Writers Running Wild in the Twenties.* New York: Random House, 2004.

Newspaper Articles

"'Show Boat' Is Owned Here." *Star Democrat* (Easton, MD). September 27, 1935.

Walsh, Winifred Walsh. "Tracing the Voyages of the Floating Theatre." *Baltimore Evening Sun*. July 16, 1991.

Woollcott, Alexander. "Edna Ferber's 'Show Boat' Is to Become a Musical Comedy." *Baltimore Sun*. November 28, 1926.

Internet Sources

Erickson, Mark St. John. "James Adams Floating Theatre Packed the Waterfront on the Chesapeake Bay." *Daily Press*. dailypress.com. October 3, 2014. https://www.dailypress. com/history/dp-nws-chesapeake-bay-showboat-20141003-story.html.

Fryar, Jack E., Jr. "James Adams' Floating Theater, a.k.a. The Showboat." *Jack's Ramblings*. jefpublications.wordpress.com. https://jefpublications.wordpress. com/carolina-chronicles-stories-from-four-centuries-of-north-carolina-history/ james-adams-floating-theater-a-k-a-the-showboat/.

James Adams Floating Theatre. floatingtheatre.org.

Livie, Kate. "The James Adams Floating Theatre." *Capturing the Chesapeake*. katelivie.com. April 16, 2014. https://katelivie.com/beautifulswimmers/ the-james-adams-floating-theatre.

Simpson, Bland. *James Adams Floating Theatre Provided a Big Show on the Sounds. Our State: Celebrating North Carolina*. ourstate.com. July 2, 2014. https://www.ourstate.com/ show-boat/.

LUCILLE FLETCHER AND DOUGLASS WALLOP

Books

Lass, A. H., Earle L. McGill, and Donald Axelrod. *Plays From Radio*. New York: Houghton Mifflin Company, 1948.

Newspaper Articles

Bready, James H. "Lucille Fletcher: The Play's Her Thing." *Baltimore Sun*. August 22, 1976.

—. "On Books and Authors." *Baltimore Sun*. April 1, 1973.

"Brinkley to Kick Off Celebration of Wallop's Works." *Star Democrat* (Easton, MD). April 30, 1986.

"Community Players Visit Author of Their New Play." *Daily Times* (Salisbury, MD). October 17, 1976.

Corddry, Mary. "Lucille Fletcher, Broadway Playwright, Lives Quiet Life on Eastern Shore." *Baltimore Sun*. March 22, 1972.

Devine, John. "Novelist Fletcher Loves Shore for Its Haunted Houses." *Star Democrat* (Easton, MD). November 2, 1990.

Emory, Pat. "Kent Folks Providing 'Atmosphere' for Film." *Star Democrat* (Easton, MD). July 12, 1984.

—. "'Space' Filming Delayed." *Star Democrat* (Easton, MD). June 29, 1984.

Hoopes, Roy. "Washington College Honors Douglas Wallop." *Star Democrat* (Easton, MD). April 18, 1986.

Howell, Peter. "She Was a Lady in the True Sense of the Word." *Star Democrat* (Easton, MD). October 6, 2000.

Lippman, Laura. "Out of Left Field." *Baltimore Sun*. April 3, 2000.

"Longtime Owners Plan to Sell Legendary Somerset Landmark." *Daily Times* (Salisbury, MD). January 13, 2002.

"Lucille Fletcher, Mystery Writer, Playwright, Dies at Age 88 in PA; Former Oxford Resident." *Star Democrat* (Easton, MD). September 7, 2000.

McCormick, Martha. *Lucille Fletcher Tells How 2-Author Household Thrives*. Star Democrat (Easton, MD). March 25, 1983.

McCulley, Jeff. "Wallop, 65, Dies at D.C. Hospital; Wrote 13 Novels." *Star Democrat* (Easton, MD). April 4, 1985.

Mills, Eric. "The Shore's First Lady of Suspense." *Star Democrat* (Easton, MD). August 5, 1988.

Myres, Karen. "Doug Wallop Talks Baseball, Sailing and His New Novel." *Star Democrat* (Easton, MD). January 23, 1981.

"Novel Features Hotel Patterned After One in Princess Anne." *Daily Times* (Salisbury, MD). June 13, 1953.

Wahls, Robert. "Footlights: Thriller-Diller Playwright." *Daily News* (New York, NY). March 5, 1972.

Wooten, Orlando. "Resort Hotel Fire Loss May Reach Half-Million." *Daily Times* (Salisbury, MD). December 15, 1969.

Internet Sources

Barnes, Bart. "*Damn Yankees'* Novelist Douglas Wallop, 64." *Washington Post*. washingtonpost.com. April 4, 1985.

"Lucille Fletcher: Radio's First Queen of Screams." *The Dagger of the Mind — Online Journal of Mystery, Suspense and Horror in Theatre, Radio, and Live Television*. October 27, 2009.

https://web.archive.org/web/20091027132313/http://geocities.com/Vienna/Stage/1045/Features/Fletcher.html.

"NASA—Wallops Island —60 Years of Exploration." *NASA*. nasa.gov. https://www.nasa.gov/vision/earth/everydaylife/wallops_60th.html.

"The Sophie Kerr Legacy." *Washington College*. washcoll.edu. https://www.washcoll.edu/academic_departments/english/sophie-kerr-legacy/index.php.

Sterling, Christopher H. "Sorry, Wrong Number ('Suspense') (May 25, 1943)." *Library of Congress*. loc.gov. https://www.loc.gov/static/programs/national-recording-preservation-board/documents/SorryWrongNumber.pdf.

ON LOCATION: DELMARVA AND OCEAN CITY

Books

Corddry, Mary. *City on the Sand: Ocean City, Maryland, and the People Who Built It*. Atglen, PA: Schiffer Publishing, 2011.

Jones, Elias. *New Revised History of Dorchester County, Maryland*. Centreville, MD: Tidewater Publishers, 1966.

Martin, Mary L., and Nathanial Wolfgang Price. *Greetings from Ocean City, Maryland*. Atglen, PA: Schiffer Publishing, 2007.

Rogner, Bud. *Tales of Delmarva and Other Places*. Bloomington, IN: Writers Club Press, 2002.

Newspaper Articles

"As an Actor—Her Pet Is a Regular Bear." *Evening Journal* (Wilmington, DE). October 27, 1915.

"Bay Island Declines." *Daily Press* (Newport News, VA). March 13, 1998.

Canforna, Susan. "Resort Hail 'Violets' Premiere." *Daily Times* (Salisbury, MD). April 14, 1986.

Childers, Stacie. "'MI:3' Filming Starts in Va." *Daily Times* (Salisbury, MD). October 2, 2005.

Cormier, Ryan. "Top Dog." *News Journal* (Wilmington, DE). July 28, 2019.

Dean, Gail. "The 'Golden Girl' Launched Her Career from Cambridge." *Star Democrat* (Easton, MD). May 21, 1986.

Diem, Jay. "Chesapeake Bay Bridge-Tunnel Stars in Latest 'Mission Impossible' Film." *Daily Times* (Salisbury, MD). May 20, 2006.

Groves, Seli. "Dale Midkiff: Finding Man inside the Image." Tribune (Coshocton, OH). April 16, 1989.

Holland, Liz. "Salisbury-Born Actor Says Dual Childhood Lifestyle Was Advantage." *Daily Times* (Salisbury, MD). April 28, 1989.

Kaltenbach, Chris. "The New Faces of 'Ping Pong Summer.'" *Baltimore Sun*. June 6, 2014.

Ladd, Jen. "'Ping Pong Summer': Being Male. Middle Class, and White." Baltimore Sun/City Paper. May 7, 2014.

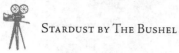

Lewis, Emory. "Bill Hinnant, 42: Actor Originated Role of Snoopy." *The Record* (Hackensack New Jersey). March 3, 1978.

"Movie People Make Good Neighbors in Ocean City." *Star Democrat* (Easton, MD). August 2, 1984.

"Native of Shore to Play Elvis." *Daily Times* (Salisbury, MD). February 6, 1988.

Oliver, Myrna. "Ray Stark, 88: Hollywood Legend, Insider Produced 'Funny Girl,' Other Classic Films." *Los Angeles Times*. January 18, 2004.

—. "William Alland; Movie Producer, Actor." *Los Angeles Times*. November 13, 1997.

Stump, Brice. "Golden Girl." *Daily Times* (Salisbury, MD). May 25, 2003.

Thomas, Bob. "New 'Trainer' Perks Ailing MGM Lion." *Honolulu Star-Bulletin*. March 25, 1971.

Thomson, David. "An obituary from Xanadu." *Guardian* (London, England). November 25, 1997.

Welsh, Jim. "A Conversation with Actor Dale Midkiff." *Daily Times* (Salisbury, MD). May 21, 1989.

Wolf, William. "Bill Hinnant, 42: of Chincoteague, Portrays Snoopy in an Off-Broadway Show Based on 'Peanuts.'" *The Baltimore Sun* (Baltimore, MD). June 25, 1967.

Wootten, Orlando. "Chincoteague Brothers Are Show Biz Successes." *Daily Times* (Salisbury, MD). September 17, 1972.

Internet Sources
Baila, Morgan. "An Ode to the Best Character in 'Once upon a Time… in Hollywood.'" *Refinery29*. Refinery29.com. July 30, 2019. https://www.refinery29.com/en-us/2019/07/239248/brandy-brad-pitt-once-upon-a-time-in-hollywood-pit-bull-character.

Bradley, Laura. "Once upon a Time … in Hollywood's Real Hero Is a Hungry, Hungry Pit Bull." *Vanity Fair*. vanityfair.com. July 26, 2019. https://www.vanityfair.com/hollywood/2019/07/once-upon-a-time-in-hollywood-dog-brandy-ending.

Chaney, Jen. "'Ping Pong Summer' Showcases an Ocean City That Hasn't Changed Much Since 1985." *Washington Post*. washingtonpost.com. June 5, 2014. https://www.washingtonpost.com/lifestyle/style/ping-pong-summer-showcases-an-ocean-city-that-hasnt-changed-much-since-1985/2014/06/05/2a52991a-ea6e-11e3-9f5c-9075d5508f0a_story.html.

Cormier, Ryan. "25 'Dead Poets Society' in Delaware Facts." Delaware Online. delawareonline.com. April 3, 2014. https://www.delawareonline.com/story/pulpculture/2014/04/03/dead-poets-society-delaware-anniversary/7252149/.

Delaware Red Pitbulls. delawareredpitbulls.com.

Emmi Shockley. emmishockley.com.

The Everett Theatre. everetttheatre.com.

Fermaglich, Kirsten. "Bea Arthur." *Jewish Women's Archive.* Jwa.org. https://jwa.org/people/arthur-bea.

Goss, Scott. "Delaware's most famous person is . . ." *Delaware Online.* delawareonline.com. April 25, 2018. https://www.delawareonline.com/story/entertainment/2018/04/25/delaware-most-famous-person/535454002/.

The Greater Ocean City, Maryland Chamber of Commerce. oceancity.org.

Haider, Arwa. "The 'Golden Girls': The most treasured TV show Ever." *BBC.* bbc.com. April 1, 2020. https://www.bbc.com/culture/article/20200401-the-golden-girls-the-most-treasured-tv-show-ever.

"Historic Sites of Ocean City, Maryland." *Preservation Maryland.* preservationmaryland. org. May 27, 2016.

Kester-McCabe, Dana. "Assateague Island's Early Beginnings." *Delmarva Almanac.* delmarva-almanac.com. http://delmarva-almanac.com/index.php/content/article/assateague_islands_early_beginnings/.

locationhub.com. DOESN'T LEAD TO ANYTHING.

https://www.locationshub.com/blog/2013/10/27/ping-pong-summer-filmed-entirely-in-ocean-city-maryland

mary-miles-minter.com

Micklos, John, Jr. "Aubrey Plaza of NBC's 'Parks and Recreation': Wilmington Native Is Building a Buzz in Hollywood." *Delaware Today.* delawaretoday.com. February 15, 2012. https://delawaretoday.com/life-style/aubrey-plaza-of-nbcs-parks-and-recreation-wilmington-native-is-building-a-buzz-in-hollywood/.

"Newman's Undercover Role on Tangier." *Daily Press.* dailypress.com. March 21, 1998. https://www.dailypress.com/news/dp-xpm-19980321-1998-03-21-9803210128-story.html.

Ocean City Life-Saving Museum. https://www.ocmuseum.org/

Pai, Tanya. "Michael Tully Talks about His Ocean City Film, 'Ping Pong Summer.'" *Washingtonian.* washingtonian.com. June 9, 2014. https://www.washingtonian.com/2014/06/09/michael-tully-talks-about-his-ocean-city-film-ping-pong-summer/.

"'Ping Pong Summer' Filmed Entirely in Ocean City, Maryland." *LocationsHub.* Locationshub.com. November 28, 2012. https://www.locationshub.com/blog/2013/10/27/ping-pong-summer-filmed-entirely-in-ocean-city-maryland.

Torres, Libby. "8 Things You Didn't Know about the Filming of ' Once upon a Time in Hollywood.'" *Insider.* insider.com. August 9, 2019.

https://www.insider.com/once-upon-a-time-in-hollywood-behind-the-scenes-2019-8

Vallance, Tom. "Obituary: William Alland." *Independent*. independent.co.uk. October 23, 2011. https://www.independent.co.uk/news/obituaries/obituary-william-alland-1288108.html.

Magazines
Rich, Joshua. "The Pick-Up Artists." *Entertainment Weekly*. July 15, 2005.

THE FIRST KISS

Books
Riskin, Victoria. *Fay Wray and Robert Riskin: A Hollywood Memoir*. New York: Pantheon Books, 2019.

Kinnard, Roy and Tony Crnkovich. *The Films of Fay Wray*. Jefferson, NC: McFarland & Company, 2005.

Newspaper Articles
Azrael, Louis. "The Free State Kiss." *Baltimore Daily Post*. N.d.

Dulaney, Carroll. "Eastern Shore Is Scene of First Kiss." *Evening Sun* (Baltimore, MD). N.d.

"Fay Wray and Gary Cooper in 'First Kiss' at Paramount." *New York Telegraph*. N.d.

"Fay Wray Flouts Movie's Plot and Weds Its Author." *Baltimore Sun*. June 16, 1928.

"Hundreds of Fans Greet Movie Stars." *Daily Times* (Salisbury, MD). June 12, 1928.

"Fay Wray's wedding was Talbot social hit in 1928." *Star-Democrat*. (Easton, MD) February 7, 1973.

"Hundreds Vote 'The First Kiss' a Very Attractive Presentation." *Star- Democrat* (Easton, MD). August 17, 1928.

Jungmeyer, Jack. "Rowland V. Lee Stepped from Stardom to Obscurity to Become Cinema Director." *Daily Times* (Salisbury, MD). November 2, 1924.

"Locale of 'The First Kiss' Filmed on the Eastern Shore Is Rich in American History." NEWSPAPER? August 22, 1928.

Maki, Greg. "Fay Wray Came to Talbot in 1928 to Film 'The First Kiss." *Star Democrat* (Easton, MD). August 12, 2004.

"Maritime museum seeks copy of 1928 movie." *Star-Democrat*. (Easton, MD) February 7, 1973.

Mills, Eric. "When Gary Cooper dredged for oysters in Chesapeake." *Star-Democrat*. (Easton, MD) December 2, 1996.

"Movie Stars to Talk from Station WSMD." *Daily Times* (Salisbury, MD). June 11, 1928.

"Natural Beauty of Talbot Provides Entire Background for 'The First Kiss' Film." *Daily Times* (Salisbury, MD). June 11, 1928.

"Paramount Players Making Film of Eastern Shore." *Daily Times* (Salisbury, MD). June 11, 1928.

"Paramount press release gives movie plot to nation's moviegoers." *Star-Democrat.* (Easton, MD) February 7, 1973.

Preston, Dickson. "Do you recall Gary Cooper's movie made in St. Michaels?" *Star Democrat.* (Easton, MD) February 7, 1973.

Valliant, Pauline. "I Remember . . . 'A First Kiss' in Talbot County." *Baltimore Sun/Sun Magazine.* May 20, 1973.

Magazines

Cooper, Dick. "Attic Treasures Tell History of Maple Hall, Claiborne." *Waterways.* Chesapeake Bay Maritime Museum Magazine. Fall 2008.

Dawson, James. "When Hollywood Came to St. Michaels: The Filming of 'The First Kiss.'" *Tidewater Times.* November 2013.

Internet Sources

http://www.arlingtoncemetery.net/tristram-tupper.htm

VIOLETS ARE BLUE

Newspaper Articles

Fleming, Dick. "Film Stars Praise Ocean City." *Daily Times* (Salisbury, MD). August 4, 1984.

—. "'Violets Are Blue' Labor of Love for Stars." *Daily Times* (Salisbury, MD). August 12, 1984.

—. "'Violets' Is a Movie Worth Seeing." Daily Times (Salisbury, MD). April 14, 1986.

"'Violets Are Blue' Premieres in Resort." *Daily Times* (Salisbury, MD). April 8, 1986.

Internet Sources

Folkart, Burt A. "James Aubrey Jr., Former Head of CBS and MGM, Dies." *Los Angeles Times.* Latimes.com. September 11, 1994. https://www.latimes.com/archives/la-xpm-1994-09-11-me-37218-story.html.

Galloway, Stephen. "When Kirk Kerkorian Hired the Most Hated Man in Hollywood." *The Hollywood Reporter.* Hollywoodreporterr.com. June 16, 2015. https://www.hollywoodreporter.com/news/kirk-kerkorian-hired-hated-man-802952.

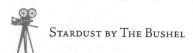

SILENT FALL

Newspaper Articles

Glielmi, Krista. "Actress Ends 3-week Stay in Talbot County." *Star- Democrat* (Easton, MD). October 31, 1993.

Greip, John. "Filming of Scenes for Movie Shifts to Estate Near Easton." *Star Democrat* (Easton, MD). October 6, 1993.

Hanks, Doug, III. "Locals Report Close Encounters with Dreyfuss." *Star- Democrat* (Easton, MD). October 15, 1993.

Kraisirideja, Sandra. *Dreyfus works with Liv Tyler for 'Fall'.* North County Times. (Oceanside, CA) October 28, 1994.

RUNAWAY BRIDE

Newspaper Articles

Bargion, Mary. "Runaway Promotion." *Daily Times* (Salisbury, MD). July 30, 1999.

Goldstein, Patrick. "'Bride's Long, Long Path to the Altar." *Los Angeles Times.* August 3, 1999.

Guy, Chris. "Spotlight on Town for Film Premiere." *Baltimore Sun.* July 30, 1999.

Mohsberg, Margot. "Berlin Plans Movie Gala." *Daily Times* (Salisbury, MD). June 14, 1999.

—. "Berlin's 'Runaway Bride' Premiere Sells Out." *Daily Times* (Salisbury, MD). July 16, 1999.

—. "'Bride' Gives Big Boost to Berlin Economy." *Daily Times* (Salisbury, MD). July 29, 1999.

—. "A Minute-by-Minute Guide to Berlin's Movie Debut." *Daily Times* (Salisbury, MD). August 1, 1999.

Waldon, David Brian. "Reverse Gere." *Daily Times* (Salisbury, MD). July 28, 1999.

Internet Sources

Bricker, Tierney. "A 'Pretty Woman' Reunion, Ben Affleck's Cold Feet and a $17 Million Payday: 20 Secrets about 'Runaway Bride' Revealed." *E.* eonline.com. July 30, 1999. https://www.eonline.com/news/1060452/a-pretty-woman-reunion-ben-affleck-s-cold-feet-and-a-17-million-payday-20-secrets-about-runaway-bride-revealed.

Sharp, Charlene. "Twentieth Anniversary of 'Runaway Bride' Celebrated This Month in Berlin." The Dispatch. mdcoastdispatch.com. August 1, 2019. https://mdcoastdispatch.com/2019/08/01/20th-anniversary-of-runaway-bride-release-celebrated-this-month-in-berlin/

FAILURE TO LAUNCH

Newspaper Articles

Buter, Shelley. "'That's a wrap' for Oxford." *Star Democrat* (Easton, MD). August 14, 2005.

Fisher, Vicki, and Sarah Ensor Pearce. "Filming under way in Oxford." *Star Democrat* (Easton, MD). August 5, 2005.

Neff, Christine. "Location Manager Takes Unique Look at Shore." *Star Democrat* (Easton, MD). August 9, 2005.

Internet Sources

Oxford-Bellevue Ferry. oxfordferry.com.

Town of Oxford, Maryland. oxfordmd.net.

GENERAL RESEARCH

Books

Brownlow, Kevin. *Hollywood: The Pioneers.* Glasgow, Scotland: William Collins, Sons, 1979.

Friedrich, Otto. *City of Nets: A Portrait of Hollywood in the 1940s.* New York: Harper & Row, 1986.

Ingraham, Prentiss. *Land of Legendary Lore: Sketches of Romance and Reality on the Eastern Shore of the Chesapeake.* Easton, MD: Gazette Publishing House, 1898.

Kael, Pauline. *5001 Nights at the Movies.* New York: Henry Holt and Company, 1991.

Lloyd, Ann (editor), and David Robinson (consultant editor). *70 Years at the Movies: From Silent Films to Today's Screen Hits.* New York: Orbis Publishing, 1988.

Norman, Barry. *The Story of Hollywood: Companion Book to Turner Network Television 10-Part TV Series.* New York: New American Library, 1988.

Preston, Dickson J. *Talbot County: A History.* Centreville, MD: Tidewater Publishing, 1983.

Shipman, David. *The Great Movie Stars: The Golden Years.* New York: Crown Publishing, 1970.

Weeks, Christopher. *Where Land and Water Intertwine.* Baltimore: Johns Hopkins University Press, 1984.

INDEX

A

Alland, William 296-297

Andrus, Leon 165-166

Arthur, Bea 287-292, 330

Assateague Island 180-183, 193, 195, 196

Avalon Theatre (Easton) 109-113, 173, 325, 347

B

Bankhead, Eugenia 84, 88, 91, 92, 97-100

Bankhead, Tallulah 3, 6, 7, 83-101, 240, 290

Barth, John 260

Beloved 300

Berlin, MD 15-23, 44-47, 168, 350

Bertinelli, Valerie 293

Blackwater Refuge, MD 137

Bledel, Alex 21

Brady, William Aloysius 5, 6, 7, 8, 9, 10

Brown, Joe David 110

Brown, John 131-132

Brynner, Yul 35

Bucktown, MD 123

Byron, Gilbert 260

C

Cain, James M. 218-241

Cambridge, MD 113-114, 122, 137, 148-150, 211, 247, 287

Cameron, James 69-71, 74-80

Centreville, MD 3, 4, 8, 9, 10

Chappell, Helen 262

Cheney, Dick 130, 215

Chesapeake Bay 4, 108, 154, 165, 173, 205, 206, 222, 245, 248, 257, 260-262, 274, 275, 277, 283, 284, 306, 319, 321, 326, 357, 364, 365

Chesapeake Film Festival 173

Chestertown, MD 219, 222, 225, 227, 236, 240, 247, 261

Cheston-on-Wye, MD 164-166

Chincoteague Island, VA 180-183, 186-189, 195-196, 198-199

Clancy, Tom 260

Clara's Heart 209, 336-342

Coates, Ta-Nehesi 259-260

Cooper, Gary 318-326

Crawford, Joan 234-236

Crisfield, MD 257, 262, 264

Cruise, Tom 284, 300

Cummings, Irving 8, 9, 10

Cummings, Priscilla 262

D

Damn Yankees   271-272, 279, 291

Days of Thunder   300

Dead Poet's Society   299-300

Delaware Bay   284

Delmarva   45, 47, 213, 264, 283, 284, 301, 312

Dodson, Debbi   358-360, 367-368

Dorchester County, MD   122, 137, 148-150

Double Indemnity   228-233

Douglass, Frederick   119, 129-132, 138, 259

Dreyfuss, Richard   77, 345-347

E

Eastern Shore   4, 16, 27, 101, 119, 120, 122, 203, 205, 219, 244, 260, 261, 283, 284, 306, 322

Easton, MD   105-115, 166, 173, 207, 211-212, 324, 346-347, 359-360

Edison, Thomas   141-142, 145-147

Emmy of Stork's Nest   298

F

Failure to Launch   363-368

Fairlee, MD   98-99

Ferber, Edna   243-257

First Kiss, The   110, 206-208, 318-327

Fitzgerald, F. Scott & Zelda   260

Flash of Genius   158, 160, 167-176

Fletcher, Lucille   262-280

Freeman, Yvette   294

G

Gere, Richard   18-19, 21, 350-352

Goldberg, Whoopi   209-211, 337, 340-342

H

Hamilton, Linda   63-81, 220, 334, 345

Hammett, Dashiell   259

Harriet   120-122, 127-128, 133, 135-136

Harris, Neil Patrick   337, 341-342

Harrison, Linda   43-60, 67, 71

Henry, Marguerite   184-189, 193, 197-199

Henry, Patrick   20-21

Heston, Charlton   44-58

Hinnant, Skip and Bill   285-286

Hit the Deck   112-113

Hurt, William   21

Hutchins, Doug   296

I

In the Land of Legendary Lore   107-109

J

James Adams Floating Theater, The   245-248, 250-257

Jones, James Earl   261

K

Keach, Stacy   261

Kearns, Robert   157-176, 299

Kearns, Tim   157-176

Kerr, Graham   275

Kerr, Sophie   261

Key, Francis Scott   260

Kingsley, Ben   21

Kline, Kevin   307-309, 328-330

L

Lifeboat   94-95

Lippman, Laura   260

Little Foxes, The   92-93

M

Man o' War   17

Marshall, Garry   18, 20, 22, 350-352

Maryland Film Office   18,19 ???

McConaughey, Matthew   363-366

Mencken, H. L.   259

Michener, James   261

Middletown, DE   299

Midkiff, Dale   286-287

Mildred Pierce   233-236

Mission Impossible III   284

Misty of Chincoteague   180, 184-195, 197, 200, 262

Mitchum, Dorothy (Spence)   29-40

Mitchum, Petrine   32, 34, 35, 38

Mitchum, Robert   26-40, 49, 112, 153, 192, 323, 330

Moloney, Marianne   337-342

Moore, Julianne   215

Morrison, Toni   300

N

Nash, Ogden   260

O

Oakley, Annie   141-154, 231

Ocean City, MD   16-17, 46-47, 55-56, 180, 267, 276, 302-315

Oxford, MD   157, 166, 173, 210, 247, 273-274, 363-365

P

Parker, Sarah Jessica   363-366

Perlman, Ron   72-74

Paterson, Katherine   262

Phillippe, Ryan   295-296

Ping Pong Summer   310-315

Planet of the Apes   44, 50-55, 58-60, 67

Plaza, Aubrey   294-295

Poe, Edgar Allen   259

Polo, Teri   296

Postman Always Rings Twice, The   236-239

Princess Anne, MD   264, 286

Q

Queen Anne's County, MD   8, 204

Queenstown, MD   4-5, 8-9, 164, 247, 254

R

Reinhold, Judge   293

Rhodes, Harry C.   8-9

Roberts, Julia   18-21, 350-352

Rothrock, Cynthia   293

Rumsfeld, Donald   130, 215

Runaway Bride   18-23, 349-352

S

Salisbury, MD   63-64, 67, 69, 71-73, 76, 264

Sayuri ("Brandy")   297-298

Schwarzenegger, Arnold   69-71, 74, 79

Shue, Elizabeth   293

Silent Fall   77, 114, 345-347

Simon, David   260

Sinclair, Upton   259-260

Sorry, Wrong Number   268-270, 279

Space   261

Spacek, Sissy   21, 306-309, 328-330, 339

Spence (Mitchum), Dorothy   29-40

St. Michaels, MD   112, 115, 129, 203-215, 247, 256, 306, 324-326, 359-360

Stanwyck, Barbara   230-234

Stars In My Crown   110-112

Styron, William   260

Swimmers   301

T

Talbot County, MD   105, 108-111, 129, 137, 157, 173, 203-215, 247, 279, 301, 319, 358

Tangier Island, VA   301-302

Terminator, The   69-71, 75

Terminator 2, 65, 74-75

Terminator 3, 78

Terminator Dark Fate   79, 80

Thomas, Sean Patrick   293-294

Tilghman, Christopher   261

Tourneur, Maurice   7, 8

Townsend, George Alfred   260, 264

Trappe, MD   33, 206

Tubman, Harriet   119-138

Tuck Everlasting   21, 168, 300

Tully, Michael   310-313

Tyler, Ann   261

Tyler, Liv   345, 347

V

Village, The   301

Violets Are Blue   307-310, 328-334

Voigt, Cynthia   262

W

Wallop, Douglass   262-280, 291

Wallops Island   181, 196, 263

Warner, William W.   261

Washington College   219-222, 225, 261

Waters, John   260

Way…Way Out   49

Wedding Crashers   211-215, 355-361

Whip, The   2-10, 85, 112

Wicomico County, MD   64, 65

Widdoes, Katherine   293

Williams, Robin   70, 169, 299

Winfrey, Oprah   73, 300

Wolfe, Tom   260

Worcester County, MD   16

Wray, Fay   318-326

Z

Zanuck, Richard   48, 49, 51, 54-57, 59